slang & sociability

slang

& sociability

In-Group Language

among College Students

CONNIE EBLE

The University of North Carolina Press

Chapel Hill and London

Library of Congress
Cataloging-in-Publication Data
Eble, Connie C.
Slang and sociability: in-group
language among college students /
Connie Eble.
     p.   cm.
Includes bibliographical references
(p.   ) and index.
ISBN 0-8078-2279-5 (cloth: alk. paper).—
ISBN 0-8078-4584-1 (pbk.: alk. paper)
1. College students—United States—
Language (New words, slang, etc.)
2. College students—United States—
Social life and customs.   3. English
language—United States—Slang.
4. Group identity—United States.
5. Americanisms.   I. Title.
PE3727.S8E255   1996
427'.973—dc20   95-47512
                              CIP

00 99 98 97 96   5 4 3 2 1

In memory of

    my mother,

    Florence Brann Eble,

    and

    my godmother,

    Adele Eble Schwegmann Ledet

CONTENTS

A project that has been in the works and on the mind for fifteen years becomes hard to extricate from daily life. I can no longer sort out in my memory all of the people who encouraged me as this book gradually took shape from hundreds and soon thousands of three-by-five cards. I am grateful for all of the responses to conference papers and community lectures, interviews with journalists, and conversations with students, colleagues, and friends that both helped me organize and interpret the data and confirmed the human interest in the topic of slang.

My first particular thanks go to my students at the University of North Carolina at Chapel Hill, those "Tar Heel voices" to whom my book *College Slang 101* is dedicated. Several of them are acknowledged in the text or in the notes when I refer to their work. Elisa Fiorenza and Kenny Levine hold a special place in my affection, for they chose during the hectic second semester of their senior year to do independent studies with me on slang. My interactions with each of them as they worked diligently and cheerfully on their projects taught me as much as I taught them.

The first linguist to encourage me to publish on slang was Charles Ruhl, who helped me impose order on the mounting piles of index cards when there were no models for studying slang. Charlie read and critiqued all of my early work on slang, and it clearly shows the influence of his monosemic view of the lexicon.

My first conference paper on slang was presented at the annual forum of the Linguistic Association of Canada and the United States in 1979. The response was so supportive that I presented a paper on slang almost every summer after that, all of which are published in the appropriate volumes of *The LACUS Forum* and listed at the end of this book. I am grateful to LACUS for granting me permission to include portions of some of those papers here. But I am even more appreciative of the collegial spirit of LACUS over the years and the personal and professional friendship I have found there. My special thanks to LACUS colleagues Victor Yngve, James Copeland, and Marcel Danesi for reading everything I have written on slang.

Richard Bernstein of the *New York Times* brought my work on slang to a general readership, and James Skardon of Spectacle

Lane Press made it available in a lighthearted paperback, *College Slang 101*.

Sandra Eisdorfer, now retired from the University of North Carolina Press, believed from our first conversation in 1987 that a university press could and should publish a book about slang, even though none had done it before. I appreciate her confidence and loyalty.

I will never forget the generosity of my university colleagues Robert Haig, Beverly Long, and Carol Reuss. They worked through much of the manuscript with me to make sure that it would be clear to readers who are not linguists. Michael Montgomery kindly read it to make sure that it would be clear to linguists too. My thanks also to Charles Lewis, who unexpectedly spent part of his vacation verifying glossary entries with me.

Thanks to bro Jonathan Lighter and sister girl Pamela Munro, who always give me a boost in their own work on slang, and to homeboy Walt Wolfram, who has boosted the spirits of all of us in North Carolina who care about sociolinguistics.

Although the word *networking* entered my vocabulary only recently, I have for more than twenty-five years of college teaching benefited from a safety net of professional women friends who have encouraged this project in hundreds of small and large ways. The network is a large one, and I cannot mention everyone I would like to, so I shall confine myself to the early Chapel Hill years: Margaret Anne O'Connor, Nancy Joyner, Carole Hines, Sue Ross, Susan Gilbert, Mary Lou Stevenson, Mary Hughes Brookhart, Boyd Davis, Jeutonne Brewer, Greta Little, Diane Leonard, Joy Kasson, Elizabeth Roth, Anne Hall, and Doris Betts.

Finally, I wish to acknowledge my family, my fellow parishioners at the Newman Catholic Student Center, and all the angels and saints who in various ways and guises helped me to create this book.

slang & sociability

Introduction

This book is about words and phrases—the words and phrases that American college students use to conduct their lives while they are about the business of earning a bachelor's degree. The vocabulary under examination here is not the vocabulary of knowledge and erudition that students learn through lectures, reading, and discussion but rather the ever changing and fashionable vocabulary of sociability that students use casually with one another, their slang.

The examples of college slang that form the foundation of this book are drawn from a collection of more than ten thousand items submitted as instances of "good, current campus slang" by undergraduates at the University of North Carolina at Chapel Hill from fall 1972 through spring 1993. The data vividly depict the linguistic behavior of this one group. These students share a cultural experience that differs in particulars from that of college students on other campuses. Moreover, as a group, college students differ in important ways from other slang-producing groups (see the end of Chapter 6). However, there is no reason to believe that in fundamental characteristics of form and effects the slang of students at the University of North Carolina is appreciably different from the slang of other American college students—or of truck drivers, hospital workers, lacrosse players, street gangs, or any other group that chooses to use a distinctive vocabulary as a means of social solidarity. Thus this book is at once a description of the nature of slang vocabulary in general and an analysis of the slang of one particular group.

Slang and Sociability selects examples from this collection of slang to describe language at work meeting the needs of a community of speakers who share the status of students at the same university. No other book-length treatment systematically examines the formal and social features of a slang corpus in this way. The underlying premise of the study is that slang is ordinary language, not a peripheral embellishment either for good or for ill. The explanation of slang offered here keeps returning to two points. First, slang is within the ordinary competence of language users. Second, the social potential inherent in language is actuated and intensified in the use of slang. The insistence that slang is part of the common core of language rather than an anomaly distinguishes this study from most other treatments of slang.

Because slang is customarily reported as the idiosyncratic and deviant vocabulary of marginalized groups, slang has never been taken seriously as a scholarly subject, one that can contribute to the understanding of language in general. Most introductions to the scientific study of language mention slang only in passing, if at all. Bloomfield (1933), Hockett (1958), Gleason (1961), and Lehmann (1976) all together devote fewer than five pages to slang. The most recent large reference grammar of contemporary English (Quirk et al. 1985) relegates slang to a footnote. Histories of the English language give slang a bit more attention, for the lexicon has long been an important part of diachronic studies. Yet some convey value judgments based on cultural attitudes rather than on linguistic evidence. Schlauch, for example, calls slang expressions "aberrations from standard English" (1959, 52). Baugh and Cable concede that "some use of slang is tolerated in the light conversation of most educated speakers" (1978, 314).

Two of America's great descriptive linguists, however, caution against discounting the importance of vernacular forms such as slang.[1] Charles Hockett writes, "We must not think of such uses of language as in any way inferior to its use in writing treatises on bacteriology or delivering lectures on civil law" (1958, 294). H. A. Gleason addresses even more specifically the issue at hand.

We have taken as normative what is really the anomalous kind of language—legal contracts, examples out of logic texts, and modern descendants from the old classical examples in grammar books. To this core we have added so much of ordinary language as is not distinct from it—or rather, so much of ordinary language as we have not yet noticed to be distinct from it. The malapropisms, poetic figures, popular language play, and ordinary double-talk we hear all around us may after all be the really typifying human language, extreme cases only of the ordinary sort of language. (1973, 32)

The two traditional and time-honored discussions of English slang are Eric Partridge's *Slang To-day and Yesterday*, which was issued in four editions from 1933 to 1970, and H. L. Mencken's chapter entitled "American Slang" in *The American Language*, most recently revised by Raven I. McDavid and David Maurer in 1963. Neither Partridge nor Mencken was an academician. Both were practical geniuses at collecting, documenting, and preserving words, and their pleasure in the oddities of vocabulary is apparent on every page. The words themselves are their central concern; the two men were not professional linguists seeking to fit the words into an overall explanation of language. They made their living by their writing, and they wrote to be read by a general audience. Partridge was a prolific maker of wordbooks—books of slang, unconventional English, catchphrases, usage, etymology, puns, and proverbs. However, his critical writing on these topics is not extensive. Mencken was a journalist, essayist, editor, and political and literary critic—possibly the most influential figure in American literary circles in the 1920s. His chapter on American slang is still commendable for its attention to history and bibliography as well as for its clear explanation of the salient characteristics of slang.

More rigorous and less discursive essays on American slang are the introductions to two important dictionaries. Stuart Berg Flexner's preface to the *Dictionary of American Slang*, edited with Harold Wentworth and first published in 1960, has become a standard and has been reprinted in subsequent editions of the dictionary as well as in anthologies for students of linguistics. The best general discussion of American slang to date, however, is Jonathan Lighter's twenty-seven-page introduction to volume 1 of his *Random House Historical Dictionary of American Slang*, published in 1994. A work of exemplary scholarship, Lighter's essay is particularly strong in discussing the history of slang and its documentation.

I hope that the present volume is as analytically sound as the work of Flexner and Lighter and yet follows in the tradition of Partridge and Mencken in making slang interesting to a general readership. With the latter aim in mind, it incorporates little secondary material and avoids technical terminology as much as possible. Although slang is valuable to the scientific study of language, *Slang and Sociability* is written more for people who are curious about language than for those who earn their living by studying and teaching about it.

The approach is fundamentally that of traditional American descriptive linguistics, analyzing a corpus of several thousand items for patterns of form and function. Although the data have implications for issues of theoretical debate, my emphasis is descriptive rather than theoretical, and I try not to use the vocabulary of any particular theory. Furthermore, because this book is a lexical study and not a phonology or syntax of slang, I discuss sounds and grammatical structure only as needed to explain the lexical items that are the heart of the study.

Still, the book does have theoretical biases. The view of language that it presents is not one that abstracts language from its users or that views language as an autonomous system. The "ideal speaker-hearer" has no place here. Meaning is not composed from semantic primes by rules, and the lexicon is seen as a complex realization fed by many sources including social and pragmatic ones. The treatment of slang offered here is consistent with lexical theories that see words and groups of words as cognitively structured and linked in webs or networks. It is likewise consistent with syntactic analysis that recognizes prefabricated units that are not generated anew with every use. Fundamental to all of these notions, of course, is the importance of social context.

The slang lexicon analyzed in this study comes from undergraduate students enrolled in introductory English linguistics courses at the University of North Carolina at Chapel Hill over a period of two decades, from fall 1972 through spring 1993. Most of the students in these classes were residents of North Carolina, between the ages of nineteen and twenty-three, white, female, and seeking certification as teachers.

The collection and the method of obtaining it began simply as a teaching device, a way to get students in an introductory English linguistics class interested in word-forming processes by having them examine the words and phrases that were currently in vogue on campus. As the starting point for discussion, students were asked to bring to class ten words or phrases that they considered examples of "good, current, campus slang." The assignment fulfilled its purpose and was repeated in subsequent semesters. By 1979 the richness of the amassed data convinced me of the potential of slang for showing how speakers readily and creatively use language for social purposes, and at the annual meeting of the Linguistic Association of Canada and the United States I presented my first paper on the topic, "Slang, Productivity, and Semantic Theory."

Over the years I have continued to collect slang from students enrolled in introductory English linguistics courses in the same way, just asking them to bring to class on separate three-by-five-inch cards ten words or expressions that they consider "good, current, campus slang." Some students cannot think of ten, and others submit eighteen or twenty. Class size has fluctuated from fifteen to forty, and the number of items collected from semester to semester has varied accordingly. By the end of the spring semester of 1993, the corpus of North Carolina slang begun in the fall of 1972 mounted to over ten thousand instances of more than forty-five hundred different words and expressions. Most of these occur only once or twice. In the entire corpus, only forty lexical items were submitted by thirty or more students. These top forty, listed in Appendix 1, constitute less than 1 percent of the lexical types but 17 percent of the total submissions; that is, one of every six items in the corpus is one of these forty. Most of them are widely used and recognized in informal varieties of American English today; half are recorded as slang in the 1992 edition of *The American Heritage Dictionary*.

Although offered as examples of campus slang, most items are neither original nor unique to the University of North Carolina. Furthermore, not every student in class is familiar with every item, and in discussion class members sometimes disagree on shades of meaning or on whether an item is still fresh or already passé. They often have different and conflicting notions about the origin of lexical items too. For example, *G* in the greeting *What's up, G?* is thought to be a shortening from a range of words from *guy* to *God*.

Sometimes students report terms that are used by their set of friends only. For instance, in the spring of 1984 one student reported that she and her friends called their suite in the residence hall *WAH*, an acronym of We Are Happy. Certainly not every such expression used by subgroups of students for social solidarity is known by or gets reported by the students in my courses. It is also possible that some students deliberately make up an item or two of slang just for the pleasure of putting one over on the teacher. Their ability to do just that simply confirms their mastery of manipulating language to distinguish the insiders from the outsiders, and a few deliberately contrived items in a corpus of this size and time span are unimportant.

For the most part, the contributors have been my own students. But in semesters when none of the introductory undergraduate English language courses has been part of my teaching assignment, I have relied on the generosity of colleagues to lend me their class for one class period. Although the students who do not know me are sometimes a bit guarded at first, by the end of the hour they are usually as eager as my own students to volunteer their favorite slang item. The general politeness of the students at North Carolina and their reluctance to risk publicly offending their teacher and fellow classmates function as a kind of censorship. As a result, the corpus probably contains many fewer degrading terms pertaining to taboo areas such as sex and race than were actually in use.

Thousands of items in the North Carolina corpus were submitted only once. For example, these terms for 'socially inept person' occur only once, in the year indicated: *nob*, 1972; *gwimp*, 1976; *pdk*, from *polyester double knit*, 1985; and *yernt* and *dweezle*, 1986. Other sets of nonce forms are *rogue*, 1984, *inch*, 1990, and *smurf*, 1991, for 'steal'; *sergeant space*, 1983, *outpost*, 1984, and *reach*, 1986, for 'someone who is out of touch with reality'; and *yam*, 1985, *squeek*, 1986, and *do the humpty-hump*, 1991, for 'engage in sex'. It cannot be determined whether such single instances were short-lived, limited to a small group, contrived for the course assignment, or simply underreported. However, the large number of unique forms suggests that at any given time many slang items are being introduced and tried out but very few get adopted by large numbers of users.

Just as it is important to understand the limitations of the slang collection itself, it is also important to be aware of the type of setting in which the slang users of this study lived, for the collegiate subculture that their slang represents is in part conditioned by the characteristics of the university that they chose to attend.[2]

The University of North Carolina at Chapel Hill welcomed its first students in 1795, making it the oldest state university in the nation. It is located in the Piedmont region of the Tar Heel State, about midway between the Atlantic Ocean and the Appalachian Mountains and about 25 miles northwest of the state capital of Raleigh. Because state law requires that at least 82 percent of the undergraduate student body be North Carolina residents, some facts about the state can help in understanding the background of the students. The 6.5 million people in North Carolina live in three distinct geographic regions—the coastal plain, the Piedmont, and the mountains—running about 500 miles east to west. The state has only ten cities with populations over 55,000 and only five cities with populations over 100,000. Charlotte, with a population under half a million, is the state's largest city. Of the towns in North Carolina, 245 have populations of 1,000 or fewer. Because the university deliberately draws its undergraduates from all 100 North Carolina counties, many students come to Chapel Hill from rural areas and small towns. For many, their freshman chemistry lecture class has more students than their entire high school did, and the university's 21,500-seat basketball arena holds twenty times as many people as the population of their hometown.

In its two-hundred-year history, the University of North Carolina at Chapel Hill has grown to 729 acres, 190 buildings, and 2,100 faculty members and has become the major research institution of the state's sixteen-campus system. It consistently ranks among the top twenty of the nation's research universities. Although the university has increased in programs, personnel, and buildings over the two decades covered by this study, the size of the student body has been held almost constant. Total enrollment is around 23,000. Of these, between 15,000 and 16,000 are undergraduates. Females outnumber males, 59 to 41 percent. Approximately 85 percent of the undergraduates are white and 10 percent black. The remaining 5 percent are Hispanic, Asian, or Native American. At least 82 percent, and usually slightly more, are North Carolinians. Fewer than 1 percent of the undergraduates are citizens of foreign countries.

Admission to the University of North Carolina at Chapel Hill is competitive. For the class entering in 1992, the mean SAT score was 1,120, and 95 percent ranked in the top 20 percent of their class. Often called a "public ivy," North Carolina offers an excellent undergraduate education. Many of its graduates gain admission to prestigious graduate and professional programs. Since 1980, nine Carolina students have been named Rhodes scholars.

Undergraduate life at Chapel Hill is traditional in many ways.

Undergraduates are required to be full-time students, carrying a minimum of twelve semester hours of course work. Although most hold some sort of part-time job on or off campus, their status as students is primary. Between 50 percent and 60 percent complete a bachelor's degree within four years, and 75 percent graduate within five years.

About 6,800 students live on campus in university residence halls. Most of the rest live in nearby sorority and fraternity houses, in a large, privately owned residence hall near campus, or in apartments in Chapel Hill and neighboring Carrboro within a thirty-minute bus ride of the university.

For more than a century, student academic and social conduct has been subject to the honor system, administered by students through the judicial branch of student government. Over the years, student government has grown large and complex, receiving student-voted fees to provide a range of nonacademic activities and services.

Another century-old tradition is the *Daily Tar Heel*, a newspaper published by students five days a week when the university is in session. It is available free to all members of the university community and is often the forum for debating issues of interest and importance to faculty, administrators, and staff as well as to students.

The crossroads of student life is the Pit—a large, sunken, bricked rectangle in the middle of the campus reached by steps on all four sides. Students congregate on the steps in good weather, and the Pit is the usual place where student groups and proselytizers for various causes give presentations, hold rallies, publicize their activities, and exercise their freedom of speech. Bordering the Pit are two libraries, a dining hall, student stores, and the student union. Student athletic facilities are just across the street.

The town's main street, Franklin Street, a ten-minute walk from the Pit, is the northern border of campus. It has movie theaters and numerous places where students can gather to eat, drink, listen to music, and dance. Socializing on Franklin Street begins after ten at night, and Thursday is the most popular evening. Social life for about 20 percent of Carolina's undergraduates is provided by affiliation with a fraternity or sorority.

Sports are an important part of life at Carolina, and a large percentage of the students participate in various club and intramural sports. About six hundred male and female students represent the university on twenty-six intercollegiate teams. Watching and talking about Carolina football and basketball is a major pastime. Basketball is the premier sport in the state of North Carolina. In the two decades covered by this study, teams from the state won the national championship in men's basketball five times; Chapel Hill's Tar Heels were NCAA national champions twice, in 1982 and in 1993.

I must admit to a romantic view of the campus. The oldest part, where many undergraduate classes are held, centers on two tree-lined quadrangles bordered by many of the loveliest buildings on campus. In the fall students make their way to classes under a blaze of gold and red leaves; when spring fever strikes, they beg their teachers to hold classes on the grass under the flowering fruit trees and a Carolina blue sky. The school colors are sky-blue and white, and a popular bumper sticker asks, "If God is not a Tar Heel, then why is the sky Carolina blue?" Many people think that the old part of campus, with its stately trees, ivy-covered buildings, and brick walkways, looks just the way a college campus is supposed to look. Many a high school senior has chosen North Carolina after a walk from the steps of Louis Round Wilson Library to Franklin Street, passing along the way such emblems of the first state university as the Old Well, the Davie Poplar, and Silent Sam, the statue of a young Confederate soldier with a rifle who stands sentry at the northern edge of campus.

It is the undergraduate culture of this tradition-rich, public, southern university during the 1970s and 1980s that the slang in this book reflects.

Anyone who writes about slang struggles with organization. The starting point is obviously exploring what slang is. From there, however, no route stretches direct or uncluttered, for slang affects or is affected by many of the aesthetic, sociological, and psychological variables that shape human language. After an opening chapter on the definition of slang, the next three chapters focus on the sine qua non of language: physical form linked with meaning. Chapter 2 classifies slang words and expressions by their form and shows that they result from the same ordinary word-building processes that give rise to the general vocabulary. Chapters 3 and 4 focus on meaning, showing in particular that slang often evokes meaning in the same ways that poetry does, by relying on the hearers' ability to make associations. The final three chapters veer from focusing on slang itself to focusing on the users of slang. Chapters entitled "Use," "Effects," and "Culture" discuss the human side of slang—where, when, and why people use it and what its use accomplishes. Throughout the book, my aim is to show that slang is vocabulary that embodies the social functions of language.

1: Definition

Slang is an ever changing set of colloquial words and phrases that speakers use to establish or reinforce social identity or cohesiveness within a group or with a trend or fashion in society at large. The existence of vocabulary of this sort within a language is possibly as old as language itself, for slang seems to be part of any language used in ordinary interaction by a community large enough and diverse enough to have identifiable subgroups.[1]

The origin of the word *slang* is unknown. Its resemblance in sound and figurative meaning to the noun and verb *sling* and the occurrence of apparently the same root in Scandinavian expressions referring to language suggest that the term *slang* is a development of a Germanic root from which the current English *sling* is derived (Partridge 1970, 2). Another conjecture is that *slang* has been formed by shortening from genitive phrases like *beggars' language* or *rogues' language*, in which the genitive suffix of the first noun attaches to the initial syllable of *language* and then the final syllable is lost (Klaeber 1926, 368). In its earliest occurrences in the eighteenth century, the word *slang* referred to the specialized vocabulary of underworld groups and was used fairly interchangeably with the terms *cant, flash,* and *argot* (McKnight 1923, 37–38).

The social and psychological complexities captured in slang vocabulary make the term difficult to define, leading Bethany Dumas and Jonathan Lighter to question whether the term is even usable for linguists. Dumas and Lighter (1978, 14–16) reject the classical formula for definition and instead propose four identifying criteria for slang.

1. Its presence will markedly lower, at least for the moment, the dignity of formal or serious speech or writing.

2. Its use implies the user's special familiarity either with the referent or with that less statusful or less responsible class of people who have such special familiarity and use the term.
3. It is a tabooed term in ordinary discourse with persons of higher social status or greater responsibility.
4. It is used in place of the well-known conventional synonym, especially in order (a) to protect the user from the discomfort caused by the conventional item or (b) to protect the user from the discomfort or annoyance of further elaboration.

They conclude that "when something fits at least two of the criteria, a linguistically sensitive audience will react to it in a certain way. This reaction, which cannot be measured, is the ultimate identifying characteristic of true slang."

Here is a selection of Dumas and Lighter's examples.

Though their dissent was not always noisy or dramatic, many Americans felt the President was a *jerk* for continuing the war.

"What should we do with the prisoners, Lieutenant?"
"*Waste* 'em."

I'd like this job, sir, because the one I have now is *shit*.

According to the criteria, *jerk*, *waste*, and *shit* all qualify as slang. *Jerk* fulfills criteria 1, 2, and 4b; *waste*, criteria 1, 2, and 4a; and *shit*, criteria 1, 2, 3, and possibly 4b (14–15).

None of the four criteria is formal, for slang is not distinct in form. And only number 3 may be said to be loosely based on meaning. But all four concern the social relationships of the participants, and the "ultimate identifying characteristic" is the consciousness of shared knowledge between speaker and hearer. Dumas and Lighter's formulation requires that the type of lexis called *slang* be recognized for its power to effect union between speaker and hearer. Whether or not the particulars of their operational definition are necessary or sufficient, in the final analysis Dumas and Lighter are right. Slang cannot be defined independent of its functions and use.

Despite the difficulty of defining the term, slang does have some consistent characteristics. Foremost, slang is ephemeral. A constant supply of new words requires the rapid change characteristic of slang. Most slang items enjoy only a brief time of popularity, bursting into existence and falling out of use at a much more rapid rate than items of the general vocabulary. Sometimes a new slang form either replaces an earlier one or provides another synonym for a notion already named in slang, like *ramped, ranked, ted* (from *wasted*), and *toe* (from *torn*) for 'drunk'; *bogel* and *hang* for 'do nothing in particular'; *bumping* and *kegging* for 'exhilarating'; *squirrel kisser* and *tree nymph* for 'someone concerned with the environment'; or *red-shirted* and *latered* for 'jilted'. Sometimes new slang extends to new areas of meaning or to areas of meaning of recent interest to the group inventing the slang, like *Tom* (from *totally obedient moron*) for 'computer'; *dangling modifier* for 'a single, long, flashy earring'; *the five-year program* (or even *the six-year program*) for 'the time it takes to complete an undergraduate degree'; or *twinkie* (yellow on the outside, white on the inside) for 'an Asian who identifies with Caucasians or has a white girlfriend or boyfriend'.

The vocabulary of college students can illustrate the ephemeral and innovative character of slang. One way to measure the ephemerality of student slang is to compare slang vocabulary at the same institution at different times. Two studies of this sort have been reported in *American Speech*. Slang items from Stanford University published in 1927 (Morse) were found to be largely out of use just five years later (Shidler 1932, 435): "In comparing the 'Stanford Expressions' of 1926 with those of 1931 I find a complete change. The place-names, and a very few characteristic Stanford words such as 'apple-polisher,' 'bawlout,' and 'rough' are the only words used as slang now—we use about fifty of the five hundred words typical of Stanford in 1926. This period of five years has had an astounding effect on our language!"

A much more ambitious and rigorous study of the staying power of college slang was undertaken in 1962 at Kansas University by Alan Dundes and Manuel R. Schonhorn, using as their point of departure an eighty-five-item list collected at Kansas thirty-six years earlier and published in *American Speech* in 1928 (Pingry and Randolph). Dundes and Schonhorn not only tested groups of more than 150 undergraduates for usage and recognition of these college slang items, but they also incorporated into their description references to the terms in dictionaries and in published accounts of slang on other campuses. Thus their study is comparative across both time and space. With regard to time, they found that thirteen items (15 percent) reported in 1926 were in use in 1962. Thirty-nine were recognizable to at least 5 members of a test group of 37 undergraduates. But thirty, more than one-third, were completely unknown, for example, *eagers* 'anxiety or haste' (1963, 175).

My sampling of the slang of students at the University of North Carolina at Chapel Hill over a fifteen-year period also attests to the rapid change in slang vocabulary (Eble, 1989b). This study tabulates the overlap of different items collected in the fall of 1972, the fall of 1980, and the fall of 1987—the dates bounding the two complete seven-year generations of college students who graduated in 1973–79 and 1982–88. The size of the collections at the three points differs: about two hundred separate items from fall 1972 and from fall 1980, and five hundred from fall 1987.

A simple headword-plus-definition comparison of the three sets bears out the ephemeral quality of the UNC-CH student vocabulary.[2] Only four of the slightly fewer than two hundred items from 1972 were submitted with the same form and meaning in both 1980 and 1987, roughly 2 percent of the types in the 1972 and 1980 collections and less than 1 percent in the 1987 collection. An additional eight occur in both 1972 and in 1987 but not in 1980. That makes a total of twelve items reported in both 1972 and 1987, about 6 percent of the types for 1972 and 2 percent for 1987. Fifteen items occur both in 1972 and in 1980, for a retention rate of about 7 percent. Twenty of the two hundred slang items from 1980 are reported still in use in 1987, about 10 percent of the 1980 corpus and about 4 percent of the 1987 corpus. Thus, within a span of fifteen years the specific items of slang vocabulary reported by UNC-CH undergraduates obviously changed to a very large extent.

Some slang words, however, maintained their form and meaning in this great flux. The four items that occur at all three sampling points are *bad* 'good'; *bummer* 'unpleasant experience'; *slide* 'easy course'; and *wheels* 'car'. Another eight occur in both 1972 and 1987 but were not submitted in 1980: *cool* 'good, in-the-know, sophisticated'; *do*, an all-purpose verb; *get real* 'be serious'; *gravy* 'easy'; *pound* 'drink heavily'; *shit*, an expression of anger or disappointment; *threads* 'clothing'; and *tough* 'good, admirable, attractive'.

A few additional items altered slightly in form or meaning. For example, *bomb out* 'fail' also shortened to *bomb*, and *jam* 'make music, dance' shifted to mean also 'perform well'. Even adding such items with altered forms or shifted meanings to the twelve slang items that have the same form and definition in 1972 and 1987, the total percentage of college slang words in this collection that lasted over a fifteen-year span is still under 10 percent.[3]

The small percentage of items that persisted should not be surprising, for here slang shows the characteristics of the language as a whole, as it does in both its word-building and semantic processes. Looking back a thousand years in English, we find that the vast majority of words have changed. Frequently used Old English verbs such as *brucan* 'enjoy', *fremman* 'do', *hatan* 'call', and *niman* 'take' have been replaced by other verbs. Nouns of kinship such as Old English *eam* and *swigra* are now expressed in the phrases *maternal uncle* and *sister's son*. The common Old English adjective *faeger* 'fair' has changed to mean 'mediocre', and its earlier meaning is now expressed in words like *pretty* and *beautiful*. In Old English the pronoun *his* was both masculine and neuter; the language subsequently developed *its* for neuter reference. Only a few words have persisted unchanged in form and meaning, for example, *mid* and *edge* (spelled *ecg* in Old English but pronounced the same). What is remarkable about the ephemerality of slang is not the percentage of terms that change but the short span of time involved.

Another feature of the comings and goings of slang is that some slang terms come back for a second and third life, the way that fashions do. For example, *cram* 'study hard at the last minute' was submitted as current in fall 1980 and fall 1987 but not in 1972 at North Carolina or in 1971 at Arkansas (Underwood). *Dead soldier*, which has been part of military slang since the eighteenth century when it meant 'empty bottle', emerged at North Carolina in 1987 with the more contemporary referent 'empty beer can'. *Out of sight* 'excellent, extraordinary' of the 1960s was felt at the time to be novel and fresh but was a reincarnation of the same form and meaning used in the Bowery in the 1890s and recorded in Stephen Crane's *Maggie: Girl of the Streets* in 1896 (Peck 1966). *Hot* 'sexually attractive' is currently in vogue for the umpteenth time, as well as *gravy* for 'an easy test or course'.

Although slang items come and go, it is easier to pinpoint, and in some instances to explain, the comings than the goings. *Ghetto blaster*, *jambox*, and *third world briefcase* naturally did not come into the language before this past decade because the 'portable stereo tape deck' had not been invented. Likewise, when a referent disappears, the slang item for it is likely to go. A striking example from college slang is the apparent loss of the most pervasive set of college slang items of the nineteenth century, words conveying the image of traveling the easy way—that is, being carried by a horse or pony—to refer to using a translation for Latin class. In the days when Latin was a required subject in British and American schools, *pony*, *horse*, and *trot* were widely known slang terms for 'a literal translation'. Because so few American college students are now compelled to study Latin, their slang no longer contains words for subverting the requirement.

However, loss of referent cannot explain the demise of these American college slang terms of the 1930s and 1940s: *flat tire* for 'unattractive girl'; *d.a.r.* (from *damned average raiser*, with the added allusion to the *Daughters of the American Revolution*) for a 'student who gets good grades'; *el foldo* 'failure'; *Jonathan Simonizer* (a synonym of *apple polisher*, in which *Jonathan* 'a kind of apple' replaces *apple* and *Simonizer* 'a brand of wax' replaces *polisher*) for 'one who curries favor'; *candidate for the plumber's degree* for 'one who takes easy (*pipe*) courses'; and *drop quiz* for 'unannounced test'. Half a century later, these slang items seem just as fresh and viable as 1992's *Air Hebrews* for 'sandals'; *garden tool* (from *hoe*, the pronunciation of *whore* with the *-r* dropped) for 'promiscuous female'; *party hat* for 'condom'; *bar golf* for 'going from bar (watering hole) to bar drinking'; *snatch 22* (from *snatch*, an old slang term for 'vulva' expanded by rhyming allusion to the Joseph Heller novel *Catch 22*) for 'an extremely ugly female'; *throw shade* for 'humiliate exceedingly'; and *Woodstock wannabe* for 'a person reminiscent of the 1960s'. The terms from the thirties and forties may not be dead but merely resting.

Ephemerality is often considered a particular attribute of slang. But not all slang is ephemeral, and not all ephemeral vocabulary is slang. *Bones* as slang for 'dice', for example, was used by Chaucer in the fourteenth century and is still slang. A comparison of words labeled slang in *Webster's Second* (1934) and *Webster's Third* (1961) shows that many slang terms have staying power, among them *beef* and *bitch* 'complain', *buck* 'dollar', *bull* 'talk insincerely', and *come again* 'repeat' (Barber 1963, 106–7). Maurer and High find that a number of terms marked slang in Grose's 1785 *Classical Dictionary of the Vulgar Tongue* are still around and still slang two hundred years later, for example, *knock off* 'to quit work' and *plant* 'to lay, place, hide' (1980, 188–89). But when slang items remain in the language for years, they often lose their slang status. Middle English *bouse*, now spelled *booze*, persists in highly informal contexts, as does *pooped* for 'exhausted', first attested in the sixteenth century. Still other slang items pass into the general vocabulary and bear little or no association with their earlier lives as slang, for example, the noun *rascal*, the verb *bluff*, and the adjective *flimsy*. *Jeopardy* from gambling and *crestfallen* from cockfighting have even acquired a learned tinge (McKnight 1923, 40–49).

Many slang terms are of course ephemeral and can even be associated with a particular era—for example, the superlative expressions *the cat's pajamas* and *the bee's knees* from the years between the first and second world wars. But other kinds of vocabulary are ephemeral too. As with slang, an item of the general vocabulary can quickly fall into disuse when its referent goes out of existence or popularity. The *isinglass* curtains of *Oklahoma*'s "Surrey with the Fringe on Top" have yielded to push-button, electronic, tinted, shatterproof automobile windows. My grandfather's *crystal set* 'early, tubeless, radio receiver' from the 1920s would now be a museum piece, and with the advance in hair care products, my grandmother would no longer need to spend hours crocheting *antimacassars* 'coverings thrown over furniture to protect it, particularly from hair oil'. The *victrola* 'record player' and *hectograph* 'device for making copies by ink impressed on a gelatin surface' of my elementary school classrooms are likewise obsolete. The metal *charge-a-plate* of the 1950s has given way to plastic *credit cards*— or just plain *plastic*. The revolutionary *LPs* so dear to the youth of the sixties are now disparagingly called *vinyls* by contrast with albums on *CDs*. Sometimes a standard word becomes obsolete even though its referent is still useful, for example, *clip* 'embrace', *fugle* 'act as a guide or a model', *lyam* 'a leash', *sain* 'make the sign of the cross for protection', and *wight* 'supernatural being'. Yet other words remain in the language but carry a rather old-fashioned flavor, like *naught* 'the grade zero', *grip* 'a small traveling bag', *the croup* 'sickness characterized by chest congestion and coughing', and the verbs *bide*, *hasten*, and *tarry*.

Slang is innovative, but so is language in general. There is no evidence that slang is created in special or unfamiliar ways (see

Chapter 2). Studies of new scientific terms (Caso 1980) and computer terminology (Covington 1981) show the same processes at work in those subject areas. Algeo's 1980 study of one thousand words from *The Barnhart Dictionary of New English since 1963* presents a rigorous taxonomy for lexical innovation that includes with refinements all the familiar morphological and semantic processes and that provides a common vocabulary to compare neologisms from various technical fields and social groups. Readers of *Time* magazine expect to imbibe a number of neologisms with their weekly dose of current events. Among possible coinages by *Time* are *culturecrats, Disneyfication, ecofreaks, megabuckers, outcumbent, petropolitics, skyjam,* and *televangelist* (Yates 1981). New words bombard us every day, and with a few exceptions they feel as comfortable and nonthreatening as the words that have been around for generations. In the 1980s *PC* (*personal computer*), *CD* (*compact disc*), and *fax* (from *facsimile*) became widespread to name new referents. *Dinks* (*double income, no kids*) described a new economic class and *nimby* (*not in my backyard*) a growing concern to protect property values. *Perestroika* 'radical change in economic policy' and *intifada* 'popular political uprising' are timely new borrowings for old notions.

Innovation is an important attribute of language; hence, innovation is an important attribute of slang too. However, the rapid rate of change in slang makes the novelty more apparent there.

Another often cited characteristic of slang is its group-identifying function (see Chapter 6). It is well documented that social groups are fertile breeding grounds for an idiosyncratic vocabulary to enhance their solidarity. Groups that operate on the periphery of society, such as con artists or drug dealers, seem particularly adept at creating slang. However, association with a group is not essential to slang. With the possibility of instant and widespread communication, the group-identifying functions of slang for the population at large may be diminishing in favor of identification with a style or an attitude rather than with a specific, easily delineated group. If items like *idiot box* 'television set', *loose cannon* 'someone who is uncontrolled and unpredictable', *shrink* 'psychiatrist', and *weirdo* 'a strange person' can be considered slang in the United States, they are a kind of national slang and say little about group identification. Robert Chapman, editor of the *New*

Dictionary of American Slang, calls this type of slang "secondary" and predicts that in the future it will be the major type of slang in America (1986, xii).

Slang must be distinguished from other subsets of the lexicon such as regionalisms or dialect words, jargon, profanity and obscenity, colloquialism, and cant or argot—although slang shares some characteristics with each of these and can overlap them. Slang is not geographically restricted vocabulary, like British *lift, serviette,* and *zed* instead of the equivalent *elevator, napkin,* and *zee* of the United States. Vocabulary that is typical of one region within the United States is likewise not slang, such as the southern use of *you all* and *y'all* as a second-person plural pronoun, or the use in the environs of New Orleans of *neutral ground* for 'median strip in a divided street', *batture* 'alluvial land between the Mississippi River and the levee', *banquette* 'sidewalk', and *krewe* 'Mardi Gras social club'. Nevertheless, just like the standard vocabulary, some slang items are associated with a particular region—for example, *bloke* with Britain and *guy* with America.

Slang is not jargon, the vocabulary used in carrying out a trade or profession or in pursuing an interest or hobby. *Ejecta* 'debris thrown by the explosion of a missile' and *jam* 'impair the enemy's electronic system' are military jargon; *cursor* 'movable indicator on a screen' and *mouse* 'box with buttons to move the cursor' belong to computer jargon; and *shot clock* and *zone defense* are basic jargon to basketball fans. But groups united by their work or a common interest can also develop a less precise slang vocabulary, which usually conveys feelings and attitudes and unity of spirit. *Chicken colonel* for 'full colonel' and *John Wayne* for 'militarily exemplary' are U.S. Army slang; *meatware* 'human body' is slang invented by computer users by analogy with the jargon *hardware* and *software*; basketball fans might call 'an official' a *zebra* or refer to a 'spectacular dunk' as *doing windows*. Sometimes words that start out as the jargon of a particular group become slang for a wider group. For example, *ice* 'diamonds' is no longer known by only jewel thieves; *gig* 'a job' is used by more than just hungry musicians; and *heavyweight* can refer to 'any important person', not just to a boxer in the highest weight classification. In other instances, words pass from the jargon of a group into the general vocabulary without ever being slang. For example, *input, output,* and *interface* are frequently used standard vocabulary items that gained their current popularity because of increased public exposure to the jargon of computer science.

Although slang synonyms abound in the taboo subjects of a culture, not all slang terms violate social propriety. *Mickey Mouse* for 'easy', *dough* for 'money', or *sleazebag* for 'unethical person' may be inappropriate in some contexts, but they are not obscene and would not be edited out of prime-time television or feature stories or cartoons in family newspapers.

Slang is largely colloquial. It belongs to the spoken part of language and is rarely written except in direct quotation of speech. But not all colloquial expressions are slang. *Shut up* for 'be quiet' is seldom written except in dialogue, but it is not slang. Neither are colloquial expressions like *stickup* and *throw up*, which contrast with neutral synonyms *robbery* and *vomit* and slang synonyms *heist* and *ralph*. In practice it is difficult to distinguish between colloquial and informal, which means vocabulary not suited to serious and important occasions. Slang words always diminish the formality of a conversation in which they occur, as in "Would you lend me some *bread?*" versus "Would you lend me some *money?*" But not all words with informal connotations are necessarily slang, like *decaf* 'decaffeinated coffee', *leak* 'unauthorized disclosure', *limo* 'limousine', or *warmups* 'clothing worn to keep the muscles warm before or during exercise'.

Although slang vocabulary carries a nuance of trendiness, Thomas J. Creswell and Virginia McDavid, in a prefatory essay in *The Random House Dictionary of the English Language* of 1987, make a distinction between slang and vogue words. Vogue words are usually new combinations or new senses of already existing words that come to national prominence very quickly from nonjocular uses in government, business, education, entertainment, and the like. Some recent examples of vogue words are *behavior disorder*, *bottom line*, *damage control*, *user-friendly*, and *wellness program*. "Vogue expressions demonstrate that their users are socially or professionally *with it*" (xxiii). The Persian Gulf War brought several words into vogue in 1990 and 1991. Suddenly elementary school children in the United States could use correctly such words as *deployment*, *sortie*, and *scud missile*, and the slangy *mother of all* ———— 'quintessence' got applied to everything from parades to pizzas.

Slang is also not an "improper" grammatical construction—like *Winstons taste good like a cigarette should* or *between you and I*—or an objectionable form like *ain't* or *irregardless*. The use of a slang term rarely violates sentence structure. For example, the slang word *bogart* 'steal' takes the regular past tense ending and functions like a verb in "Joey *bogarted* my sweatpants again." Objections to the use of slang are matters of social appropriateness and not grammar.

Cant or argot, the specialized and sometimes secret language of thieves and other groups that operate on the fringes of the law, has contributed many items to the general slang and colloquial vocabulary of English (Maurer 1981, 195–233). The argot of the racetrack, for instance, is responsible for *piker* 'small time gambler', *ringer* 'illegally substituted horse', *shoo-in* 'fixed race, easy win', and others. Often words acquired from argot have lost their specific connection with the questionable activity that gave rise to them. Today one can *OD* 'overdose' on legal substances like ice cream as well as on drugs. Other generalized expressions that originated in argot are *clip joint* 'business establishment that overcharges', *close to the vest* 'incommunicative', *cold turkey* 'total and abrupt deprivation', *junkie* 'addict', and *stool pigeon* 'informer'. But not all groups that contribute to the slang or colloquial vocabulary of English are associated with the underworld. For example, *in the cellar* 'in last place' comes from sports fans, *tubular* 'excellent' from surfers, *scuttlebutt* 'gossip' from sailors, and *Smokey the Bear* 'highway patrol officer' from truckers.

Slang is mainly words or groups of words, though body language and the sounds used are often important in conveying the meaning of slang expressions. For instance, the term *L7* for 'a socially inept person, a *square*' should be accompanied by the thumb and index finger of one hand (shaped like an *L*) joining the index finger and thumb of the other (shaped like a *7*) to form a square. Other expressions must be said with specific combinations of pitch, stress, and pauses. *Gouda, gouda, gouda,* a signal that someone who is *cheezy* (an *L7*) is approaching, is intoned in measured alternations of stressed and unstressed syllables to imitate a pulsing alarm. Although, for the most part, slang items conform to the general constraints on sound combinations that govern the English language, the venturesome spirit behind much slang includes playing with sounds (see Chapter 2). Onomatopoeia or echoism, mock dialect and foreign pronunciations, and rhyming account for many slang terms. The intonation with which something is said can indicate to the hearer that it is to be taken as slang: in their slang interpretations a *wicked* car, a *mean* machine, and a *bad* dress are all 'good'.

Syntax, or sentence structure, is not important in defining slang. Slang expressions are not composed in word order sequences idiosyncratic to slang, and individual slang words and phrases typically fit into an appropriate grammatical slot in an established pattern. For example, the slang verb *bum out* 'cause or experience unpleasant feelings or bad reactions' behaves syntactically like any transitive phrasal verb.

> That bad call *bummed out* the whole team.
> That bad call *bummed* the whole team *out*.
> That bad call *bummed* them *out*.

Nevertheless, UCLA students have found several features of "slang syntax" noteworthy and one or two idiosyncratic, for example, "an unusual affective use of the definite article," as in "Susan set me up with her big brother. She's *the* homie" (Munro 1990, 13).

Users of American English who want to know whether a given word is or is not slang are destined for disappointment. Dictionaries, the ordinary repositories of information about words, are ill equipped to record slang.[4] In large part, slang is short-lived, slippery in meaning, characteristic of marginalized groups, oral, and, most important, defined by social context and situation — all characteristics that militate against slang's showing up frequently and consistently in the files on which dictionaries are based. Nevertheless, *slang* is a label in almost all contemporary American dictionaries of English, although just what the label means and its relationship to other usage labels can vary widely.

In his overview article "American Lexicology, 1942–1973," James B. McMillan pinpoints the source of the labeling problem as a faulty definition of the term *slang*: "Until slang can be objectively identified and segregated . . . or until more precise subcategories replace the catchall label SLANG, little can be done to analyze linguistically this kind of lexis, or to study its historical change, or to account for it in sociolinguistic and psycholinguistic contexts" (1978, 146).

My study of fifty items in *Webster's Third*, five desk dictionaries, and three collections of new words (Eble 1985) confirms the difficulty of categorizing by a system of labels lexical items such as *beat it* 'leave'; *bummer* 'bad experience'; *chow down* 'eat'; *haul ass* 'leave'; and *zap* 'kill, defeat'. Of the fifty items surveyed, only six are labeled *slang* in all sources in which they appear: *boss* 'excellent'; *bread* 'money'; *ice* 'diamonds'; *ralph* 'vomit'; *schmo* 'oaf'; and *toke* 'drag on a marijuana cigarette'.

Sidney Landau, in *Dictionaries: The Art and Craft of Lexicography*, offers an explanation of the situation. "[Slang] is sometimes grouped with the style labels ('formal/informal') and sometimes with the status labels ('standard/nonstandard'), but it does not comfortably fit with either. Slang does not represent a vocabulary that one can adopt to suit a social situation, as one can with terms on the 'formal/informal' index. . . . Slang is deliberately nonstandard" (1984, 189).

The dictionaries of Merriam-Webster use the label *slang* most sparingly, leaving entirely unlabeled lexical items such as *guts* 'courage'; *mooch* 'beg, cadge'; *put down* 'criticize'; and *rap* 'converse'. The absence of a label implies that the word or phrase belongs to the general unremarkable vocabulary of English, whose use conveys no social implications. For example, the absence of labels gives no hint of the nuances signaled by the diction in a sentence like "They were bitching because those macho jocks aced the econ exam," no words of which bear a label in *Merriam-Webster's Tenth*.

The three editions of *The American Heritage Dictionary* (1969, 1982, 1992) and in particular the second unabridged *Random House Dictionary* (1987) edited by Stuart Berg Flexner do better at explaining the nature of slang in the prefatory matter and apply the label more often. For instance, *floozy* 'a gaudily dressed, usually immoral woman'; *fuzz* 'police'; the verb *gold brick* 'loaf'; *jerk* 'fatuous or foolish person'; *scarf* 'eat voraciously'; *schlep* 'lug, move slowly'; *stud* 'virile male'; and *suds* 'beer' are all designated *slang* in both *AHD* and *RHD2* but carry no label in *Merriam-Webster's Tenth*.

Dictionary labeling practices merely confirm the difficulty of categorizing by a system of labels lexical items whose unselfconscious use often depends on attitudinal and situational factors. Although he mentions slang only briefly, in his essay "On Specifying Context: How to Label Contexts and Varieties of Usage" R. R. K. Hartmann calls for the lexicographical treatment of precisely the dimensions that are salient in slang. He suggests that a pragmatic approach to context can provide a unified way to classify the covariance of linguistic form with style, register, regional dialect, sociolect, and the like (1983, 118). Regardless of the exact shape that such a pragmatic approach would take, or the methodology that it would entail, it could then accommodate slang as akin to other linguistic phenomena.

If grammars and dictionaries are to explain language accurately, they must find ways to describe slang. Thus, the definition of slang used by both linguists and lexicographers must incorporate the social, contextual, and rhetorical dimensions inherent in this type of vocabulary.

2: Form

Language, in essence, is the coming together of form and meaning. In other words, sounds intentionally produced using the human vocal organs (form) somehow evoke an interpretation (meaning). Of form and meaning, only form is directly observable, and scientific descriptions of language must take form into account.

The forms, or shapes, of words and expressions in a language usually reveal recurring patterns of organization. Such patterns give speakers the resources to create new forms based on forms already in the language rather than having to coin new words directly from sounds. An example of a productive formal process in English is the addition of the suffix *-er* to a verb to give a noun that means 'one who or that which performs the action of the verb'. Thus, a *programmer* is 'one who programs'; a *surfer* is 'one who surfs'; a *recorder* is 'that which records'; and so forth.

In any language, most new words are formed productively, that is, in conformity with patterns already established in the language rather than by coinage—the invention of a word merely by putting sounds together. Coinage accounts for almost no new words in English. One standard English word often cited as an example of coinage is *blurb* 'a brief publicity notice, as on a book jacket'. American humorist Gelett Burgess is credited with coining *blurb*, which was first attested in 1914. Almost all new words recycle words or parts of words that are already in the language. Words that have recently come into common parlance with the widespread use of computers can illustrate this. *Computer* is a noun formed from the English verb *compute* (which was originally borrowed from Latin) by the addition of the suffix *-er* 'that which'. *Computerize* adds another suffix that changes the derived noun into a different verb. The shortened form *compu-* has become the first part of such words as

compucenter and *compupaper*. The form *computer* has been shortened to merely the letter *c* in *PC*, for *personal computer*. All of
these new words entered English in regular and predictable ways,
making use of productive processes. Moreover, a new word enters
as part of a grammatically related set, or paradigm. Speakers auto-
matically add the correct inflectional suffix required by the context; thus *computerize* becomes *computerizes* 'third person singu-
lar present tense', *computerized* 'past tense and passive participle',
and *computerizing* 'progressive participle'. In addition, *computerize* joins the set of verbs that become nouns by the addition of the
suffix *-ation*, like *organize/organization*.

The slang portion of vocabulary acts no differently. New slang
words and expressions usually arise productively too. Slang ex-
ploits existing forms and their current meanings in various ways,
drawing on and often mixing resources from the sound system,
the word-building processes, paradigms, and the speakers' knowledge of the culture. Thus the general vocabulary item *fraternity*
'brotherhood', for example, yields in slang *frat, fratty, fratty-bagger,
fratrat, fratdom*, and *frat out*—all referring in some way to the
stereotypical behavior of members of a particular kind of male
social organization.

ORDINARY WORD-BUILDING PROCESSES

Some processes mainly entail altering the shape of a word, with
predictable effects on meaning. For English the most important
of these ordinary word-building processes, in descending order of
frequency, are compounding, affixation, functional shift, shortening, and blending (Algeo and Algeo 1991).[1]

Compounding
Compounds are words consisting of parts that are themselves
words, for example, *overdose, piggy bank*, and *night-blooming*.
Speakers generally signal that the two separate words are to be interpreted as a unit by a characteristic pattern of stress in which the
first element is uttered with greater intensity and with no pause or
change in pitch before the second element: *greenhouse* is a compound in "We grew orchids in the *greenhouse*," but *green* and
house are separate words in "We live in the *green house*, not the
white one." The standard written language has no clear-cut rules

for the writing of compound words; they can be written as one word (*overdose*), as two separate words (*piggy bank*), or hyphenated (*night-blooming*). Compound words that modify a following noun are the most likely to be hyphenated: *open-heart surgery, nit-picking regulations, close-captioned programming.* However, reliable dictionaries often differ on the written forms of compounds, for example, *double talk* or *double-talk.*

Compounding is an ancient word-building process in English, evidently already well established when the language was first brought to England by Germanic settlers in the mid-fifth century. Throughout the period of recorded Old English — from roughly the eighth through the eleventh century — compounds were frequent in both poetry and prose. Some English compounds of that era were *daegraed* (day + red) = 'dawn'; *mildheortness* (mild + heartness) = 'mercy'; and *modcraeft* (mind + skill) = 'intelligence'. Many words that were compounds in Old English have remained in the language but are no longer obviously compounds. Normal changes in the sounds over the years have hidden their separate components. Thus, current English *lord* no longer functions as a compound word, though it is the development of the compound *hlafweard* 'bread keeper' from Old English. Other compounds in which the identity of the individual elements has been lost are *gospel*, from *god* + *spel* 'good + tale'; *sheriff*, from *scir* + *gerefa* 'shire + reeve'; and *steward*, from *sti* + *weard* 'sty + keeper'. In some instances the second elements of compounds have acquired the characteristics of a productive suffix rather than a freestanding form. *Full* and *less* are independent words in current English but with more generalized meanings are also productive suffixes. For example, *-ful* occurs as an adjective-forming suffix in *careful, mindful, mournful,* and *skillful.* *-Less* is a suffix indicating 'lacking in' in *careless, childless, fearless,* and *speechless.*

Compounds can be created from individual words of various parts of speech. Probably the most common type is the NOUN + NOUN pattern: *girlfriend, homeroom, music box, tennis court, wind sock.* Other ordinary patterns are ADJECTIVE + NOUN: *big toe, blacktop, heavy water, short story*; and NOUN + VERB: *baby-sit, clockwork, heart attack, headache, home run, placekick.*

Although they are usually classified as phrases rather than as compound words, many vocabulary items in current English are made from a word of any part of speech plus a short, invariant word like *down, up, in, out*. The same words serve as prepositions or adverbs in other contexts but are usually called particles in this construction. Everyday examples of one of these words functioning as a unit with another word are *slowdown* ("The entire staff participated in the work *slowdown* yesterday"); *look up* ("We looked up his phone number"); *pencil in* ("He asked me to *pencil in* the date for the play"); and *printout* ("The *printout* has the wrong information"). In informal spoken English today the word *out* is added to almost any noun or a verb in its passive participle form, or in a mock passive participle form, to mean 'sated with': "After three hours trying to call up that lost file, I'm *computered out*." "One late flight, a missed connection, and lost luggage — I'm *Eastern Airlined out*" (Canine 1986).

Even though compounds are straightforward in form (WORD + WORD = COMPOUND), that very simplicity gives rise to complexity in meaning. Compounds are underspecified: the elements are merely juxtaposed with few or no clues about the grammatical or semantic relationship between the parts. They are like shrunken sentences with nonessential words omitted; information that can be readily inferred is not specified. In a compound made of a NOUN + VERB, for example, the noun could be in a subject relation to the verb, as in *headache* (from someone's *head* [subject] *aches* [verb]); in an object relation to the verb, as in *nitpick* (from someone *picks* [verb] *nits* [object]); or in a locational relation to the verb, as in *waterski* (from someone *skis* [verb] on the *water* [object of locative preposition]). Similarly, the reverse order of grammatical elements, VERB + NOUN, yields, for example, the adjective meaning 'rapid, dangerous' in *breakneck* (from someone *breaks* [verb] *neck* [object]) and the noun *floatplane* (from the *plane* [subject] *floats* [verb]). Compounds of a NOUN + NOUN have an even greater range of relational possibilities, particularly because noun and verb forms can be identical. Thus compounds made of nouns can have unspecified subject-verb and object-verb relationships, as in *raindrop* (the *rain* [subject] *drops* [verb]) and *beartrap* (something *traps* [verb] *bears* [object]). In a compound like *speed bump*, the *bump* [subject] hinders *speed* [object]. Sometimes the unspecified information for a compound is more complicated: a *box score* is a statistical record, or *score*, of a sporting event presented in tabular form in a rectangle, or *box*, in a newspaper; that is, the *box* [subject] contains the *scores* [object].

In a series of compounds with the same last element, the relationship with the first element can differ. An *iceman* is someone who brings ice, but a *trashman* is someone who takes trash away; movement is not specified in either compound, and the formally similar *chairman* implies no movement at all. A *steamboat* is a boat powered by steam and a *sailboat* is a boat powered by wind caught in a sail, but a *shrimpboat* is a boat for catching shrimp, and a *gravy boat* is not a boat at all but a dish shaped like a boat that holds gravy.

In addition, compounds in English are often figurative, like *lame duck* 'an official in office between the election and the inauguration of a successor'; *hot-blooded* 'passionate'; *red herring* 'distraction from the real issue'; *soap opera* 'a kind of radio or television drama'; *turncoat* 'traitor'; and several already cited above. For many compounds, the meaning depends on specific cultural knowledge. A *no-hitter* in baseball is not simply a game in which batting players have failed to hit the pitched ball; it is a game in which no base hits have been charged against the pitcher.

The ordinary, everyday processes of compounding—with all of their attendant complexities—are a major source of new words in college slang. For many slang items, the WORD + WORD structure is obvious, and in context the meaning can be fairly easily derived from the parts: *all-nighter* 'a session of studying or writing that lasts all night'; *court party* 'a party at Big or Little Fraternity Court on the UNC-CH campus'; *do-right* 'a helpful deed'; *dough-brain* 'someone who acts stupidly or as if not thinking'.

Because college students like to use slang to give freshness to old or predictable information, they will often take a word that can stand by itself and arbitrarily attach it to other words. In its widespread and spontaneous use, the free form tends to lose its specific referent in favor of a more general meaning that can be attached to a wide range of words. In its meaning and its propensity for combining with other forms, the second member of the compound becomes more like a suffix than a free form. For example, the element -*city* indicates merely 'a presence or abundance of', not 'a metropolis', and can be added to almost any kind of word: *cram city* ("Mid-terms next week—*cram city!*"); *dweeb city* ("It's *dweeb city* around here"); *jewelry city* ("Even when she plays tennis, Janis is *jewelry city*"); *tan city* ("The day after spring break it was *tan city*").

Other nouns that operate productively as the second member

of compounds are -*action* 'activity' ("I'm ready for some Chinese *food action*"); -*animal* 'one who does something excessively' ("The *study animals* are complaining about the noise"); -*dude* 'person' ("Somebody pay the *pizza dude*"); -*dweller* 'someone who frequents a particular place' ("I could hardly get into Lenoir Hall because of the *step dwellers*"); -*head* 'person' ("The *potheads* were in the corner mellowing out"); -*machine* 'enthusiast, devotee' ("That *sex-machine* keeps phoning Karen even though I told him she went home this weekend"); -*queen* 'an enthusiast who is female' ("The *datequeen* slept through class this morning and then wanted to copy my notes"); -*wad* 'dense, foolish person (usually attached to a proper noun)' ("*Mikewad* here locked himself out of his room").

A very large number of verbs in slang are formed by the addition of a short, invariant word like *out* or *off* to a word of any part of speech. Although English has dozens of particles available for word building, almost all of the examples in college slang use *out, on, off*, and *up*: *sue out* 'act like a sorority member, or *Sue*'; *harsh on* 'criticize, belittle'; *blow off* 'miss class, ignore responsibility'; *mommy up* 'love, hug, comfort'. In college slang *out* is the most productive particle: *beam out* 'daydream'; *blow out* 'shock, embarrass'; *bomb out* 'fail, perform poorly'; *bum out* 'cause or experience unpleasant feelings or bad reactions'; *burn out* 'become mentally or physically exhausted'; *check out* 'look at, scrutinize'; *chill out* 'relax, calm down'; *crank out* 'produce large amounts of work, energy, volume'; *geek out* 'study hard'; *goob out* 'cause repulsion or disgust'; *jell out* 'relax by doing nothing'; *lay out* 'sunbathe'; *lude out* 'become unable to function or physically incapacitated, sometimes because of drugs'; *phase out* 'become unaware, as if asleep'; *pie out* 'become drunk'; *plastic out* 'assume temporarily an artificial behavior or personality'; *rag out* 'become tired'; *raunch out* 'offend by making sexual remarks or using offensive language'; *rock out* 'play music loudly'; *schiz out* 'lose emotional control, act crazed'; *snort out* 'overeat'; *spaz out* 'lose mental control'; *sue out* 'dress and look like a typical sorority member'; *tang out* 'abandon, put an end to'; *trip out* 'strike as funny, crazy, or extraordinary'; *weird out* 'feel confused and at a loss because of someone's or something's strangeness'; *wig out* 'become astonished'; *wimp out* 'let someone down, fail to live up to a commitment'; *z-out* 'go to sleep'.

Sometimes the word + particle construction is typical of and strengthens the synonymy of a group of related verbs: *blimp out, chow down, grease down, hone out, mow on, munch out, pig out, pork out, snort out, throw down,* and *trough out* all mean 'to eat, usually quickly or in great quantity'.

As in the general vocabulary of English, slang permits the compounding of words of various grammatical classes, with the exact relationship between the parts unspecified. NOUN + NOUN is the dominant pattern: the verb *batcave* 'sleep' (*bat* [subject] lives in a *cave* [object of locative phrase]); *bowhead* 'stereotypical sorority member' (she wears a *bow* [object] on her *head* [object of locative phrase]); *cheeseman* 'socially inept person' (*man* [subject] is *cheezy* [adjective]); *earth daddy* 'older-than-average college-age male with sixties values' (*daddy* 'male of older generation' [subject] values the *earth* [object]); *legman* 'ladies' man' (*man* [subject] admires females' *legs* [object]). Often the second part of a NOUN + NOUN compound is derived from a verb by the suffix *-er*: *buzz crusher* 'anything that destroys a feeling of euphoria' (something *crushes* [verb] one's *buzz* [object]); *ghetto blaster* 'portable stereo tape deck' (the music *blasts* [verb] throughout the *ghetto* [object of locative phrase]); *mountain climber* 'high induced by drugs' (someone *climbs* [verb] *mountain* [object]); *rice burner* 'Japanese motorcycle' (motorcycle *burns* [verb] *rice* [object]). *Redneck* 'stereotypical rural southerner' and *big time* 'to a superlative degree' show the ADJECTIVE + NOUN pattern. *Jambox* and *boogiebox*, both meaning 'portable stereo tape deck', combine VERB + NOUN. Some compounds are grammatically ambiguous. *Facerape* 'kiss passionately' can be analyzed NOUN + VERB or NOUN + NOUN. *Lose move* 'stupid action' can be VERB + VERB or VERB + NOUN.

The underspecified relationship between the words that constitute a compound makes the compound a likely form for figurative interpretation, and compounds in slang often rely on metaphor, metonymy, allusion, cultural knowledge, and other kinds of indirect reference. *Dead soldier* is a metaphor for 'empty beer container' and *wounded soldier* for 'a partially emptied' one. *Plastic cow* 'nondairy creamer' is built on the metonymic connection between *cow* and *cream*. *Sofa spud* 'person who lies around doing nothing' alludes to the well-established *couch potato*, whereas *lunchbox* 'someone who is out of touch with reality' is a development from the synonymous *out to lunch*. *Ozone ranger*, a synonym of *lunchbox*, alludes to the radio and television character the Lone Ranger. Figurative meaning in slang is discussed more fully in Chapter 3.

Affixation

Affixation by prefixes and suffixes allows the English language limitless opportunities for the development of open-ended sets such as *reassemble, reconvene, reissue, resubmit,* based on the prefix *re-,* or *cautiously, deeply, quickly, vacantly,* based on the suffix *-ly.* Slang uses many of the same prefixes and suffixes as general purpose English does but sometimes with greater freedom and slightly different meanings or grammatical consequences.

Prefixes in English tend to have easily paraphrased meanings, like *anti-* 'against' in *antiaircraft; inter-* 'between' in *interstate; pre-* 'before' in *predate;* and *un-* 'not' in *unconvincing.* Many English prefixes are the result of borrowing from Greek or Latin, like *bio-* 'life' in *biostatistics; geo-* 'earth' in *geophysics; semi-* 'half' in *semicircle;* and *trans-* 'across' in *transcontinental.* Often words built with such prefixes are part of the learned or technical vocabulary of the language.

Two productive prefixes in recent use in college slang are *mega-* 'a great amount of' and *perma-* 'permanent'. *Mega-* (from Greek *megas* 'great') has long had a place in English in learned words like *megalith* and in scientific vocabulary like *megacycle* and *megahertz.* In college slang *mega-* combines freely with a large range of ordinary words to yield such results as *megabitch* ("That teacher is such a *megabitch*"), *megabooks, megabucks, meganap, megawash,* and *megawork. Perma-,* a shortening of *permanent,* is a combining form with the same meaning in *permafrost* and *permapress.* In college slang it inspires *permagrin* ("After just two beers she had *permagrin*"), *permagross, permanerve,* and *permaproblem.*

English tends to encode grammatical information at the ends of words. Thus suffixes are likely to give information about the grammatical class of a word. For example, the suffix *-ness* indicates that a noun has been made from an adjective, as in *kindness, thoroughness,* and *thoughtfulness; -ize* marks verbs, as in *computerize, evangelize,* and *legalize; -al* changes a noun into an adjective, as in *central, national,* and *remedial.*

The favorite productive suffix of college slang is a favorite in the general vocabulary as well, the noun-forming *-er* 'one who or that which'. Some of the slang items built by the addition of *-er* are *bummer* ('that which *bums* one *out*') 'depressing experience' ("Studying on Thursday nights is a *bummer*"); *crasher* 'one who cannot tolerate alcohol'; *cruiser* 'one who is seeking the company of a member of the opposite sex'; *doper* 'that which is associated with marijuana smoking' ("The *doper* music is loud tonight"); *killer* 'excellent' ("That guy has one *killer* jump shot"); and *wanker* 'undesirable person, thing, or situation' ("Don't read that book—it's a real *wanker*"). Another frequently used suffix is adjective-forming *-y*, equivalent to the *-y* that changes the noun *trend* into the adjective *trendy*. College slang has *dorky, fratty, freaky, geeky, groovy, lunchy, spacey, squirrelly*, and others.

In the mid- and late 1980s the suffix *-age* in college slang gave rise to many spontaneous locutions, often preceded by the qualifiers *major* or *massive*: *foodage* ("I'm desperate for *foodage*"); *fundage* ("My parents didn't come through with the *fundage*"); *scoopage* 'potential date material' ("Is Joe *scoopage*?"); *studyage* ("I have to do some massive *studyage* tonight"); *rainage* (Q: "How's the weather?" A: "*Rainage*"). It is difficult to extract a consistent meaning for *-age* in these uses, except for the effect of changing the word to which it is added into an abstract and mass noun. Two suffixes appear to be indicators of repetition or intensity: *-omatic*, as in *cramomatic* ("I have to *cramomatic* for Dr. O'Connor's English test"), *dunkomatic, jamomatic, jogomatic*; and *-orama*, as in *barforama* ("She gave us a fourteen-page take-home test—*barforama*!"), *funorama, geekorama*, and *sexorama*.

Other productive suffixes used to form in-group vocabulary are *-aholic* 'a person who indulges excessively in the noun to which the suffix is attached', as in *bookaholic, caffeinaholic, foodaholic*, and *hoopaholic*; *-dom* 'the domain of', as in *fratdom, geekdom*, and *jockdom*; and *-fest* 'an abundance of', as in *beerfest, pizzafest*, and *sleepfest*.

Functional Shift

The vocabulary resources of the English language are made more flexible by the ability of English words to shift in grammatical function without undergoing an alteration in form. English is amenable to functional shift because current English has relatively few forms that identify a word as belonging to a particular grammatical category. For instance, a word like *step* gives no formal clues about its grammar. Examined out of context simply as a form, *step* could be a verb, noun, adjective, or adverb. In context as a verb, "*Step* to the right, please," or as a noun, "Be careful of the broken *step*," the form is identical. For this reason, a word that enters English as a member of one grammatical class can quickly shift to another class. Historically, this is what happened with *instance*, *loot*, *stucco*, and *trash*, all of which entered English as nouns but have become verbs as well. *Export*, *shiver*, and *read*, by contrast, entered as verbs and took on an additional function as nouns. The shifting from one grammatical category to another without change in form is considered clumsy usage by some authorities, who object to the use of words such as *contact* and *impact* as verbs because they were established in the language as nouns and also because verbs meaning the same thing already exist.

Speakers of English often make use of functional shift in conversation when they shift the part of speech of a word with no lasting effects on the vocabulary. The most common spontaneous shift is from noun to verb: "I *aspirined* myself enough to make it through the rehearsal"; "He *saxophoned* his way across the South"; "I just *pigstied* my apartment all during exams." In writing, such creative shifts are usually contrived for effect, but in the spoken language they are much less deliberate and not likely to be repeated.

Yet sometimes a shifted form does catch on, in slang just as in the language in general. Nouns shift to verbs in *flag* 'make the grade F' ("I'm afraid I *flagged* that test"); *scope* 'look for members of the opposite sex' ("Mack spent the afternoon sitting on Jock Wall *scoping*"); *potato* 'lie around doing nothing' ("I just want to *potato* all weekend"); and *x* 'stop or eliminate' ("My mom *x-ed* my idea about hitchhiking to Florida"). In *my bust* 'my fault'; *raise* 'parents'; and *skips* 'tennis shoes' verbs have shifted to nouns. An adjective shifts to a noun in *my bad* 'my fault' and to a verb in *harsh* 'criticize, belittle' ("I can't stand the way that James keeps *harshing* on Carole"). A more complicated shift results in the adjective/adverb *later* becoming a verb meaning 'put an end to a relationship', as in "Jennifer's boyfriend *latered* her the week before the pledge formal." It most likely derives from the popular use of *later* for 'good-bye', a shortened form of the nonliteral farewell *see you later*. Another devious derivation that relies on functional shift is presented by the adjective *hulked* 'angry', as in "I was so *hulked* at John for breaking the exercise bike." It is formed on the passive participle of a verb in the same way that adjectives like *painted, locked,* and *closed* are. The verb must be *hulk,* functionally shifted from the noun *hulk.* The meaning 'angry' for *hulked* was inspired by a television character who was transformed by anger into a being of superhuman size and strength in *The Incredible Hulk.*

Shortening

By the process of shortening, sounds are eliminated from words without an immediate change in meaning. Everyday English is filled with such abbreviated forms: *phone* from *telephone, TV* from *television, radar* from *radio detecting and ranging,* and many others. Shortened forms are often less formal than the longer sources from which they are derived and thus can convey a casual and sometimes sardonic attitude toward the subject. An *anthro exam* does not seem so daunting as an *anthropology examination*; a *hyper* child does not seem so pathological as a *hyperactive* one. *Veep,* from *vice president,* and *CREEP,* from the *Committee to Re-Elect the President,* may be suitable for headlines but not for letterhead. Because of association with the less formal and less carefully crafted levels of language use, the process of shortening has been condemned as slovenly and imprecise by language guardians over the centuries. The noun *mob* was quite objectionable in the early eighteenth century when the literate were still aware that *mob* was a shortening of the Latin phrase *mobile vulgus* 'moving crowd'. And even at present, some dictionaries and usage guides warn against use of the shortened *quote* as an acceptable substitute for *quotation.*

When words are shortened, sounds can be eliminated from the beginning (*airplane* > *plane*) or end (*graduate* > *grad*) or both (*influenza* > *flu*). Sometimes, over the years, the newer shortened form and the original longer form diverge in meaning. For instance, *fan* and *fanatic* are no longer synonyms, even though many fans are fanatic; and in American English a *van* is a 'large, one-compartment, covered vehicle for transporting people or equipment', whereas a *caravan* is 'a procession of vehicles or pack animals'.

In an extreme form of shortening, words are made from the initial letters of the words in a phrase. Words like *IRS* (*Internal Revenue Service*), *NBA* (*National Basketball Association*), and

SAT (*Scholastic Aptitude Test*) are pronounced by naming the individual letters. In others, like *AIDS* (*acquired immune deficiency syndrome*), *HUD* (*Housing and Urban Development*), and *zip code* (*zone improvement plan code*), the letters are pronounced together as a word.

All types of shortening are evident in college slang. The most frequent pattern of clipping is the loss of sounds from the ends of words: *bod*, from *body*; *boheme* and *boho*, from *bohemian*; *bourgie*, from *bourgeois* 'someone who is bourgeois, superficial, pretending to be with it'; *bro* and *broth*, from *brother*; *cazh*, from *casual*; *coke*, from *cocaine*; *feeb*, from *feeble* 'dull-witted or absent-minded person'; *friz*, from *Frisbee*; *ho*, from *whore* 'promiscuous or seductively dressed female'; *home*, from *homeboy* or *homegirl* 'person from the same hometown, good friend'; *hyper*, from *hyperactive*; *j*, from *joint* 'marijuana cigarette'; *joe*, from *Joseph Schlitz Brewing Company* 'beer'; *max*, from *maximum*; *mesc*, from *mescaline*; *narc*, from *narcotics agent*; *obno*, from *obnoxious*; *presh*, from *precious* 'favorable, enjoyable'; *rad* 'excellent', from *radical*; *spaz*, from *spastic* 'clumsy person, usually said jokingly'; *vibes*, from *vibrations* 'inaudible signals that people and places emit'; *vid*, from *videotape*.

Slang words formed by clipping sounds from the beginning of the word are *brary*, from *library*; *do*, from *hairdo*; *file* 'show off, dress up', from *profile*; *rents*, from *parents*; *ted* 'drunk', from *wasted*; *tives*, from *relatives*; the verb *use*, from *abuse*; *za*, from *pizza*; *zoid* 'fan of punk rock music and styles', from *freakazoid*. *Preesh*, from *appreciate*; *twize*, which rhymes with *wise*, from the pronunciation of *-dweise-* in *Budweiser*; and *welk*, from *you're welcome*, show clipping from both directions. *A-box*, from *attitude box*, shows clipping from the first word in a compound; it refers to someone who is *throwing attitude*, or who is 'in a bad mood'. *Rotic*, from *romantic*, has dropped *man* from the middle and means 'romantic without the man', as in "This sunset is very rotic."

Two kinds of shortening reduce words to letters. The dominant type in college slang is initialism, which names the individual letters: *BFE* (*bum fucking Egypt*) 'in the middle of nowhere, far away'; *DDFMG* (*drop dead fuck me gorgeous*) 'very attractive member of the opposite sex'; *DHC* (*deep, heavy conversation*); *DTR* (*defining the relationship*); *GH* (the soap opera *General Hospital*); *GQ* (*Gentlemen's Quarterly*) 'fashionably dressed'; *HD* (military designation *husband dependent*) 'male who mooches off a female'; *KO* (*kick off*) 'die'; *MDG* (*mutual desire to grope*) 'strong physical attraction'; *MLA* (*massive lip action*) 'passionate kissing'; *MRA* (*massive reeb action*) 'unsociable behavior'; *NBD* (*no big deal*); *NC* (*no class*) 'a boorish person'; *NCAA* (*no class at all*), pronounced NC Double A, an allusion to the acronym for the National Collegiate Athletic Association; *NTO* (*not the one*) 'date who does not come up to expectations'; *NTS* (*name tag shaker*) 'an attractive male that makes a female's heart beat so fast that her name tag shakes'; *OOC* (*out of control*) 'drunk, high on drugs, or acting crazy'; *OTL* (*out to lunch*) 'inattentive, unaware'; *OTR* (*on the rag*, allusion to menstruation) 'snappish, in a bad mood'; *PDK* (*polyester double knit*) 'someone who is out of date or out of touch'; *PIB* (*people in black*) 'brooding, gloomy teenager who wears dark clothes and listens to alternative music about death'; *PMS* (*premenstrual syndrome* or *putting up with men's shit*) 'feel annoyed'; *PQ* (*polyester queen*) 'someone who is out of date'; *R&I* (*radical and intense*) 'extremely exciting or enjoyable'; *SAB* (*social airhead bitch*); *SOL* (*shit out of luck*); *TSH* (*that shit happens*); *VPL* (*visible panty lines*).

Acronyms in which the letters are pronounced together as a word are much less frequent: *fubar* (*fucked up beyond all recognition*) 'unattractive, suffering the ill effects or alcohol or drugs'; *moto* (*master of the obvious*); *nail* (*nice ass in Levi's*) 'well-built male'; *Rotsi* (*Reserve Officers Training Corps*); *tan* (*tough as nails*); *tom* (*totally obedient moron*) 'computer'; and *The Ugly* (*the undergraduate library*). *Phat*, which students always insist is spelled with *ph-* rather than *f-*, means 'having a curvaceous figure' and is said to be from either *pretty hips and thighs* or *pretty hips, ass, tits*. The acronym of *No shit, Sherlock* 'too bad' is cleverly NS^2, pronounced N-S-Squared.

In a reverse process, an established acronym or letter name can be expanded. *ABC store* (from *Alcoholic Beverage Control Store*) becomes *Aunt Betsy's Cookie Store*, *MD* (from *Mogen David 20/20*) becomes *Mad Dog*, and *WG's* for 'clothes issued by *Wollen Gym*' have become *Weegies*. *Ace* 'the grade A', *Dog* 'the grade D', and *Zoo* 'the lowest grade possible, Z' are straightforward expansions. *Flag* for 'the grade F' relies on the shape of the letter as well, but *Hook* for 'the grade C' refers only to the shape and is not an expanded acronym.

Blending

A combination of shortening and compounding, the process of blending puts together pieces of words and their meanings. Thus *brunch* is formed from *breakfast* and *lunch* and means 'a meal that combines breakfast and lunch'. Blends are currently popular in English in names created for food products, for example, *beanburger*, *charbroiled* burgers, *cranapple* juice, and *croissan'wich*. Although blends are fashionable in the marketplace, college slang makes little use of this process of word formation, with only about a dozen examples collected since 1972: *buel* (*body* + *fuel*) 'food, to eat voraciously'; *droned* (*drunk* + *stoned*) 'unaware because of alcohol or drugs'; *froyo* (*frozen yogurt*); *homechop* (*homeboy/homegirl* + *lambchop*) 'endearing term for a close friend, usually of the opposite sex'; *polislide* (*political science* + *slide*) 'easy political science course'; *scrump* (*screw* + *bump*) 'have sex'; *spadet* (*space* + *cadet*) 'student preoccupied with studies'; *slorch* (*slut* + *whore* + *bitch*); *spork* (*spoon* + *fork*) 'eating implement'; *sweave* (*swerve* + *weave*); *trendinistas* (*trendy* + *Sandinistas*) 'political or social activists who combine heightened political consciousness with stylish clothing'; *vomatose* (*vomit* + *comatose*) 'disgusting'.

BORROWING

An important source of new words throughout the documented history of English has been borrowing. In standard dictionaries of English, only a minority of the words listed have developed from native sources. Most come instead—in whole or in part—from Latin, Greek, or French. In general, the more formal and technical vocabulary of English has been either borrowed directly or constructed by compounding or affixation from forms that were originally Greek or Latin—words like *aesthetics*, *aerodynamics*, *canine*, *ego*, *fluorocarbon*, *literature*, *pedestrian*, *permutation*, and *photography*. Such words tend to be used in writing and for the transmission of information rather than for phatic communication and are usually learned in the classroom or by reading. Most current English words from foreign sources are well established in the language, for acquisition of new words by borrowing has diminished in recent centuries. In the Algeos' accounting of the sources of new words in American English, 1941–91, borrowing is responsible for only 2 percent (1991, 14).

Borrowing from foreign languages is not a feature of slang in general or of college slang. This is not surprising. By its very nature slang is not outreaching and cosmopolitan, for its primary function is to bind people of similar persuasions. Scholarly borrowings such as those from Greek and Latin that so increased the standard and technical vocabulary of English simply have no place in slang, not even in the slang of earnest university students. Foreign borrowings in college slang are, for the most part, confined to greetings and playful mispronunciations and are reminders of beginning classes in foreign language when students are trying desperately to make sense of and remember the strange jumble of sounds inundating them. Thus they take into their slang expressions like *osmosis amoebas* 'good-bye', formed on the Spanish farewell *adios amigos*.

Slang does borrow from a second language that is part of the culture, but for American English only Yiddish has been a noteworthy contributor. Dialect borrowing has been the most important type of borrowing in American slang, with the largest number and best-known items coming from African American speech communities. Borrowing in slang is discussed more fully in Chapter 4.

PROCESSES PARTICULARLY SUITED TO SLANG

Although the same ordinary word-building processes that give rise to the general vocabulary also shape slang expressions, the form of slang items can be additionally affected by other linguistic factors particularly suited to the aims of slang. This section discusses three kinds of pressure to which slang forms are susceptible — patterns of sounds, patterns of meanings, and multiple and mistaken etymology. The last two are semantic phenomena that can be important in determining the shape that a slang term will have.

Playing with Sounds

The role of phonology as a productive impetus in slang should not be underestimated. Manipulating sounds for fun is consistent with the flippant, venturesome spirit of much slang use. Hence the polite apology *Excuse me* is playfully pronounced *Screws me*, *Squeeze me*, or *Exsqueeze me*. The farewell *Later* expands by rhyme to the improbable *Later, tater!* (undoubtedly also motivated by the picturesque "See you later, alligator. After while, crocodile" made popular by a 1950s rock-n-roll song by Bill Haley and the Comets).

The dormitory named *Granville Towers* has two bynames, depending on which syllable is altered—*Grand Vile* and *Grossville*.

Onomatopoeia, or echoism or imitation of sound, accounts for many slang terms, including these for 'vomit'—*barf, buick, earl, ralph,* and *yuke*. Other echoic forms from college slang are *jing* 'money' (from *jingle*) and *sssss*—, a hissing sound to indicate that an *airhead* 'someone who lacks common sense' is emitting the contents of his or her brain, air. Linguist Roger Wescott (1977, 1978) has noticed that some sounds appear to give words a slangier flavor—most noticeably *z* in words like *zazzy* from *jazzy, scuz* from *scum,* and *zap* from *slap* or *whap*; and the sound of *oo* replacing a vowel in words such as *cigaroot* from *cigarette* and *bazooms* from *bosom* or added to the end of a word like *smasheroo* from *smasher*.

Wescott is an advocate of phonosemy, or sound symbolism— the notion that particular sounds may of themselves correlate with particular meanings.[2] He suggests that sounds made with the lips (labials) and sounds made at the back of the mouth (velars) often connote derogation. He shows that in sets of terms for tabooed objects and actions and in derogatory terms for ethnic, racial, and other stigmatized groups, the degree of labiality and velarity is greater than that occurring in most semantic domains (1971, 123–25). A word like *gook,* for example, which in general English can refer to 'gooey or sticky stuff' or can be an offensive term for 'an Asian', begins and ends with a velar consonant and has a back vowel pronounced with lip rounding. The phonology itself signals that the meaning of the form includes unpleasant or derogatory connotations. Wescott strengthens his claim by pointing out that a particular term may have more than one denotation, yet the connotations are consistently negative. For example, whether *bum* is a verb meaning 'feel depressed' or a noun referring to 'an unemployed drifter' or 'the buttocks', the connotations are still unfavorable (125).

Because slang tends to be negative, it is not surprising that many slang terms contain labial and velar sounds. A canonical example from college slang is *wanker* 'an undesirable person, situation, or thing' and the related retort *wank!,* supposedly formed in imitation of the buzzer on the television show *Truth or Consequences. Wank* begins with a consonant that is both labial and velar and ends with two velar consonants. In the hostile college slang expression *bunk you,* a euphemism for *fuck you, bunk* begins with a labial and ends with two velars. The verb *bungo* 'seriously mistreat or inflict injury on' is similar in both sound and meaning to *bunk*. Many slang synonyms for 'loser' likewise contain labial and velar sounds: *goob*, a clipping of *goober*, begins with a velar consonant and ends with a labial with a back, lip-rounded vowel in between; *gweeb* begins with a velar *g* and a labio-velar *w* and ends with a labial *b*; *quad* begins with velar *k* and labio-velar *w*. In *wimp* 'weak, indecisive person' and *feeb* 'dull-witted or absent-minded person' all of the consonants are labials. *Punk* 'someone or something worthless' begins with a labial and ends with two velars, whereas *quimp* 'socially inept person' begins velar and ends labial. The adjective *bogus* 'undesirable, unappealing' has a labial and a velar consonant joined by a lip-rounded back vowel. *Dook* 'something unpleasant or worthless' and *dookie* 'someone obnoxious' omit the front glide pronounced before the vowel in *duke* (as in rival Duke University) to make the word sound more derogatory. Labio-velarity is prominent in college slang. Additional examples can be found in many subject areas, particularly in terms for members of the opposite sex (*babe*, *hunk*) and for sex (*boff*, *bong*, *bonk*, *bop*, *bump uglies*, *grub*, and *pork*). In matters pertaining to sex the prevailing contemptuous attitude appears to be aided by the prevalence of forms containing labial and velar sounds.

Rhyming is the favorite sound effect of slang. For example, from general American slang come *brain drain* 'the loss of intellectual and educated people from a community because of a lack of opportunity' and *boob tube* 'television'. The rhymers par excellence have been the Cockneys from London, who have developed an elaborate and colorful repertoire of slang terms based on rhyme. Straightforward examples are *trouble and strife* for 'wife' and *mince pies* for 'eyes'. But most Cockney rhyming slang involves a shortening process in which the rhyme word is not expressed: *elephant* means 'drunk', from *elephant's trunk*; *plates* means 'feet', from *plates of meat*; and *Godfer* means 'child', from *God forbid*, which rhymes with 'kid' (Ashley 1977, 124–27). Examples of rhyme from college slang are *balls to the walls* 'a tense if not frantic time or situation that requires the ability to fight back'; *beat the feet* 'hurry up'; *cheesy, sleazy, greasy* 'female of questionable reputation'; *dressed to impress* 'well-dressed'; *fag hag* 'heterosexual female who associates with gay males'; *fake and bake* 'get a tan in a tanning booth'; *godsquad* 'people who evangelize on campus'; *groomed to zoom* 'well-dressed'; *hell dwell* 'have a good time drinking and partying at local pubs'; *jap scrap* 'motorcycle; appliance made in Japan'; *nutter butter* 'someone who is unaware or inattentive'; *pit sit* 'sit on the steps of the Pit between classes'; *pop tops* 'drink beer'; *rocks for jocks* 'an easy geology course'; *sight delight* 'good-looking male'; *slop shop* 'any campus snack bar'; *stylin' and profilin'* 'very well dressed and groomed'; *take a chill pill* 'calm down, relax'; *tighty whities* 'men's briefs'; *whatever floats your boat*, an expression of acceptance 'okay'.

Alliteration marks *bad bongos* 'situation in which things do not go well'; *Bible beater* 'evangelizing fundamentalist Christian'; *Birkenstock buddy* 'environmentalist'; *blimp boat* 'obese person'; *brain burp* 'random thought'; *Carolina Crunge* 'contagious flu-like illness that spreads throughout campus a couple of times a year'; *group gropes* 'encounter groups'; *peace person* 'someone who identifies with the antiwar movement of the 1960s'; *polyester princess* 'female who dresses out of fashion'; *rip the rug* 'dance'; *romper room* 'place to get rowdy'; *thunder thighs* 'overweight person'; *virgin vault* 'residence hall for females'; and *Woodstock wannabe* 'someone with the sensibilities and style of the 1960s'. The repetition of vowel sounds can be heard in *lose move* 'stupid act', *scooby-doo* 'someone who eats a lot and never gains weight', *space case* 'someone who is out of touch with reality', and *waste case* 'drunkard'. Vowel alternation is heard in *schnicky-schnacky* 'public display of affection'. Indeed, a kind of ablaut (as in the alternating vowels of current English *sing, sang, sung,* and other irregular verbs) seems to characterize variant forms for the same notion. For example, the slightly different *ook, yuke, yuck,* and *yak* all mean 'vomit'; and *whipped* (from *pussy-whipped*) has inspired *whooped* and *whupped* too for 'unduly controlled by a female'.

Although most North Carolina students have a distinctly regional accent themselves, they enjoy mock dialect pronunciations and spellings like *wrought iron* for the exclamation *Right on!*; *Raw's* for *Roy Rogers Restaurant*; and *shoot the peel* for 'play basketball', in which *peel* is a dialect approximation of *pill*, a metaphor for the ball. They also enjoy creating mock learned words that sound like polysyllabic borrowings from Greek or Latin: *motivate* or *motorvate* 'move around socializing in a group, leave'; *matriculate* 'start a trip'; *emboosticated* 'embarrassed'. Superfluous combining forms like *-age* ("I'll have to ask my parents for more *fundage"*) and *-factor* 'the abundance of' ("What is the *book-factor* for English 36?") are modeled on and poke fun at overblown bureaucratic or learned usage.

The choice of pronunciation for a slang term can be conditioned by the sound of a form already in the language. There need be no semantic link. This seems the situation in the expression *Come in, Berlin*, which simply means 'pay attention', where *Berlin* is chosen not merely for its distance but mainly for its rhyme. *Brr rabbit* is a complaint about the cold. It expands the common *brr* that imitates shivering from the cold by means of matching it to one of the few set constructions in English that contains the sound /br/, the name of that clever inhabitant of the brier patch, *Br'er Rabbit*. *Rabbit* has no other significance in the complaint about the cold. *Ozone ranger* 'a person who is up in the ozone, out of touch with reality' undoubtedly acquired the element *ranger* by association via rhyme with the *Lone Ranger*. *Gril* 'an affectionate noun of address to another female' playfully reverses the internal sounds of *girl*, much like deliberately pronouncing *pervert* with the second and third sounds reversed as *prevert*. Sometimes the connection to the already existing sequence of sounds that triggers a slang term is not entirely arbitrary. *Stupid Health* and *Student Hell* for 'Student Health Services' are phonological deviations that convey students' frustrations with their medical care. *Out of state*, a synonym formed on *out of sight*, may be merely an already established, phonologically proximate sequence handy as a target form. However, on a campus at which the status *out-of-state* is likely to be expensive, the link with *out of sight* may not be purely arbitrary. In North Carolina, where there is no distinction between the pronunciation of *pin* and *pen*, it is probably inevitable that *Spencer Dormitory* for women would be called *Spinster Dormitory*. The pronunciation of the acronym for Reserve Officers Training Corps (*ROTC*) as /rotsi/ with the first syllable the same as *rot* can hardly escape pejorative connotations.

Semantic Fields

Just as associations between forms influence productivity, so do links in meaning.[3] Vocabulary items that evoke some common element of meaning can be said to belong to the same semantic field; thus words as different as *raft, bicycle, bus, train, floatplane, moped*, and *747* are all realizations of the unifying abstraction, or semantic field, of transportation. Once a concept is expressed in the vocabulary of a given semantic field, that field provides a related set of vocabulary items that are readily available, with some innovation and alteration in form, for use in expressing related concepts. For example, from the semantic field health foods comes the name of a kind of nutritious cereal, *granola*, to refer to 'someone who identifies with the styles and concerns of the 1960s'. *Granola* triggers an association with other kinds of health foods, which in turn inspire alternate forms for indicating 'someone who identifies with the styles and concerns of the 1960s': *granola-groid, crunchy granola, crunchy, grape nut, nut-n-berry, rice-and-beaner, earth biscuit,* and *earth muffin.* As another example, *wasted* is a kind of destruction used to characterize 'suffering the effects of alcohol or drugs'. *Toxic waste dump* and *waste product* are associated with the verb *waste* and become synonyms, along with *wasted,* for 'drunk'. The possibility that a semantic field provides an established framework for and somehow shapes the proliferation of vocabulary items is suggested in college slang by the large percentage of terms that can be assigned to a handful of semantic fields. At least 20 percent of the items in my corpus of UNC-CH slang occur in the six large semantic fields air and space, animals, destruction, edibles, motion, and temperature.

The field that I call destruction is the largest and encompasses several hundred slang items built on forms that in general usage refer to kinds of injury, harm, decomposition, or incapacitation: *bite on* 'imitate', *bomb* 'fail', *busted* 'arrested', *crack* 'witty person', *crash and burn* 'sleep', *hit on* 'make sexual overtures', *obliterated* 'drunk', *tore out of the frame* 'drunk', *smashed* 'drunk', *toxic waste dump* 'person who uses drugs', and others. Although the meanings associated with many of these pictures of destruction are scattered in subject area—*crunch* a collective noun for 'females', *eat up* 'fatigued', *eat your heart out* 'be envious', *hit one's head on the ceiling* 'make a mistake', *ripped off* 'cheated', *trash your act* 'stop'—the majority of expressions in this semantic field pertain either to the consequences of indulging in alcohol or drugs or to performing well or poorly in academics or athletics. The semantic field of destruction, therefore, appears to offer producers of slang a ready-made source for the creation of vocabulary to talk about drinking, drugs, and success or failure in schoolwork or sports.

Overindulgers in alcohol or drugs are pictured as the objects of various kinds of destructive processes: heat (*baked, burnt out, toasted*), explosion (*blasted, blown out, blown up, bombed*), breaking (*ripped, smashed, tore out of the frame, wrecked*), and others. In the subject area of schoolwork, the destruction terms can indicate either failure or success. "I *bombed* that last test" means 'did poorly'. "I *blitzed* that last test" means 'performed well'. In other words, the test destroys the taker, or the taker destroys the test. Likewise, to *smoke* a test means 'to do well', and a test that is itself *smokin'*, or is a *smoker*, is 'a difficult one' — one that *kicks ass* 'prevail over something or someone'. Success or failure in performance extends to athletic endeavors as well. When the UNC Tar Heels are *smoking* NC State, the Tar Heels are winning; if they *get smoked*, they have lost. Sometimes the same expression can be used for several of these meanings. *Wasted*, for example, can picture the destructive power of alcohol, drugs, schoolwork, or sports.

The meaning that is most frequently realized by a term from the semantic field destruction is 'drunk or otherwise suffering the effects of alcohol'. Among the synonyms for drunk are *blind, blitzkrieged, blown out, crispy, flipped out, fried, invertebrated, juiced, laid out, messed up, obliterated, ploughed, polluted, ripped out of one's gourd, ripped to the tits, saturated, slammed, smashed, totaled out, trashed, toasted, whipped,* and *wiped out*. Coherence among the terms for 'drunk' is provided not only by the semantic field but also by form. Most of these terms are passive participles in form and grammar: "He was *obliterated* (by two beers)." Often the passive participle is augmented by a particle, usually *out* or *up*: *wiped out, messed up*. Such patterns are probably responsible in part for the creation of other slang synonyms for 'drunk' that are not terms of destruction and have no meaning in the general vocabulary but do conform to some of the phonological characteristics associated with slang and derogatory terms, for example, *smuckered, snockered,* and *zoolooed*.

The use of a semantic field such as destruction for the motivation of terms for a given subject is merely a tendency. The semantic field destruction does not necessarily imply 'drunk', because not every destruction term means 'drunk'. But any destruction term might mean 'drunk' tomorrow. Conversely, not every term for 'drunk' pictures destruction, but the chances are that the next new one will. For English slang the connection between the semantic field destruction and the meaning 'drunk', while far from necessary, lessens the arbitrariness of the connection between form and meaning and predisposes creative users of the language to choose a form for the meaning 'drunk' from a restricted set of already existing forms.

Multiple and Folk Etymology

Form can also be affected by the speakers' notions of the etymology of a word or expression. Sometimes more than one explanation of the origin of a word is plausible—multiple etymology. In other instances speakers make sense of an unfamiliar form by a plausible but incorrect guess at its etymology—mistaken etymology, traditionally called folk etymology.

In "Lexical Polygenesis: Words as Resultants of Multiple Linguistic Pressures," Roger Wescott questions the assumption that every word derives from a single ancestral item and that when several sources seem possible, all except one are false etymologies. Instead, he not only permits but finds more plausible multiple etymology, contending that "in the absence of a plurality of overlapping or mutually reinforcing source forms, most lexemes would not develop or, having developed, would not persist" (1979, 84). Slang and proper names are two lexical areas in which Wescott finds multiple origins most conspicuous.

In the UNC-CH slang collection, for example, *brutus* is 'a mean, ugly person'. Clearly it is related to *brute* 'animal'. But why is the form *brutus* rather than *bruto* or *brutage*? Possibly the allusion is to the treacherous assassin of Julius Caesar or to the stereotypical use of *brutus* as the name for a mean, ugly dog. The likelihood is that all of these sources reinforce each other and contribute to the form and meaning of the term. Another slang term in which multiple etymology seems to be operating is *rents* for 'parents'. It became popular in UNC-CH slang in the early 1980s as a clipping of *parental units*, mock sociological jargon from the Coneheads skit on the television program *Saturday Night Live*. A variant clipped form is *rental unit*, making explicit the financial dependence of students on their parents. The multiple etymology of *rents* is all the more compelling given the national trend of adult, college-educated children of the middle class moving back to their parents' home for financial reasons. The process of making sense of *rents* seems to have gone a step further for some high school students. Teresa Labov reports that one of her subjects in Pennsylvania said that in high school the term was *wrens* (1992, 347). For many American speakers who regularly simplify final consonant clusters, *rents* sounds just like *wrens* and, as a term for parents, must make as much sense. Multiple etymology may likewise be at work in shaping the form and meaning of *zod* 'a person who is stupid or not up on the latest'. *Zod* rhymes with *odd* and with *quad*, which is geometrically related to *square*, which is a well-established slang term that means basically the same thing as *zod*. But *zod* could also be a clipping of *Izod*, the brand of shirts at the height of college fashion a decade ago but now out of style.

Mistaken etymology, better known as folk etymology, is a kind of analogy—a cognitive strategy that makes the unknown fit the pattern of the known, that treats the unfamiliar as familiar or believable. Folk etymology is in essence the same impulse that gives such humorous mistakes from children as *and lead us not into Penn Station* instead of *and lead us not into temptation*, or the parable of *the goodest American* rather than *the good Samaritan*. Malapropisms are simply adult versions of the same attempt to make sense out of new or unfamiliar words. Thus someone unfamiliar with tennis understands that Steffi Graf is *top seated* instead of *top seeded*. As a process affecting the general vocabulary of English, folk etymology applies mostly to foreign words, learned or old-fashioned words, scientific names, and place-names. Trying to hear something familiar in the name of the insect the Spanish named *cucaracha* led English speakers to analyze it as *cockroach*. The second syllable of Old English *aecern* got interpreted as the grain name *corn* in current English *acorn*. And the hybrid primrose technically called *polyanthus* (from the Greek meaning 'many flowers') becomes instead the more familiar woman's name *Polly Andrews* (Palmer 1904).

Folk etymology as just described with reference to the general vocabulary seldom operates in slang, for slang rarely admits foreign, learned, or scientific words—except in jest. But because newness is a prized feature of slang vocabulary, the probability of a slang term being unknown to the hearer is high, triggering the same tendency to reshape form or meaning as do foreign or learned words.

A possible example of folk etymology from college slang is the development of the form *crib course* for 'an easy course'.[4] The phrase *crip course* had been well established in college slang for decades, formed as a clipping of a *cripples' course*, or perhaps a *crippled course*. At the time *crip course* was created, the noun *cripple* for 'someone who is lame' was common. Fashioned from the verb *creep*, the noun *cripple* had been part of the English language for at least six centuries. In the latter half of the twentieth century, the noun *cripple* diminished in use in favor of the adjective *handicapped*, a twentieth-century creation that focuses on the afflicted person's disadvantageous position in society. When the more recent generations of American college students learned *crip course*, they did not make an immediate association with the seldom-used noun *cripple*. Eventually they changed the form to a very similar one, *crib*, for which they could supply a plausible explanation. Jonathan Lighter cites a 1987 University of Tennessee student theme that explains the logic: "The easy courses are called *crib courses* because even a baby could pass them" (1994, 521). In another instance of interpreting the unfamiliar by the familiar, *deep six* 'to put an end to something' has acquired the meaning 'to finish a six-pack of beer'. The notion of 'finish' has been retained from the earlier meaning of the expression, but to those of college age, the most familiar association evoked by the number *six* is beer, not a grave.

The shape of slang expressions is not what makes the slang segment of the English lexicon distinctive. The forms of slang result from the same ordinary word-building processes that produce the general vocabulary.

3: Meaning

Chapter 1 on the definition of slang shows that the characteristics distinguishing slang from other kinds of vocabulary are fundamentally social, and Chapter 2 shows that the slang forms that
bring about such social effects are the result of ordinary processes
of word formation. This chapter on the meaning of slang asks two
questions. What do slang terms mean? How do slang terms get to
mean what they do? The answers to these two questions show that
the meaning of slang supports the characterization of slang as ordinary language with the social implications enhanced.

WHAT DO SLANG ITEMS MEAN?

Slang usually provides an alternative vocabulary for referents
already named in the language. Thus *boob tube* and *idiot box*
entered the English language after *television*, and *to nuke* followed
to microwave. In these examples and others, slang tends to provide
fresh and catchy alternatives laden with connotations and cultural
associations. For instance, 'a dependent spouse or child' can be
called a *crumbsnatcher*; and one slang synonym for 'moped' is *DWI
Harley*, implying that using the less powerful mode of transportation is the result of having one's license revoked for driving while
intoxicated.

Within the vast semantic territory covered by the lexicon, slang
items do not develop in equal distribution. Terms that are not likely
to be used in social and light-hearted contexts are not likely to
beget slang equivalents — for example, abstractions like *trinity* and
oligarchy, technical terms like *chromosome* and *calibrate*, physical phenomena like *gravity* and *evaporation*, and countless words
from specialized subject areas, like *petroglyph* from archaeology

and *phoneme* from linguistics. Of course, if any seemingly neutral or even sacred notion gets tied up with the attitudes, emotions, and self-esteem of people who casually or regularly talk about it together, that notion is liable to trigger slang. Thus hospital personnel who work and talk together in stressful life-and-death situations often develop slang to signal solidarity with one another, like *box* or *tube* for 'die' or *deep fry* for 'chemotherapy'. Slang serves the human and not the occupational needs of the users. Slang in occupational areas—such as computer science, gambling, medicine, navigation, and warfare—varies in particulars that are pertinent to their common activity. Thus *Ada from Decatur* for 'point eight in craps' is useful among dice gamblers, whereas *growzy* to describe a program or machine that is 'slow' is part of the slang of computer users. Such occupational slang generally coexists with a large and precise jargon developed to get the job done.

Slang with nontechnical referents tends to be fairly predictable in its range of meanings, mostly pertaining to relationships with other people. Slang provides users with words for emotional highs (*jamming*) and lows (*bumming*), succeeding (*acing*) and failing (*being throwed*), expressing approval (*killer!*) and disapproval (*no way*). Evaluative terms are plentiful, as slang tends to judge rather than to define (*slimebucket* 'objectionable person', *geek* 'one who studies excessively', *jerk* 'socially inept person'). Slang vocabulary connotes polarities (*awesome* 'superlative' vs. *zero* 'someone with no redeeming virtues') with little gradation on the evaluative scale. Slang rarely takes the middle ground, except for the universally accepted *OK*, which has not inspired a string of synonyms. Derogatory terms for outsiders are common. For instance, a *porch monkey* is a 'black person'; a *soda cracker*, a 'white person'; *UYB* ,'uppity Yankee bitch'; a *frat rat*, a 'member of a fraternity'; and a *Bible beater*, an 'evangelical Christian'. Almost all groups that cultivate slang, even female college students, create or acquire derogatory words for 'women', picturing them as objects (*bacon, box, hosebag, slampiece*) or as animals (*bitch, chick, dog, fox*).

Slang often violates the linguistic taboos of the general culture. For English, the flouting of social norms shows up in the proliferation of slang terms for intimate body parts, bodily elimination, and sex. Current slang terms built on *ass* and *butt* defy the convention that in polite conversation one does not speak about the buttocks. Thus *asshole* and *butthead* are common offensive designations for 'an obnoxious person'. *Buttloads* and *up the butt* mean 'in great quantity', as in "I have buttloads of homework this weekend" or "I have homework up the butt this weekend." The compound *poop-butt* for 'an undesirable person' doubly defies taboo by combining a word for 'excrement' with one for 'buttocks'. Typical of the anti-intellectual bent of slang, mental faculties are also described with words for bodily elimination. A *brain burp* is 'a random thought' ("That was a brain burp if I ever heard one—what in the world are you thinking about?"); and a *brain fart* is a 'temporary loss of memory' ("I'm having such a brain fart—I can't think of my own phone number"). Words that originally referred to the penis are frequent in slang. For instance, a *dork* is 'someone who does not fit in', and most current users are not aware of its original reference to the male anatomy. *Dick*, on the other hand, retains clear association with maleness in the expression *a dick thing*, which means 'characteristically associated with males'. Slang provides numerous verbs for 'to engage in sexual intercourse'. Among those recently in use on college campuses are *bounce refrigerators, bump uglies, do the naked pretzel, get paid, knock boots, scrog,* and *scrump*.

The slang of a group proliferates around topics of importance to that group. Thus prisoners develop terms for one another based on the type of crime for which they are incarcerated. *Baby raper* and *chicken hawk* mean 'child molester'; *crib burglar*, 'someone convicted of breaking and entering a domicile'; and *digger*, 'pick-pocket'. College students, who are perennially preoccupied with the quest for a partner for romance or sex, *cruise, put it in cruise mode, check it out, scam, scope,* or *troll*. Slang users are rarely satisfied with one or two variants. Instead they constantly replenish the store of words to capture the same limited range of meanings with fresh language. The result is a large number of synonyms or near synonyms. These are a few of the many ways that a college student can say 'leave': *blow, blow this popsicle stand, bolt, book, dust, get the heck out of Dodge, jet, motivate, poof,* and *split*.

In a statistical study of the slang items submitted by North Carolina students in twenty-nine consecutive semesters, from fall 1976 through fall 1991, Elisa Fiorenza (1992) identified twenty-seven categories of meaning into which ninety-three of the most frequently submitted slang items fall. In descending order by the number of different slang items per meaning, the meanings can be glossed as 'excellent', 'socially inept person', 'drunk', 'attractive person', 'to insult', 'to relax', 'hello', 'attractive', 'to do well', 'fraternity or sorority member', 'to have a good time', 'to leave', 'to kiss passionately', 'to disregard', 'to eat rapidly', 'exhausted', 'to fail', 'good-bye', 'to get in touch with reality', 'to lose control', 'out of touch', 'person out of touch', 'to pursue for sex', 'to study hard and late', 'worst situation'. In addition, three slang items can be classified as fads (*not* a negation, 'no'; *psyche* 'fooled you'; and *word up* 'I agree') and two others as intensifiers (——— *from hell* and *mega-*) (see Appendix 2).

The range of meanings evoked by the most frequently used college slang items is narrow. Most pertain to types of people and to relationships between and among people. Standards of behavior that one does or does not live up to are implied, as more than one-third of the slang items can be classified as judgments of acceptance or rejection. In meaning, then, college slang reflects the users' preoccupation with sociability.

The meaning of contemporary slang tends to replicate the meaning of slang of the past, except for a small number of slang names for new things. Thus *froyo* for 'frozen yogurt', *microbeer* for 'seven-ounce beer', and *nuke and puke* for 'microwave meal' are fairly recent additions to American eating habits and to slang as well. Francis Grose's 1796 edition of *A Classical Dictionary of the Vulgar Tongue* lists among the expressions used by beggars, thieves, and various sorts of rogues many semantic equivalents of current campus slang. The words are different, but the meanings are the same. When today's college students 'vomit', they *shoot cookies*; similarly indisposed eighteenth-century speakers *shot the cat*. Today's money is *duckies*; in Captain Grose's time 'money' was *balsam*. A 'forward or wanton woman' of the 1990s is a *whoredog*; in the eighteenth century she was a *cleaver*. Intoxicated persons are now *hammered*, whereas two hundred years ago they were *mauled*. The image of being beaten is the same, for *mauled* is ultimately from Latin *malleus*, which means 'hammer'. Indelicate terms for parts of the human anatomy always have a place in slang: *knockers* is one current term for 'woman's bosom', whereas *apple dumplin' shop* was one eighteenth-century variant.

The question "What do slang items mean?" is only partly answered by categorizing their denotations. The raison d'être of slang is its power to evoke connotations based on human associations. Chapter 5 on the use of slang further develops its social dimensions.

The simplest definition of language is the coming together in some mysterious way of meaning and sounds produced by the human vocal apparatus. No one knows exactly how this takes place. In the connection between sound (or form) and meaning— the very essence of language—both form and meaning are in flux. While form changes, the meaning associated with it can change as well, sometimes slightly and sometimes dramatically. Thus over the past thousand years, *disk* and *dish* have diverged slightly in form and meaning, both having developed in English from Latin *discus*. Diverging only slightly in form but drastically in meaning are *bleach* and *black*, which developed from the same Proto-Indo-European root of several millennia ago. Diverging drastically are *colony* and *wheel*, which have changed both in form and meaning since Proto-Indo-European times, when they had an identical source. These realignments between form and meaning took place over many years. But changes in the correspondence between form and meaning are current and ongoing too and take place both in the standard vocabulary and in slang. In the past decade the forms *crack* and *aids*, which were already in the language meaning 'opening' and 'helps', have become associated with a lethal drug and the ravaging, incurable AIDS. The word *hurl*, which in the general vocabulary means 'to throw with force', has been appropriated in slang as one of the many synonyms for 'to vomit'.

Because most slang items are identical in form to words and expressions in the general vocabulary, the meaning of a slang term can be described as a series of increasing divergences from general usage. Describing the meaning of a slang term in such a comparative way is basically the same process as describing the acquisition of new senses for a word from one point in time to another. Historical semantic change is not merely random but is cognitively guided. For instance, it makes sense for the name of an individual with a salient characteristic to become a common noun applying to other people with that characteristic. Thus from Ebenezer Scrooge of Charles Dickens's *Christmas Carol* comes the common noun *scrooge* for 'a miserly person'. Slang makes use of the same type of logic, as when *Ken*, the well-groomed and -clothed male doll companion to *Barbie*, becomes the noun for 'a painstakingly fashionably dressed and groomed male'.

The least apparent change in meaning occurs when a lexical item is used more frequently in slang than in general usage. The form and denotation of the word are essentially unaltered, but the use of the word in an increasing number of contexts carries meaning in itself. Although *gross* for 'coarse in nature or behavior, vulgar' barely changes in denotation in slang, its application as a negative evaluation in so many contexts from reaction to raw liver to reaction to outmoded clothing adds triteness to its meaning.

A slight change in meaning is occasioned by a shift in part of speech or subcategory, which permits a word to occur in new contexts. *Scope* for 'to look at' and *daze* for 'to daydream' both occur in college slang as verbs rather than nouns ("I was just scoping the crowd and dazing when I heard my mother's voice behind me"). *Raise* 'parents' becomes a noun rather than a verb ("The raise want me to pay my own car insurance"); *harsh* 'mistreat' a verb rather than an adjective ("Sean really harshed me when he didn't get me a Grateful Dead ticket"); and *hulked* 'angry' an adjective rather than a verb ("Rob got so hulked when the teacher didn't show up for their conference"). In such instances, the divergence in meaning from general usage may be attributed to the difference in meaning between the grammatical classes noun, verb, and adjective.

Other semantic shifts range from small to considerable. In college slang *bizarre* means 'beyond the norm' ("It was totally bizarre how John talked the cop out of giving him a ticket"). *Heinous* 'terrible' can describe objects ("My hair looks heinous"). *Plastic* means 'artificial, fake' ("Pass me the plastic cream"). *Bogus* conveys a negative evaluation ("What a bogus assignment!"); and *radical* means 'excellent' ("Kevin's new CD is radical"). *Perpetrate* means 'pretend' ("She's not engaged — she's just perpetrating"). The shifting of meaning by degree is only one of a number of semantic processes that operate over time in the language at large and in slang as well.[1]

Another ordinary way in which the connection between form and meaning changes is by either an increase or a decrease in the number of referents a form designates. These opposing processes are called generalization and specialization, and they are at work in all living languages.

In generalization, terms acquire wider ranges of referents. Many English words have arrived at their current meaning by the process of generalization. For example, the word *meander* originally designated a particular winding river in Asia Minor; it has by now generalized to mean 'to wander aimlessly'. In the American South the term *coke* can refer to 'any carbonated beverage', not just Coca-Cola. Brand names, whether or not they are registered trademarks, often generalize: *hoover* 'vacuum cleaner', *kleenex* 'facial tissue', *scotch tape* 'cellophane adhesive tape', *windex* 'cleaning solution for glass', and *xerox* 'photocopy'. Although most of these enter the language as nouns, they soon become verbs as well ("Please hand me the windex" vs. "I windexed the mirror in the bathroom"; "Where's the scotch tape?" vs. "I need to scotch tape the flap of this envelope"). The legal holders of protected names like these prevent competing products from using them. Yet ordinary speakers ignore proprietary rights to specific form-meaning associations and, in time-honored tradition, continue to generalize product names when it suits them.

Slang items likewise show generalization. *Homeboy* and its derivatives now refer to 'a friend or someone who appears friendly', not just to 'someone from the same hometown or high school'. To *spaz* is 'to act silly or strange' in any way, not restricted to 'exhibiting muscle spasms'. *Get a job* is a command to 'act mature', that is, act in the mature way expected of someone who has the responsibility of a job. *Rape* can mean 'put a damper on things', as in "Man, are you doing anything special—are we raping you?" In the expression *rape my buzz*, *buzz* is generalized from the 'pleasant euphoric feeling caused by drinking a small amount of alcohol' to 'a generally happy or pleasant feeling', as in "My dad phoned this morning and raped my buzz." *Get the heck out of Dodge* means to 'leave any place'. *Smegma*, a Latinate term for bodily secretions, in slang means 'anything disgusting and slimy', as in "I scrubbed the smegma from the bathtub." The proper name *Jody* has come to be 'the generic male that a husband or boyfriend accuses a female of cheating with', as in "Why are you running to answer the phone—are you worried it's Jody?"

Perhaps the best current example of generalization is the word *dude*. When it started cropping up in American English in the 1880s, *dude* meant 'a man extremely fastidious in dress and manner'. By one route of development a *dude* became associated with city life and fashion and then with the East. By the 1920s this meaning was captured in the expression *dude ranch*, which is still in use. In another route of development, the notion of dressing sharply dominated, and *dude* became 'a man who dressed stylishly or flamboyantly', a meaning preserved among black speakers, who also generalized *dude* to 'any male'. With the stereotypical use of *dude* by black entertainers in the 1970s and 1980s, this meaning became widely known, if not used. By the early 1990s, thanks in large part to the popular television character Bart Simpson, *dude* became even more general, referring to males and females, adults and children.

A loss of force or vividness often takes place in conjunction with generalization. Intensifiers and hyperbolic expressions are particularly susceptible to such loss, a process sometimes called emptying. In the 1980s the word *awesome* generalized to the point of emptiness because of the speech of adolescents popularized by films, television, and advertising. A word can be emptied of its specific meaning and retain only a positive or negative value; common examples in standard English are intensifiers such as *very, quite, awfully, terrifically,* and *terribly.*

At any given time, slang has a number of expressions at various stages of generalizing. The following functionally synonymous slang terms from two school years, 1990–91 and 1991–92, all mean 'excellent, worthy of approval': *awesome, bad, bitching, booming, brilliant, buddha, candy, chicalean, choice, classic, cool, critical, decent, def, diva, gnarly, hype, keeva, kegging, kicking, killer, outrageous, righteous, ripping, slamming,* and *sweet.* Functioning as intensifiers equivalent to *very* at the same time were *butt, major, power, totally,* and *way.*

Many phrases are built on verbs of generalized meaning such as *do, get, make,* and *take.* The verbs themselves contribute little to the specific referential meaning of expressions such as *get along with someone; get away with something; get off a horse/plane/train;* and *get through the day/week/month.* Slang also builds phrases on generalized verbs. The verb phrases *get a clue, get a grip, get a job, get a life, get with the program* all mean 'act in an aware or responsible manner'. *Get down* means 'dance'; *get the heck out of Dodge,* 'leave'; *get over it,* 'adapt to a situation'; *get up with,* 'meet'; and *get you some,* 'have sex'. Many phrases formed around *get* are fixed expressions that show disbelief (*get outta here, get out of town*), encouragement (*get it, get some*), or admiration (*get back, get off, get up*).

The opposite of generalization is specialization, in which the range of referents decreases. Specialization has played a major role in the form-meaning connection of many current English words. The word *starve* in Old English meant 'die' but now means 'suffer or die from lack of food'. *Tide* a thousand years ago referred to time periods of various lengths and kinds and is preserved in words like *Yuletide*. But now *tide* is used almost exclusively with reference to water—to the times between the high and low water levels along the shores of oceans and seas. *Timber* a thousand years ago was related to a verb that meant 'to build' and referred to any kind of building materials; now it designates only one type, wood. *Cassette* originally designated 'a small box'; today the word is used almost exclusively for the plastic containers for electronic tapes or even, by association, to the tape recording itself.

Many slang terms can also be explained as instances of specialization. An *all-nighter* is not just an activity that lasts all night but specifically 'a night-long stretch without sleep to study hard or to write a paper': "I had to pull an all-nighter just to finish the last chapter." *Cruise, hunt,* and *scope* all involve moving and looking, but particularly to find a partner for romance or sex: "Kathy's scoping tonight—she needs a date for the formal." If the search is successful, one *hooks* or *hooks up*: "Kathy finally hooked with that guy from her biology class." *Grass* or *the weed* is specifically 'marijuana'. A *late-night* is a 'party, usually at a fraternity house, that does not get started until around one in the morning and usually gets very big': "The late-night was so crowded that we couldn't get past the porch." *Mine* means 'my fault': "The phone is disconnected—I forgot to pay the phone bill. Mine." *Story* refers to 'an afternoon television soap opera': "I don't take afternoon classes—I can't miss my stories." *The walk of shame* is the walk back to her residence hall by a female early in the morning after having spent the night out with a male. She usually has an unkempt appearance, wearing wrinkled, unsuitable clothing or the male's old shorts and T-shirt. At the University of North Carolina, *the yard* is specifically the area between the undergraduate library and Greenlaw and Bingham Halls where students congregate midmorning to see and be seen. Among college students the verb *hold* has narrowed to mean 'possess or have access to one particular substance, marijuana', as in "I'd love to get stoned. Are you holding?"

For many terms a specialized and a generalized meaning exist concurrently. *Ace* means 'to make an A on a test' and 'to perform any action well'; *home* can actually be 'someone from the same hometown' or, more generally, 'a friend'; *jam* can mean 'to have a good time dancing' or 'to have a good time at a party'; *jones* can be 'a craving for drugs' or 'a craving for anything'.

Connotation, important to the meaning of a lexical item, also figures into the alignment between form and meaning. Sometimes the connotation associated with a term becomes more favorable or less favorable, opposing processes called amelioration and pejoration.

Amelioration over time accounts for the current meaning of many English words. For example, *dizzy*, which once meant 'foolish, stupid', now means 'having the sensation of whirling or falling'. The ancestors of *knights* were 'boys', and the *steward* was the 'guardian of the pig sty'. *Chivalrous* had to do with 'horses', and *prestige* with 'magic'.

Amelioration is widespread in slang, perhaps because the generally negative tone of a large portion of the slang vocabulary offers many opportunities for words to acquire more positive or elevated associations. Many words enter slang from the taboo terms of subcultures. *Jock*, now a widespread informal designation for 'athlete', developed via *jockstrap* 'athletic supporter', in which *jock* meant 'penis'. The verb *boogie* 'move, dance, perform' originally referred to 'syphilis' and entered the informal language of the mainstream from *boogie-woogie* of black musicians. The world of black music was also responsible for popularizing the ameliorated meanings of *jam, jazz,* and *juke*—all of which originally had sexual referents.

Many negative and derogatory terms in the general informal vocabulary of English and in slang originated as blunt and coarse references to sexual acts, body parts, and bodily functions. With increased use in a variety of contexts, such terms lose their shock effect, sometimes even becoming euphemistic. *Shit*, for example, can have downright positive connotations, as in "That dude really knew his shit for the quiz today." In 1990 students used *the shit* to mean 'the best': "I went to Busch Gardens last weekend and rode the Big Bad Wolf—that's the shit." As a productive second element *-freak* has ameliorated to mean 'extremely interested in or overly fond of': "Debbie is a real popcorn-freak." Like many verbs that designate 'sexual intercourse', *fuck* and *screw* can also mean 'mistreat, swindle': "I really got screwed on that econ exam." A jarring example of amelioration during the 1980s was the sudden and widespread use of *suck* 'fellatio' to mean merely 'stupid, unpleasant, or objectionable', as in "Getting up at 5 A.M. sucks" or "All this rainy weather sucks." For some items an ameliorated meaning coexists with an earlier or derived negative meaning. The common *jerk* 'socially inept and unlikable person' retains its earlier meaning of 'masturbate' in the general slang expression *jerk off. Bitchin'*, an adjective derived from *bitch*, can mean either 'difficult' or, when applied to females, 'good-looking': "What a bitchin' exam!" versus "What a bitchin' girl!" *Slut* has ameliorated in college slang and can be used affectionately as a noun of address among female friends or as the second part of a compound meaning 'female habitué'. Thus a *pit slut* is a 'female who sits around the Pit to meet friends and see people'.

The opposite of amelioration is pejoration, in which the connotations evoked by a form become less favorable. Pejoration has shaped the current meaning of many English words. *Ghost* once meant simply 'spirit', as it still does in the *Holy Ghost*. A thousand years ago the etymon of *silly* meant 'happy, blessed', and *lore* was associated with 'learning, doctrine, preaching'. In the history of the English language, a disproportionate number of words referring to females have undergone pejoration. *Hussy* 'a lewd or brazen woman' developed from *housewife*. *Biddy* 'hen', *bitch* 'female dog', and *vixen* 'female fox' have all become derogatory terms focusing on alleged objectionable behavioral traits in women. *Fairy* has become a derogatory term for a 'male homosexual'.

In the slang portion of the lexicon, pejoration is less evident than amelioration. Because of the generally negative tone of slang, words likely to undergo pejoration — that is, words with positive or at least neutral connotations — have little reason to be adopted in slang in the first place. Derogatory epithets abound, for example, *butthead, cracker jack, cretin, crud, dildo, dimwit, dingleberry, dip, donut hole, dork, geek, groover, gweeb, jerk face, nob, punk, quimp, reeb, scuzbag, tang, three dollar bill, tool, twerp, twink, ween, wimp, wuss*, and *yo-yo*. It is characteristic of slang that new items are used quite frequently in a short period of time; a widening sphere of use leads to wider acceptability, a situation that favors amelioration rather than pejoration.

Nevertheless, pejoration has affected some items of college slang. A *future* is 'an unattractive male'. Three geometric terms — *straight, square*, and *quad* — are all are derogatory epithets that designate with various connotations 'a person who does not fit in with the prevailing college life style'. A *facial* is 'an insult or rebuff', as in "Ben got turned down by that girl again—what a facial!" *Polyester*, once the miracle fabric for the nonwrinkled look, has fallen out of fashion in clothing and has come to stand for 'something out-of-style or fake', as in "That salesman was so polyester." *Attitude* has specialized and pejorated to mean 'an uncooperative or condescending attitude': "When he drinks and starts talking about his wealthy family, the room just reeks of attitude." A pair of pejorated terms in use in 1990 makes one of the few allusions in college slang to academic pursuits. *Booked* means 'ugly', and *published* means 'very ugly': "You might think that guy is booked. Well, his roommate is published."

The cognitive processes that give rise to generalization/specialization and amelioration/pejoration do not operate in isolation from each other. Ordinarily in the history of a word a combination of these and other processes applies. Two representative examples from current campus slang can illustrate this.

Ace means 'the grade A' or 'to perform well'. The word originally referred to a Roman coin. It entered English in the Middle Ages from French in the context of gaming and meant 'a single mark on a card, die, or domino'. In racquet sports and golf, positive connotations accrued to the use of *ace* for a point scored by a single stroke. In World War I, a pilot who shot down five or more enemy aircraft was called an *ace*, with the term soon generalizing to designate a person of extraordinary skill in any competitive activity. By the 1930s *ace* meant 'of high or first rank or quality', the meaning it has in the black slang *ace boon coon* 'best friend' and in college slang *ace* for 'the grade A'. From there it was a small step to using *ace* as a verb meaning 'perform well'.

The English word *queen* goes back to an ancient root for 'woman', a meaning that it had in Old English alongside the specialized and ameliorated meaning 'female ruler, wife of the king'. This meaning shifted to 'highest-ranking woman, epitome of' in uses of *queen* such as *beauty queen* or *queen of the silver screen*. It persists in the slang of high school and college students, though usually with some intended sarcasm, as the productive second element in expressions like *shag-queen* for 'female who dances the shag well' and *taco-queen* for 'female who is proficient at preparing or eating tacos'. By early Middle English the neutral meaning 'woman' also specialized in another way and pejorated to *quean,* 'a disreputable woman, a prostitute'.[2] Early-twentieth-century citations show it further specialized to a male acting like a woman, 'an effeminate homosexual'. This meaning of *queen* persists in slang, along with a derivative *queeny* 'effeminate'.

Language often refers indirectly. If someone in the checkout line at a grocery says "I'm parked across the street," the hearer realizes with no puzzlement that it is not the speaker but the speaker's vehicle that is across the street. Everyday, ordinary language is filled with meaning derived from implied connections. We get the children off to school *on automatic pilot.* At work we try to *forge links* or *plow new ground,* always mindful to express our ideas *concretely.* We *pencil in* a tentative appointment with a friend and are too *chicken* to make an appointment with the dentist. The traffic is a *nightmare.* The evening news informs us of the latest dismal proclamation from the *Oval Office.* But we can end the day *on a high note* watching *reruns* of our favorite sitcom. The ability to make complex and multiple connections between form and meaning is central to human cognitive and linguistic ability, and most of the time we are unaware of the series of semantic transfers that the interpretation of a word or phrase requires. The phrase *Oval Office,* for example, must be interpreted as a proper noun—a particular office that is oval shaped, the one in the house where the president of the United States lives; although another person may actually utter the words and may do so in another office, a proclamation from the *Oval Office* is a message from the president. For many words of current standard English, connections of this sort have long passed from the conscious awareness of the users, and the form evokes meaning directly. The word *rehearse,* for example, originally meant 'to harrow again' and captured in a single word the image of a harrow breaking up and leveling ground that had been plowed. The learned *regurgitate* for 'vomit' has its origin in Latin *gurges* 'whirlpool'. Current English *balance* has developed from the image of two scales in the Latin word *bilanx,* a combination of *bi-* 'two' and *lanx* 'scale'.

Although often taken for granted in ordinary language, the types of indirection illustrated by the examples above have long been recognized as an important feature of the diction of poetry. They are important in slang as well. The terms that have been used for centuries to describe figurative language in poetry can also be applied to everyday language and to slang: *metonymy, synecdoche, irony*, and *metaphor*.[3]

Metonymy makes reference by association. "Metonymic concepts allow us to conceptualize one thing by means of its relation to something else" (Lakoff and Johnson 1980, 39). For example, 'journalists' are called *the press* because of the machinery used in the printing process. This type of oblique connection between form and meaning underlies many ordinary words and expressions in current English. Most of the names for nonprimary colors, for example, have arisen as a result of metonymy. *Orange, peach*, and *avocado* are the colors associated with those fruits. The color *turquoise* comes from the gemstone, which itself was named metonymically by its place of discovery, Turkestan. *Aqua* is the blue-green color of seawater. *Lavender* and *violet* are shades of purple that take their names from flowering plants. *Navy*, from the color of British naval uniforms, is ultimately associated with the Latin word for 'ship', *navis*. The list of metonymic color terms goes on: *cream, ebony, ivory, lime, rose*, and others.

Metonymy triggers semantic shifts of various types and degrees throughout the lexicon. A simple and frequent kind of metonymy associates an instrument with the action performed with that instrument. Current English *probe*, for example, either can refer to 'a device or instrument used to investigate' or, metonymically, can be a noun meaning 'investigation' or a verb meaning 'to investigate'. The proverb *the pen is mightier than the sword* evokes its meaning in a similar way. *The pen* is an instrument of reasoned persuasion, and *the sword* is an instrument of coercion. The proverb is really about the power of reason over force, not about pens and swords. New expressions can also be metonymic. A *recycling igloo* is a 'sturdy plastic crate in which recyclable items like newspapers and aluminum cans are placed for curbside pickup'. It is called an *igloo* because it is about the same size, shape, and material as ice chests, one popular brand of which is *Igloo*. The brand name itself derives its meaning by association with the type of Eskimo house made of thick blocks of ice that serve as insulation.

Often metonymic connections get lost over a period of years or from one language to another. Current English *picayune* 'of little value' developed from the name of a Spanish coin of little value in circulation in the southern United States in the nineteenth century. The word itself is a development of a French dialect word that may have originated in imitation of the jingle of coins. Users of the word *zest* have no reason to associate the 'feeling of enhanced pleasure' with its original connection to 'the piquant taste of lemon or orange peel'. The stringed instrument called the *dulcimer* takes its name from the Latin word for 'sweet' because of the sweet sound associated with it. A North American bird of red plumage is a *cardinal* by association with the color of the robes worn by Roman Catholic ecclesiastic officials who are called *cardinals*, derived from the Latin word for 'principal'. The verb *blanche* 'scald or parboil vegetables or fruits in hot water or steam' developed from the French 'to whiten, lose color' because one effect of pouring boiling water on vegetables is the diluting of their color.

Slang vocabulary likewise grows by metonymy. A 'beer' is called a *brew* and its derived form *brewski* because of the process of manufacture, a *chill* or a *cold one* because of its serving temperature, *suds* or *head* because of the foam at the top of a glass, some *tin* because it comes in cans, or a *ha-ha* because of the pleasure of drinking it. 'Athletic shoes' are called *kicks*, *skips*, or *quick starts* because of the physical activity associated with them and *chucks* from the Converse brand endorsed by Chuck Taylor. The game 'basketball' is *hoops* because of the circular metal frame that holds the net. The shape of the letter *F* inspires the term *flag* for a 'failing grade'. 'Environmentalists' love trees and are thus called *tree-huggers* and *tree nymphs*. In the early 1970s when Earth Day was established and environmental concerns were reflected in the dress, food, and music of college students, the term *organic* meant 'fashionable' and carried positive connotations, as in "Wearing Earth shoes is organic." In the eighties and nineties people who clung to the styles of the earlier decade were described with gentle disparagement by things associated with the back-to-earth movement, for example, *earth muffins, ferns, granolas, grape-nuts, groovers*, and *hey-wows*.

College students in the early 1990s called 'money' metonymically *bank* or *paper*, as in "I've got to get some bank/paper before I leave town." The noun *lamp*, from *street lamp*, the stereotypical prop for lounging idly, became a verb meaning 'do nothing in particular', as in "We were just lamping on Franklin Street last night." A 'disappointing social event' was a *Maybelline waste*, not worth the effort of putting on makeup (Maybelline is an inexpensive brand of cosmetics), as in "That's the last time I'll go to that

Maybelline waste." *Jar pot* was one way of referring to 'particularly strong marijuana', because it had to be stored in a jar to contain the odor. *Jar pot* then inspired, by association with *mason jar*, the synonyms *Benny Mason* and *Mr. Mason*.

On college campuses, items of clothing or accessories associated with a group can be used for naming the group. Thus 'a stereotypical fraternity member' has for years been called a *fratty-bagger* or a *bagger* because of a style of pants once fashionable, and for a few years he was called a *gator* because of the alligator emblem on the once popular Izod shirts. Now he is a *hat*, from the fashion of wearing baseball caps. 'Stereotypical sorority members' are *bowheads* because of the hair bows in style in the late eighties and *slickies* because of the shiny fabric of the Umbro soccer shorts they are fond of wearing. *PDK*'s are 'out of style, not aware of what's going on' because they still wear *polyester double knit*. A *suit* is a 'properly attired businessman'.

The stereotypical element in these and many other slang expressions supports George Lakoff's characterization of stereotypes as kinds of metonyms. "Social stereotypes are cases of metonymy — where a subcategory has a socially recognized status as standing for the category as a whole, usually for the purpose of making quick judgments about people" (Lakoff 1987, 79). In social situations where fitting in is a constant concern, like college campuses, it is not surprising that the in-group language is filled with metonymic expressions.

Often hard to distinguish from metonymy and therefore sometimes considered a kind of metonymy is the figure of speech called synecdoche. Synecdoche names the whole by the part or, less frequently, the part by the whole. An example in ordinary language is the use of the body part *hand* to signify 'worker' or 'help in performing work', as in "farmhand" or "give me a hand with this heavy box." A *monorail* is named for a significant part of the equipment used in that type of transportation; the verbs *sail, skate*, and *ski* similarly signify the whole by the name of an important part. In informal language and slang, synecdoche accounts for *brain*, 'intelligent person'; *caf up*, 'drink coffee or eat something containing caffeine for energy'; *threads*, 'clothing'; *tube*, 'television'; *tunes*, 'music'; and *wheels*, 'automobile'. Typical part-by-whole synecdoche designates representatives by the entity they are representing, as is common when talking about team sports. Thus in the sentence "North Carolina is on the line for two shots," *North Carolina* refers to 'a basketball player on the team representing the University of North Carolina'.

Metonymy is also the basis of many allusions in slang. *Mickey D's Rainbow Steakhouse*, for example, refers to McDonald's restaurant by a combination of things associated with the fast-food chain—its nickname, the shape of the arches that are its identifying symbol, and, sarcastically, the beef served there. A complete appreciation of the expression depends on knowing the allusions, a topic discussed in the next chapter.

Another literary trope useful for analyzing the semantics of slang is verbal irony, the use of words to convey the opposite of their ordinary meanings, like the vernacular *big deal* to signify that something is not important. Context signals that an expression is to be interpreted ironically rather than straightforwardly. In speech, a peculiar sound pattern also cues the hearer. Because irony depends on sufficient shared knowledge to infer the speaker's intention to be ironic, irony often goes undetected (Muecke 1973; Tanaka 1973).

Ironic interpretation, according to linguist Eva Kittay, is similar to metonymy. Both metonymy and irony involve the transfer of meaning within a semantic field rather than across distinct domains (1987, 291). In irony the transfer is to the opposite meaning within a semantically linked set. Thus, ironically, *bad* means 'good'.

Irony is the linguistic representation of the conflict between appearance and reality, a theme that is important in the slang of many groups, including college students. College slang always has several lexical items that criticize those who give false appearances. These examples are from the early 1990s. A *poser* was 'someone who pretends to be something he or she isn't', as in "She tries to be cool, but she's just a Suzi-poser" (a *Suzi* is a stereotypical sorority member). *Poser*, and the derived adjective *posey*, also had a more specialized reference to 'someone who tries to act sophisticated', as in "I hate that dance club—everyone there is so posey." 'Someone who acts as if he or she is better than others' was a *pomp*, a clipping of *pompous*. Similar in meaning to *poser* and *pomp* was the noun *wannabe*, made popular by the Spike Lee film *School Daze* and the television program *Saturday Night Live*, as in "My friend Chris is such a frat boy wannabe." More generally a *wannabe* was 'an imitation of something better, a phony', as in "Don't let John introduce you to his roommate—he's a definite wannabe" or "Since I can't afford a real diamond, I guess I'll settle for that wannabe." *Pseudo-* could attach to almost any noun ("I'm sick of this pseudo-food/pseudo-class/pseudo-music"). *Perpetrate* was a verb meaning 'pretend to be something one isn't', as in "I knew you in high school, so don't perpetrate around me."

College students' fondness for juxtaposing appearance and reality is shown in their use of a sentence pattern in which a statement presented as fact is immediately retracted by the use of a word like *fake* or *psych*, as in "Your econ prof phoned—she wants to see you. Fake!" A similar structure to indicate negation—adding *not* after a statement said in a serious tone—became immensely popular during 1990–91 because of its use on the "Wayne's World" skit on the television program *Saturday Night Live*, as in "I really know a lot about morphemes and allomorphs for this test—not." By 1992 the distinctive use of *not* of "Wayne's World" had spread to newspaper headlines, advertising copy, and national television commercials and was already judged outdated on college campuses.

In the least complicated kind of verbal irony, some terms mean the opposite of their meaning in standard usage. *Bad* means 'good' ("M. C. Hammer gave a bad concert last night"). *Mean* and *wicked* likewise have positive values and mean 'good, admirable' ("He drives a mean/wicked machine"). *Sick* means 'great' ("I'd love to live in Atlanta—it's the sickest city"). *Killer* is an exclamation of approval ("I made an A—killer!") or a positive evaluation ("That new song is killer"). *Killer weed* is 'extremely high quality marijuana'. *Intellectual hour* is 'soap opera time'; *lifer* is 'someone who has commited a trivial offense'; a *rocket scientist* is 'someone who is stupid'; and *Student Death* refers to Student Health Services. In its ironic use *love* means 'trying, difficult' ("That was a love exam"). Slang even comments ironically on itself. *Groover*, a positive term that meant 'someone with it, in the know' in the 1960s, indicated 'someone or something out of date or fashion' in the 1980s, like someone who would say the outmoded adjective *groovy*.

Many times a term will have both a positive and a negative meaning. *Trip*, for example, means 'overwhelmingly either pleasant or disgusting'. Compare these two exchanges. A: "That was the best movie I ever saw." B: "Yeah, it was a trip." versus A: "Dr. Smith says that he expects everyone to flunk the exam." B: "Yeah, the man's a trip." Although *shit* and its derivatives are ordinarily negative ("You don't know shit about it" or "I have all this shit to do for my English class"), in some contexts *shit* can have a positive value ("I know my shit for that English 36 test"); and *the shit* can mean 'the best' ("Michael's new BMW is the shit"). *The junk* also means 'great, the best' ("I'm happy that you got early acceptance to med school—yo, that's the junk"). As a verb, *bitch* is usually negative ("I wish you wouldn't bitch about the mess in my half of the room"). But when used in its adjective form *bitching*, it means either 'good-looking, excellent' ("What a bitchin' chick!") or 'unattractive, objectionable' ("What a bitchin' exam!").

A number of set expressions used to characterize a situation are ironic. Most of them are said with the sarcastic intonation that conveys irony in English generally. They are considered slang here rather than simply colloquial language because their college student users considered them slang. *That's fair* is a sarcastic expression that means 'that's unfair' ("You're tired of dating me? That's fair"). The phrase *that's close* is used to discourage an unreasonable request or to refute an outrageous statement and means 'that's not close to the real situation' (A: "Lend me $10." B: "That's close"). Similarly, *probably* can mean 'probably not' (A: "James is going to call her tonight to ask her to the game." B: "Yeah, probably"). *Shocker* is a comment on something that is not surprising ("You're going out tonight? Shocker! You go out every night"). *I hate that* can be 'a sincere expression of sympathy', as in "I hate that your grandmother is in the hospital," or, in its slang use, an ironic expression meaning 'I love that', as in "My afternoon class was canceled today. I hate that because I'll have to lay out by the pool instead."

Another type of indirect reference is metaphor. Metaphor as a tool of poets has been discussed since the time of Aristotle. Observers over the centuries have marveled at the potential of metaphor in literature to push at the boundaries of human thought and experience. The great twentieth-century American poet Robert Frost puts it this way: "Poetry begins in trivial metaphors, pretty metaphors, 'grace' metaphors, and goes on to the profoundest thinking that we have. Poetry provides the one permissible way of saying one thing and meaning another" (1966, 36).

Linguists have long noticed that metaphor is widespread in ordinary, nonliterary uses of language as well (Bloomfield 1933, 443; Thomas 1969, 25). Yet only in the past two decades have theoretical concerns led to scrutiny of metaphor by linguists. Eva Kittay, in *Metaphor: Its Cognitive Force and Linguistic Structure*, carefully explores the claim that metaphors are conceptual and provide members of a linguistic community with structures for perceiving and understanding the world (1987, 2–3). Kittay maintains that

> the cognitive force of metaphor comes, not from providing new information about the world, rather from a (re)conceptualization of information that is already available to us.
>
> Metaphor is a primary way in which we accommodate and assimilate information and experience to our conceptual organization of the world. In particular, it is the primary way we accommodate new experience. Hence it is at the source of our capacity to learn and at the center of our creative thought. (39)

Unlike metonymy, which involves reassignment of form and meaning within a set of associated concepts, metaphor crosses content domains and names one thing by something in another domain, calling forth a likeness or analogy between things that are fundamentally different. Thus 'the data storage capacity of a computer' is called *memory* because of its resemblance to the human mental faculty; 'a list of alternative directives in a computer program' is a *menu* because the listing and choice features are similar to the method of selecting food and drink in a restaurant.

For the most part, language users easily adjust the link between sound and meaning required by metaphor. Speakers of English, for example, have no trouble applying the word *garbage* to 'useless and inaccurate data generated by a faulty computer program or error'. Over time or with frequent use, the metaphoric origin of words and expressions is sometimes forgotten. Such words and phrases are called dead metaphors. English words that contain the base -*ject* started as metaphoric uses of the Latin word for 'throw': *conjecture* 'throw together', *dejection* 'throw down', *project* 'throw forth', *reject* 'throw back'. An *expired* driver's license or subscription now seldom calls to mind the original meaning of 'breathe out', as in one's last breath. Current speakers of English have no reason to be aware that *dependent* is a development of Latin components meaning 'hang down'. Even expressions whose metaphoric origins are not buried in foreign etymologies often escape notice—for example, "the *eye* of a needle," "the *heart* of the matter," "the *leg* of a chair," "the *tongue* of a shoe."

Perhaps the most obvious set of metaphoric words in English applies the characteristics of animals to humans and their activities. The straightforward transfer of a name from an animal to a person includes *dinosaur*, 'an old-fashioned, out-of-date person'; *magpie*, 'a talkative person'; *night owl*, 'person who stays up late at night'; and *shrew*, 'mean-spirited person'. *Batty, bearish, bullish, catty, mousy*, and *waspish* are adjectives derived from the names of animals; *drone on, ferret out, hound*, and *lionize* are verbs similarly derived. The compound *catnap* implies the simile 'nap like a cat', and *dogear* means 'the turned-down corner of a page of a book' that looks like a dog's ear. Few passengers aboard a 747 associate the pilots' *cockpit* with a hole where cocks fight, but the connections with the animal kingdom are still apparent in *cat-and-mouse game, dog days of summer, dog-eat-dog world, play possum*, and many others.

Given the tendency of the general vocabulary toward metaphor, it is not surprising that metaphor abounds in slang. As an obvious instance, the pattern of animal metaphors well established in general English occurs also in slang. In college slang an *animal* is an 'athlete' or, as the second member of a compound or phrase, an 'enthusiast', for example, *party animal, heavy metal animal*, and *skiing animal. The Beast* is 'Milwaukee's Best', a popular inexpensive brand of beer. A *fox* is 'an attractive female', and a *stud* is 'an attractive male'. A *turkey* is 'a person who acts stupid or never seems to do things right', and a *snake* is 'a person who steals something, particularly another's date'. A *rat bitch* is 'an undependable lab partner', and a *study mongrel* is 'someone who studies hard'. A *coyote date* is 'a woman who is so ugly that when her companion for the night wakes up the next morning and she is asleep on his arm, he would rather chew off his arm than wake her up'. *Plastic cow* is 'nondairy creamer', and *roach* is 'the butt of a marijuana cigarette'. To *bat cave* is 'to sleep'; to *bug out* is 'to act frantic or crazy'; to *gator* is 'to wallow in beer while doing a dance in imitation of an alligator'; and to *hawk* is 'to participate in an athletic activity for fun'. One who acts *squirrelly* acts 'crazy, nuts, or insane'.

Recent college slang has elaborated extensively on dog metaphors. *Dog* itself can have various related negative meanings. As a noun or adjective it labels someone or something as 'unattractive or unappealing' ("Avocado bubblegum is dog"). As a verb *dog* specializes in context to mean 'make the grade D or do poorly' ("After all that studying, I dogged the test anyway"); 'defeat soundly' ("I dogged him in racquetball"); or 'treat unfairly, dismiss' ("Mark didn't call you back like he said he would—he's dogging you"). Ironically, *dog* can also mean 'do something fast, hard, or well' ("Ted said he didn't study but ended up dogging the test and blowing the curve"; "We were dogging that food"). *Dog out* means 'betray, neglect, treat with disrespect'. *Call the dogs* means 'to vomit'. *Dog* is often the second member of a compound or phrase: *brary dog* 'someone who studies in the library'; *brew dog, chilly dog* 'beer'; *corn dog* 'someone who is socially inept or acts weird'; *hooch dog, jimmy dog, james earl dog* 'marijuana cigarette'; *mad dog* 'cheap wine'; *pig dog* 'someone who eats a lot'; *shroom dog* 'someone who uses hallucinogens'; *wimp dog* 'male with little personality'. As with many slang words for animals, *dog* and its spinoffs often have sexual implications. A *bowser, bow-wow,* or *mud puppy* is 'an ugly female'. To *dog it* is 'for a female to act sexually loose or promiscuous', and *whore dog* and its younger equivalent *slut puppy* refer to 'a sexually promiscuous female'. The male counterpart is a *hound*. To act *like a big dog* is to do something 'with intensity' ("I was running like a big dog to catch my bus"). To *run with the big dogs* is 'to do anything that anyone else can, rise to a challenge' ("I think I can run with the big dogs in honors English").

Another productive source of metaphors in college slang is food. In the late 1980s and early 1990s, the nationally recognized *couch potato* for 'someone who lies around doing nothing more energetic than eating and watching television' was still in use, along with its synonymous offspring *sofa spud* and *sofa yam* and the verbs *potato* and *veg*. *Banana factory* was a 'hectic, horrible, or futile situation', and *duck soup* was 'something easy'. *Cheese* became a metaphor for 'something unattractive or undesirable' and gave rise to *cheeseball, cheezy, velveeta, cheese whiz,* the personified *Captain Cheddar,* and the French equivalent, *fromage. Cool whip* was 'something very new and appealing', while *granola* was 'something out of date'. *Jellybeans* were 'painkillers' and *sugar* 'cocaine'. *Soda cracker* was 'a white person'. A 'girlfriend or boyfriend' was a *snackbar,* and *go for sushi* meant 'kiss passionately'.

Although subject areas like animals and food tend to provide vehicles for the proliferation of slang metaphors, a sampling of metaphors from college slang from the late 1980s and early 1990s shows that their inspiration is diverse. *Batting practice* means 'the custom of going from bar to bar drinking until drunk'. *Cool breeze*, 'person who is sharp-witted, athletic, well-liked'. *Crumb*, 'feel sad or depressed'. *Daisy chain*, 'the connection between people who have had sex with the same partners at different times'. *Dope*, 'stylish, exciting, admirable'. *Double-bagger*, 'ugly female' (the female is so ugly that both she and her date must wear bags on their heads). *Drive the porcelain bus* or *ride the porcelain Honda*, 'vomit'. *Dump-truck date*, 'overweight female'. *Fake bake* 'get a tan in a tanning salon'. *Ghetto blaster* or *third world briefcase*, 'portable stereo tape deck'. *Gunslinger*, 'female who rejects a male's attentions rudely'. *Hemorrhoid*, 'annoying person'. *Play tonsil hockey*, 'kiss passionately'. *Pill* or *rock*, 'basketball'. *Popsicle stand*, 'current location'. *Ride the E Train*, 'feel the effects of the drug Ecstasy'. *Toast*, 'in big trouble'. *Toxic waste dump*, 'someone who is drunk'. *White bread*, 'characteristic of white suburbia'. *Wide load*, 'someone with large hips and buttocks'.

Many metaphors used in slang enhance their meaning by cultural allusions. *Wide load* for 'someone with large hips and buttocks', for example, alludes to the required signs on oversized trailers and cargo in transit on public roads and applies the image of a slow-moving, cumbersome vehicle to a person. *Easter bunny* for 'a benefactor, someone who does a favor' mimics a 1991 M&M candy commercial. Additional examples of metaphors that elicit meaning by allusion are discussed in the next chapter.

In content, the metaphors of college slang parallel closely the metaphoric patterns for general American English described by Lakoff and others. For example, slang images pertaining to lust fall right into the domains identified by Lakoff (1987, 409–15). HUNGER: 'A sexy female' is *bacon*; 'a sexy male' is *beef-a-roni*; and 'to kiss passionately' is to *go for sushi*. ANIMALS: A *fox* and a *stud* are attractive members of each sex. HEAT: Having one's *burners on high* is to be 'sexually excited'. INSANITY: 'To have sex' is to *rage* or *do the wild thing*. MACHINES: 'To seek a member of the opposite sex' is to *put it in cruise mode* or to *put it in overdrive*. GAMES: 'To kiss passionately' is to *play tonsil hockey*, and 'to have sex' is to *score* or *hit a home run*. WAR: The 'penis' is a *heat-seeking missile*. PHYSICAL FORCES: One *hits on* members of the opposite sex, potential *slampieces*, and winds up *throwing down, knocking boots*, or *banging* them. Although the particular forms may be different in slang, the cognitive patterns that give rise to them are the same as for the general vocabulary.

Marcel Danesi's insightful semiotic analysis of language use within a group of middle-class teenagers in Toronto further supports the link between figurative language and cognition in contexts in which the social dimensions of language are paramount. *Cool: The Signs and Meanings of Adolescence* (1994) more fully develops Danesi's earlier hypothesis that "teenagers live and act in a world largely called into existence by the categories of their own speech" (1988, 440). In teenagers' speech Danesi finds three basic discourse programming categories: emotive, connotative, and clique coded. The connotative category, "at the core of the adolescent's verbal modelling of reality," is based largely on metaphor (1994, 102).

Metaphor is at once new and old—a reconceptualization, or new way of thinking, based on prior knowledge shared by a linguistic community. The creative dimension makes metaphor appropriate to poetry; the social dimension makes metaphor appropriate to slang. Experiments by psychologists even suggest that the social functions of slang make slang metaphors more readily understandable and memorable than their literal equivalents (Gibbs and Nagaoka 1985).

The processes that describe how slang means often overlap and operate in conjunction with one another. For instance, the phrase *out to lunch* in general colloquial English means 'away from the job to have a meal'. But in slang the phrase has generalized to mean not just 'away from the job' but 'away from whatever is going on'. *Lunch* is a clipping of the phrase and serves as the base for the derived adjective *lunchy* 'unaware'. *Lunch* is related by metonymy to *lunchbox* (one carries *lunch* in a *lunchbox*), and *lunchbox* is a metaphor for 'someone who is not in touch with reality'.

Several expressions that mean 'vomit' also show how circuitous the route to meaning can be. *Talk to Ralph on the big white phone* is a clever embellishment of *ralph*, which means 'to vomit' and which probably originated as an onomatopoeic approximation. *Ralph* as a personification can *talk*. *Phone* is associated metonymically as an instrument that transmits *talk*. *Big white phone* is a metaphor for toilet. A similar expression for 'vomit' is *worship the porcelain goddess*. The metaphor for toilet is *porcelain goddess*. The meaning 'vomit' for the entire expression can be arrived at by a series of metonyms: a posture associated with worship is kneeling with a bowed head; kneeling with the head bowed over a toilet is associated with vomiting.

The traditional terminology of semantic change and literary analysis used in this chapter is often inadequate to describe the semantics of slang items. For instance, since metonymy sometimes relies on a remote association with a number of possible relationships to the original concept, metonymic connections can be puzzling. Take, for example, *gut course* for 'easy course'. Couldn't a *gut course* just as plausibly be 'a hard course, one that requires guts'? To arrive at the meaning 'easy course' for *gut course*, the need for guts must be construed as an exclusive one. That's all you need for a gut course — no studying, no research, no papers, just visceral stamina.

Another kind of indirectness expected in literary language is allusion, reference to a historical or literary event, person, place, or the like. Because allusion relies on shared knowledge that can serve as a sign of belonging to a limited circle of people, allusion is important in slang. The specific kinds of allusions that are used in college slang are discussed in the next chapter.

4: Borrowing & Allusion

Borrowing and allusion are treated together here because in these two processes the creators of slang go beyond their small circles of peers to acquire vocabulary. This chapter shows how even these two seemingly outward-directed processes suit the fundamentally inward-directed social aims of slang. Often when users of slang seem to reach out to groups unlike themselves, they are in reality strengthening their own in-group ties.

BORROWING

In borrowing, one language variety acquires a new lexical item from another language variety, either a dialect or a foreign language. Usually the borrowed word or expression changes in form or in meaning, or in both, in the transfer. For example, the original French form *levee*, the passive participle of the verb 'raise', has become the English noun *levee* 'an embankment along a river', changing in placement of accent, vowel sounds, and meaning.

In generalizing about borrowing in English, it is useful to differentiate between cultural borrowing (different languages) and dialect borrowing (same language). Within cultural borrowing two types are distinguishable, ordinary and intimate (Bloomfield 1933, 461).

By means of ordinary cultural borrowing, English has acquired from other languages thousands of names for things and experiences once unknown to speakers of English. *Chimpanzee* is from Kongo; *demitasse*, from French; *khaki*, from Hindi; *mediator*, from Latin; *tepee*, from Dakota; *sofa*, from Arabic; and *thermometer*, from Greek.[1] Ordinary cultural borrowing reflects an openness to new, different, or exciting areas of experience from outside the culture of the borrowing speech community.

By contrast, intimate cultural borrowing involves different languages that are spoken in the same place. Typically one language is the language of those in power and thus carries prestige. The less powerful speakers of the other language borrow from the prestige language. For English, the most dramatic instance of intimate cultural borrowing endures in the enormous layer of French vocabulary added to English during the Middle English period (ca. 1100–1500), including words that no longer seem foreign, like *carry*, *country, fruit, join, male*, and *move*.

The third kind of borrowing takes place between mutually intelligible varieties of the same language and is therefore called dialect borrowing. Current examples are the use of northern *you guys* in southern *you all* territory and in positive sentences the expansion of *anymore* meaning 'nowadays' beyond the Midland dialect region, as in "Anymore you see round bales of hay in the fields."

Intimate cultural borrowing and dialect borrowing are similar because they imply negotiation of the status of the groups doing the linguistic borrowing and lending. Borrowing ordinarily goes from the more privileged group to the less privileged group, the have-nots imitating the haves. But, as Bloomfield points out, the direction can be reversed "facetiously" (1933, 471), the dominant language or dialect speakers borrowing downward for reasons of levity, humor, or rhetorical effect. A current example is the adoption of the noun *dude* into many colloquial varieties of standard English from the dialects of African Americans, as in "Some dude was scalping tickets in front of the Dean Dome and got arrested."

Although borrowing from foreign languages has been a major source of new vocabulary in the documented history of English, the percentage of new words entering from foreign languages in the past half century has been quite small (Algeo and Algeo 1991, 14). Likewise, borrowing from foreign languages has been a negligible source of slang. A sampling of 10 percent of the entries in Chapman's *New Dictionary of American Slang* (1986) turns up fewer than twenty-five instances of ordinary cultural borrowing. Among them are *bum* 'someone who does not work', from German; *fu* 'marijuana', from Portuguese; *greefa* 'marijuana', from Mexican Spanish; *old Siwash* 'archetypical small college', from Chinook jargon; *snoose* 'snuff', from Swedish; and *toney* 'stylish, elegant', from French.

The only foreign language that has contributed more than a sprinkling of slang terms is Yiddish, from which English has borrowed such varied informal vocabulary as *fin* 'five dollar bill', *hock* 'to pester', *klutz* 'a clumsy person', *kvetch* 'to whine, complain', and *smack* 'heroin'. Many Yiddish borrowings begin with the initial sound of the word *shoe*, spelled *sch-* or *sh-*, like *schlock* 'inferior merchandise', *schmaltzy* 'sentimental', and *schnook* 'an ineffectual person'. Initial *schm-* associated with Yiddish borrowings is used productively to form derisive rhyming compounds, like *fancy-schmancy*, *nice-schmice*, or *glad-schmad*. It is debatable whether Yiddish words in American slang should be classified as intimate cultural borrowings (from a foreign language) or as dialect borrowings (from another variety of English). Perhaps early borrowings came into slang directly from Yiddish, but it is likely that more recent borrowings are from English dialects that have been influenced by Yiddish. Take, for instance, *schlep* 'lug, carry clumsily', which has spread from the dialect of metropolitan New York to become part of general American slang.

The low incidence of borrowing not only follows the trend in the English language as a whole but is also consistent with the function of slang to enhance solidarity among like-minded people rather than to reach out to different sorts. Thus examination of those slang items that originate in the languages and dialects of other groups can be instructive. In the twenty-year collection of college slang at the University of North Carolina, about two hundred items at most can be classified as borrowing, about half from foreign languages and about half from dialects, mostly African American varieties of English.[2] Even for many of these two hundred, the foreign connection is problematic.

In the UNC-CH corpus, borrowings from other languages can be grouped into a series of categories based on the degree of foreignness. Many are not original to college slang and are already sufficiently a part of English to be listed in dictionaries. Some are not even slang, like *siesta* 'afternoon nap', but for a while at least they were part of the vogue vocabulary on campus and reported by students as examples of good, current campus slang.

Two sets of the borrowed words are already at home in English. Foreign words listed as ordinary words without usage labels in standard English dictionaries are *beau* 'boyfriend', *diva* 'prima donna', *mousse* 'foamy preparation for the hair', and *pissoir* 'public toilet'. A clipped form *gig*, from *gigolo*, has changed in meaning to 'a male who dates many women', and *mousse* becomes a verb with the addition of the particle *up*. *Alter ego*, a Latin phrase in general English, in slang has come to mean 'identification', sometimes called *I.D.*, or *ID*, an allusion to Freudian psychology.

Other foreign words are already part of the slang and informal vocabulary of English and appear in either slang or conventional dictionaries. These are *capeesh* 'understand', *chutzpah* 'brashness', *ducats* 'money', *ganja* 'marijuana', *hombre* 'guy', *macho* 'aggressively masculine', *politico* 'politician', *schlock* 'inferior merchandise', *schmuck* 'detestable person', and *shekel* 'money'. Of these, *politico* has specialized to 'a campus political figure'. *Schlock* has shifted slightly to mean 'out of fashion, trite' and has inspired *nonschlock*, which means 'avant-garde'. *Shekel* has shifted to a verb meaning 'give, hand out', as in "Shekel me some of those Scoobie snacks." Other established items of slang that entered as borrowings have changed more drastically in meaning. *Blitzkrieg* and *blitz*, from German *Blitz* 'lightning', mean 'defeat' or 'drunk' in general slang, but in college slang they also mean 'to perform well on a test'. *Commando*, 'overeager person' in general slang, in the phrase *go commando* means 'without underwear'. *Gonzo* 'insane, wild' becomes one of the many synonyms for 'drunk' in college slang.

A handful of college slang expressions are common foreign words that retain the meaning and the approximate form of the source language: *chica* and *chiquita* 'girl'; *beaucoup* /buku/ and *beaucoups* /bukuz/ 'a large quantity'; *tres* 'very'; *ciao* 'good-bye'; *grazie* 'thanks'; and *qué pasa* 'how are you?'. These are simply sprinkled into the conversation in place of an English equivalent.

Other borrowings are more complicated. *Faux* /fo/, a clipping of *faux pas*, is a noun or a verb: "That was a real faux."/"I really fauxed that time." *Fois* /fwa/, from French 'time, instance', means 'reminiscent of European style': "How do you like my fois sweater?" A few borrowings are translations into a foreign language of American slang expressions. In college slang, French *fromage* is occasioned by slang *cheese* 'objectionable', and *legume* translates slang *vegetable*. Spanish *luego* replaces the farewell *later*, and French *mange* becomes a regular verb for 'eat': "We manged peanut butter and jelly sandwiches at midnight." The passage of time can add complications. In 1974 the Nazi motto *sieg heil* for students was merely an affirmative response to "How are you?" In the 1990s with the rise of neo-Nazism the expression is not a matter of levity and is not used as slang by college students.

At least two French expressions have preserved form but with meanings entirely different from their sources. *La vogue*, which means 'fashion, style' in French, as college slang means 'the women's toilet'. *Escargot*, 'snail' in French, in a play on *his cargo* or *his car go* in English means 'male walking arm in arm with his date'. In four instances, a foreign proper name is used. *Ponch*, a clipping of the name of the Cisco Kid's sidekick *Poncho*, is 'a noun of address for males'; and *guido* means 'macho'. Capitalizing on the sounds of foreign names are *sarajevo* 'good-bye', from the site of the 1984 winter Olympics (and possibly influenced by Japanese *sayonara*), and *gorbachev*, a substitute for *gesundheit* when someone sneezes.

The foreignness of the sound seems to be a large part of the appeal of borrowing in slang. Mock Latin *doscus* and its clipped derivatives *dosc* and *dosh* mean 'fool', as does their pompous-sounding synonym *dorkus pretentious*. *Schlub* 'fight'; *schmiel/schmielage* 'female'; *schmiel on* 'act nice in order to pick up a female'; and *schnack* and *schnicky-schnacky* 'affection' sound like mock Yiddish. *Schmegma* 'gross, slimy' is a mock Yiddish rendering of the clinical *smegma*. An endearing suffix from the non-WASP-sounding name *Rosenblatt* is *-blatt*, as in *dudeblatt*. *Mongo* 'huge' and the term of endearment *mongolito* are perhaps mock Spanish. *Mutile* is phony French for 'an incapacitated, immobile person', and the French pronunciation of the suffix *-ment* in *solidment* makes the affirmative response *solid* more emphatic. *Chicalean* 'very fashionable or appealing' is built on French *chic*. Campus cafeterias *Lenoir* and *Chase* are ironically associated with French cuisine by the mock French pronunciations *Lenwah* and *LaChaise*. German *meister* 'master' has become a popular second element in compounds like *slackmeister*. Made popular by the television program *Saturday Night Live*, the suffixes *-meister* and the Japanese *-san* are added to proper names to convey familiarity. For example, the name *Mary Walsh* becomes *Marysan* or *the Walshmeister*. *Brewski* has long been a slang term for 'beer', but the Polish-sounding *-ski* is also a suffix added to the name of a person who does something stupid: "Toddski, you went away for the weekend with my car keys in your pocket."

A term submitted in 1992 as an example of campus slang comments on the way that students play with sounds from other dialects. The verb phrase *Cajun talk* means 'pronounce any word ending in -*(t)ion* as *shawn* (such as educa*shawn*), in imitation of the way Cajuns speak'. In the most drastic alterations of foreign expressions, approximate English phonetic equivalents are substituted, often resulting in nonsense. Almost all of these are based on phrases learned in introductory foreign language classes. The meaning of the expression comes from the source language, not from the English words. Three blendlike expressions retain Spanish elements: *hasta la bye bye, hasta hasta pasta,* and *adios amoebas* mean 'good-bye'. *Hasta mañana* 'see you tomorrow' inspires *hasty bananas. S'il vous plaît* 'please', *silver plate* and *seafood plate. Adios, amigos* 'good-bye friends', *osmosis amoebas. Merci beaucoup* 'thank you very much', *mercy buckets* and *mercy buttercups. Au revoir* 'good-bye', *o'river* and *Paul Revere. Auf wiedersehen* 'good-bye', *my feet are staying.* As English forms with no allusion to the source language, these make no sense. Pronouncing foreign sound sequences as identifiable English words, even though the resultant phrase is nonsense, is similar to the process of folk etymology that yields *cockroach* from Spanish *cucaracha* (see Chapter 2). It is a means of making the unfamiliar familiar.

Some slang items are malapropisms and pseudolearned imitations. These are not borrowings, but they play on the phonological shape of learned borrowings in English. Among the slang items that seem to derive their humor from the polysyllabic Latin- and Greek-based elements of the vocabulary are *sleazoid* 'a promiscuous female', *motivate* 'leave', *laminite* 'a phony', *somnambulance* 'someone who is funny, likable, crazy', *hypnotist* 'crazy person', *arbitrary* 'insignificant', and *fratosororalingoid* 'obnoxious fraternity or sorority member'.

Taken together, the borrowings from foreign languages in college slang do not indicate acceptance or admiration of things foreign. For the most part, college slang is ethnocentric. It conveys the notion that a foreign language is somehow not worthwhile because it does not sound like English. Forcing the foreign sounds to approximate words in English becomes for many college students the basis of humor. When the foreign expressions are those associated with classroom experiences of foreign language learning, the attitude is also anti-intellectual. Mock foreign expressions rely on stereotypes, generalizations about a group that are likewise consistent with the us-versus-other social function of slang.

Dialect borrowing is more prevalent in slang than is borrowing from foreign languages. However, only a handful of slang items are borrowed from regional dialects. The dialects that supply slang are social dialects, the linguistic varieties developed by groups united by class, education, ethnic background, occupation, and the like. Many such groups—like enlisted military personnel, carnival workers, and drug addicts—live on the margins of society without ready access to prestige or power. In a reverse of the pattern of creating a standard lexicon, in which the less powerful borrow linguistically from the more powerful, slang has always borrowed heavily from the dialects of subcultures.

In the twentieth century, African American dialects have most influenced general American slang.[3] According to Robert L. Chapman, editor of the *New Dictionary of American Slang*, "close analysis would probably show that, what with the prominence of black people in the armed forces, in music, in the entertainment world, and in street and ghetto life, the black influence on American slang has been more pervasive in recent times than that of any other ethnic group in history" (1986, xi).

Chapman's 1986 dictionary includes among its 17,000 entries only about 500 that are associated with African Americans (designated in the dictionary as *black*). Of these, about 60 are ethnic slurs or are outsiders' perceptions of African American culture and are unlikely to have been originated by African American speakers—for example, *porch monkey* or *Hershey bar* for 'an African American'; *African golf* for 'the game of craps'; and *Ethiopian heaven* for 'topmost balcony in a segregated theater'. The remaining 435 or so are African American in origin or use, or both, and can be analyzed from various perspectives to give a picture of African American contributions to American slang.

Etymologically, only 6 of the 435 have definite or plausible origins in African languages: *buckra* 'white man'; *jive* 'banter'; *juke* 'dance'; *jumbo* 'huge'; *mojo* 'amulet, power'; and *swank* 'well dressed'. As is true with slang in general, the overwhelming majority of African American slang terms have originated in the ordinary ways by which English generates new vocabulary. For example, compounding is shown by *crumbsnatcher* 'baby' and *walkboy* 'good male friend'. *Burner* 'one who performs (*burns*) well' and *funkiness* and *funkified* (from *funky*) are formed by suffixation. *Do* and *tude* are shortenings of *hairdo* and *attitude*. Rhyming is operative in *honky-tonk* and *boon-coon* 'best friend'. *Eyeball* 'to look at' and *off* 'to kill' are verbs formed by functional shift from another part of speech. Semantic shifts of various types and degrees account for large numbers of African American slang items. *Bottoms* 'shoes'; *chimney* 'the head'; and *skin* 'palm of the hand' are metonyms. Metaphors include *forks* 'fingers'; *lemon* 'light-skinned black woman'; and *piano* 'section of spare ribs'.

Because ephemerality is often characteristic of slang, dates associated with entries are also worth noting. More than 20 percent of the African American entries carry a dating phrase that shows "the time of origin and/or special currency of the terms" (xxxiv). Many from more than fifty years ago are still in use in informal varieties of American English, sometimes with a slightly different meaning—for example, *uppity, white trash, truck, Joe Blow, reefer,* and *latch on to.* The two decades with the greatest number of entries are the 1930s, the golden age of radio and nightclubs when black entertainers began achieving national prominence, and the 1960s, the decade of the civil rights struggles to end legal segregation. Terms from the 1930s include *alligator* 'devotee of swing and jive'; *gasser* 'anything amusing';[4] and *jam* 'have a good time'. Almost all of the terms that rose to popularity in the 1960s are still in general informal use, though many speakers may no longer be aware of their African American origins, for example *bug* 'to pester'; *the nitty-gritty* 'harsh reality'; *ripoff* 'theft'; and *do one's own thing* 'follow one's own inclination'. Several terms borrowed over the years from Black Vernacular are synonyms. Of *bad, mean, serious,* and *righteous* for 'excellent', only *righteous* marks its user as a throwback to an earlier era. *Slide, truck,* and *split* all mean 'to leave', and all can still be recognized and used, although they are not so current as *peace out* and *Audi 5000.* Because fewer than one-fourth of the items are dated and because the dating of slang items is fraught with imprecision, these data can be only suggestive.

Another uncertainty in using dictionary entries as data is tracking the progression of use of a term, particularly in slang. Some terms originate within one group but by use become identified with another. *The Hound* and *the Dog* for 'Greyhound bus' are associated with African Americans and students, though they originated among truckers. In student slang at the University of North

Carolina, *case nickel* and *case quarter*, for 'a single coin worth five cents' and 'a single coin worth twenty-five cents', were popularized by African American students and thus on campus are considered black slang. Yet older and rural North Carolinians of both races use the terms. *Uncle Tom* for 'a black who is overly subservient' is widely known to be from the title character of Harriet Beecher Stowe's novel, but its shortened form *tom*, particularly when it functions as a verb, is marked as black usage. Many terms that originated among African Americans remain for the most part in that community, like *conk* 'to straighten hair'; *have papers on* 'to be married to'; and *Up-South* 'the North'. Others move into general American slang and informal usage, retaining various degrees of association with African American speakers, for example, *uptight* 'nervous'; *chill out* 'relax'; and *tude* 'a negative attitude'. And when an expression like *crunch time* bursts into popularity in the 1980s with no associations with African Americans, should it be linked to an outdated black slang source, here *crunch* meaning 'crisis', and categorized as an African American contribution to the language?

Another characteristic of the African American dictionary entries in Chapman is that 15 percent are accompanied by "impact symbols" marking them as offensive (xxxiii). That so many slang terms are objectionable in public and polite usage is consistent with slang's irreverent nature. Slang is where the language can name what is distasteful to speak about. Two important taboo areas in American culture are sex and race. Of the 64 items with impact labels almost all refer to sex or race, for example *lay pipe* 'copulate'; *poontang* 'black woman regarded as a sex object'; and *peckerwood* 'a poor southern white'. Marginalized groups have less to lose in violating the taboos of society, and it is not surprising that general slang reaches into the vocabulary of these groups for offensive words. The availability of offensive vocabulary in the dialects of marginal groups confirms the entrenched position of the mainstream, which stereotypically pictures such groups as preoccupied with unrestrained behavior such as sexual promiscuity, drinking, dancing, and having a good time.

From the perspective of subject matter, African American contributions do not present a version of general slang in miniature. The meanings are far more limited. Most striking is the lack of terms for drinking and drunk. There are only 7 in 435: *conk-buster*, *ink*, *King Kong*, and *kong* all refer to cheap varieties of wine and liquor; *taste* means 'a drink of liquor'; and *ripped* and *teed up* mean 'drunk'. Similarly, only three terms mean 'marijuana', *gage*, *reefer*, and *tea*; and *floating* is 'a drug-induced high'. There are no terms of African American origin recorded by 1986 for cocaine, heroine, or hallucinogens. Violence is not prominent either. Five terms mean 'kill': *chill, kiss-off, off, vamp,* and *waste*. A single term, *bill*, means 'knife', and *popper* means 'gun'. Nevertheless, there are 8 terms for 'policeman', including *bluebird, Irvin,* and *skull-buster*.

More than three-fourths of the 435 terms fall into a handful of broad and sometimes overlapping categories. The area of inter-personal relationships includes *gatemouth* 'a person who knows and tells everyone else's business'; *homeboy* 'a person from some-one's hometown or a friend'; *run a game on someone* 'take advantage of someone, particularly by deception'; and *walk soft* 'behave quietly and peacefully'. Matters of sex and women account for 43 terms, for example, *flavor* 'a sexually attractive woman'; *george* 'invite to sexual activity'; and *ground rations* 'copulation'. Another 45 refer to personal appearance, including skin color, for example, *do-rag* 'a scarf worn over a processed hairdo'; *headlight* 'a light-skinned black person'; and *righteous moss* 'nonkinky hair'. A slightly smaller set encompasses music, dancing, having a good time, and performing well. For example, *rug-cut* means 'dance at a rent party or other cheap occasion'; an *all-originals scene* is 'a party where only blacks are present'; and *tcb* (*take care of business*) means 'perform stylishly and effectively'. More than 20 terms are negative or positive evaluations. *Lame* means 'an old-fashioned conventional person', and *L7* 'someone who is not with it' is the graphic representation of a *square. Toast* means 'excellent', and *stone* means 'thorough, perfect'. About 70 items refer to whites or African Americans or to relationships between them. A *marshmal-low* is a 'white'; a *bleed* is a 'fellow black'; and *feel a draft* means 'sense racial prejudice'.

Taken as a group, the image conveyed by the 435 words as-sociated with African Americans in general American slang is a pleasant one, suggesting that blacks like to get all dressed up and to get together having a good time dancing and laughing and greeting one another. On the surface the vocabulary items seem to depict a group of lower status as appealing and worthy of imitation. Yet a closer look shows that the borrowings from African American ver-naculars are fairly cautious and are filtered by the stereotypes held by mainstream society. These patterns in general slang hold up for college slang as well.

Only about 100 items in the University of North Carolina corpus are associated with African Americans. But at least 7 of these are among the 40 most frequently submitted campus slang terms 1972–93: *jam, diss, bad, homeboy/homey, dude, word/word up*, and *fox/foxy*. At least one-third of the 100 are sufficiently established that they are listed and labeled in dictionaries as black in origin or usage. Examples are *ace buddy* 'best friend'; *attitude* 'resentful, hostile manner'; *blood* 'black person'; *blow* 'sing'; the verb *boogie* 'party'; *bourgie/boojie* 'middle class'; *boss* 'excellent'; *clean* 'well dressed'; *crib* 'house, room'; *dig* 'understand'; *dude* 'male'; *eagle flies* 'payday'; *fly* 'attractive'; *fox* 'sexy female'; *hawk* 'cold wind'; *homeboy* 'someone from the same hometown'; *jam* 'dance, perform'; *jive* 'deceptive talk'; *rap* 'converse'; *slave* 'job'; and *word up* 'an exclamation of agreement'.

Most of these classical borrowings from Black Vernacular English are connected with the world of jazz and blues music or the music of hip-hop. Well established by the early 1970s when the University of North Carolina corpus begins, these items are tame. They do not suggest an image of African Americans who had just won a difficult civil rights struggle, securing their right to attend a traditionally white university. They summon a less threatening image of entertainers such as Louie Armstrong, Cab Calloway, and others who brought an exciting new sound to American popular music in the 1930s and 1940s.[5]

As for form, more than half of the African American terms in the corpus are monosyllables. Several appear to be the result of shortening processes. *Ace* 'friend' is from *ace buddy*; *A.D.* 'leave', from *Audi 5000*; *blood*, from *blood brother*; *bone* 'have sex', from *do the bone dance*; *boogie*, from *boogie-woogie*; *bourgie/boojie*, from *bourgeois*; *dap*, from *dapper*; *def*, from *definitely*; *diss*, from *disrespect*; *file*, from *profile*; *fly*, from *flychick*; *ho*, from *whore*; *home, homey*, from *homeboy*; *psych*, from *psychology*; and *tude*, from *attitude*. *Phat* 'voluptuous' is said by students to be an acronym of Pretty Hips and Thighs/Tits. The acronym *OPP* 'someone else's partner', from rap music, is euphemistically said to be from the phrase *other people's property*; other versions of the source phrase are *other people's pussy* and *other people's prick*. There is no instance of suffixation to build a new word, and there are only about

10 compounds, including 3 with particles—*peace up* and *word up* 'good-bye' and *down with* 'agree'. Some of the more recent items are prefabricated phrases acquired from musical lyrics (*cold busted* 'caught in the act') or television shows (*go on, girl,* an expression of encouragement; *homey don't play dat,* a refusal to cooperate).

Two phrases are clearly in imitation of Black Vernacular—the greeting *what it is* and *we be X-ing,* as in "We be joking." *What it is* is used by most students on campus. But intended as slang *We be X-ing* is used mostly by white students in imitation of African Americans, usually in sentences depicting energetic, fun-filled activities, as "We be jamming to the music," "We be dancing," or "We be shootin' some hoops."

Categorized by meaning, the African American borrowings in college slang are even more limited in semantic range than is college slang in general. Most of the items pertain to personal and social relationships—verifying group membership and personal ties (*ace buddy, blood, dap, homeboy, main squeeze* 'best girlfriend or boyfriend', *posse* 'group of friends'); looking sexy (*clean, fly, foxy, stone fox, phat*); giving a good appearance (*file, front, perpetrate*); and having a good time (*boogie, jam, jive*). There are evaluative terms, of course, some of which are ironic: *bad, wicked, stupid.* There are no words for academic matters, none for drinking or drunk or vomiting, or for performing poorly. Unlike college slang in general, the words borrowed into college slang from Black Vernacular are not overwhelmingly negative, or judgmental, or sexist.

African American borrowings are far more prominent in the speech of college students than the relatively small number of African American students and borrowings from them would suggest. What college students seem to enjoy are the expressive features of Black Vernacular—the high-fiving, extreme ranges in intonation, nouns of address, irony, and one-upmanship with language. Recent borrowings of vocabulary and African American verbal style are more likely instigated by media performers such as Arsenio Hall and Public Enemy No. 1 than by fellow students. Eddie Murphy was responsible for the popularity of the exclamation *Psyche!* meaning 'I tricked you' in the late 1980s, but *psyche* in the same sense was reported as current student slang at the black Lincoln University in 1934 (Sebastian 1934). Some of the expressive features of Black Vernacular—like *dude* as a noun of address—have been appropriated and popularized by nonblack media figures. *Party on, dude* was the slogan of two white teenagers in the film *Bill and Ted's Excellent Adventure*; and *Cowabunga, dude,* a combination of surfer and black styles, was learned by schoolchildren throughout the nation from the television cartoon character Bart Simpson. *Wannabe* 'a phony' became popular after Spike Lee's film *School Daze* (1988) applied the term to a group of African American students who 'want to be' white. The influence of Black Vernacular styles on the in-group language of white college students is a particular instance of a greater pattern of black influence on American popular culture.

ALLUSION

Another way of reaching beyond the immediate situation to apply knowledge from another context is allusion. Like the other figures of speech—metonymy, irony, and metaphor—allusion evokes meaning indirectly. Allusion briefly refers to a person, place, or event outside the immediate context to elicit associations already in the minds of the audience. Thus calling someone who is crude or boorish *Neanderthal* triggers associations with a specific stage of prehuman development untouched by civilization.

Figurative language always depends on at least a rudimentary understanding of a second referent known by both the user of the figure of speech and the audience. A simple metaphor like *garbage* for 'nonsense generated by a computer' relies on a common understanding among speakers of English of the nature of household refuse referred to as *garbage*. A simple metonymy like the widely used *plastic* for 'credit card' assumes knowledge of the material that credit cards are made of. Often it is difficult, or simply not worthwhile, to distinguish allusion from other kinds of verbal indirection. Allusions, however, usually require specific rather than general information—knowledge of particular people, places, and events.

As a literary device, allusion enriches meaning, for it activates the imagination, allowing the audience to make connections and to experience the pleasure of recognition. Literary allusions usually tap the type of knowledge acquired from books or formal education rather than from the popular culture. In American and British literature, for example, allusions are often classical or biblical. Thus the title of Edgar Allan Poe's "To Helen" immediately brings to the reading of Poe's poem a comparison with Helen of Troy of the Greek epics. And T. S. Eliot's title "The Journey of the Magi" prompts the image of the three wise men from the East who followed the star to Bethlehem in the Gospel of Matthew. Allusion often consists of direct quotation or obvious paraphrase or imitation. For example, the opening line of Robert Browning's "The Bishop Orders His Tomb at St. Praxed's" is "Vanity, saith the preacher, vanity!" It readily calls to mind "Vanity of vanities, saith Qoheleth, vanity of vanities" (Eccles. 1:2). Literary works in turn provide allusions for several expressions in informal English. For example, *to have an albatross around one's neck*, meaning 'to carry a constant, onerous burden', comes from Samuel Taylor Coleridge's *The Rime of the Ancient Mariner*.

Although allusion is expected in literature, it is plentiful in standard, nonliterary language as well. A *Jonah* 'one believed to bring bad luck' refers to the Old Testament prophet; a *pyrrhic victory* 'victory won at tremendous costs', to Greek victories over the Romans in the third century B.C.E.; and a *waterloo* 'any crushing defeat', to the place in Belgium where Napoleon met his final defeat in 1815. As with other kinds of indirection, the original referent can become remote. In explaining the *hail mary* strategy in the Persian Gulf War in 1991, General Norman Schwarzkopf was alluding to a desperation play in football, in which the quarterback throws a high pass toward the end zone into a crowd of jostling receivers and defenders with the prayer that one of his wide receivers will be able to get there and will catch it for a touchdown. The need for heavenly intervention for a play of that sort to succeed had caused the play be named for the prayer "Hail Mary." Sometimes the allusion becomes so cryptic that the audience cannot be expected to make the connection. The popular style of music from southern Louisiana known as *zydeco* is a phonetic approximation of the Louisiana French *les haricots*, which alludes to an old saying *les haricots sont pas sale* 'the beans are not salty'. The expression meant that money was scarce, and beans had to be cooked without salt meat for seasoning. Zydeco music has its roots in the hard times, when one of the instruments used was an ordinary old scrub board.

Allusion is not only a way of enhancing meaning by bringing ancillary knowledge to interpretation; it also provides a way of excluding those who do not have the knowledge. An allusion can be missed; an audience can fail to make the connection. A speaker of current English can understand and effectively use *an albatross around my neck* without catching the allusion to Coleridge. Allusions in literature are often deliberately arcane, known and discoverable only to those steeped in the literary high culture. Slang too capitalizes on the fact that the knowledge required by an allusion may be privileged. Instead of relying on learned culture, however, slang usually alludes to vernacular and popular culture.

Many informal and slang expressions in current American English allude to popular leisure-time pursuits such as playing or watching sports and watching films and television. As the following examples from ball games illustrate, everyday, purposeful conversation is often couched in such vocabulary. Public officials are judged on how well they *field hardball* questions. A major snowstorm forces the post office to *play catch up*. A town manager offers a *ballpark* figure for the cost of a recycling program. Students who skip class and do not turn in assignments have *two strikes against them* at examination time. Someone who wants a fair chance to compete in any type of venture asks for a *level playing field*. Examples from other sports and games include *ace up one's sleeve* from cards, *dark horse* from horse racing, *on the ropes* from boxing, *playing for keeps* from marbles, and the retort *Go to jail. Go directly to jail* from the board game Monopoly.

The slang of college students likewise draws its allusions from leisure activities, in particular from the areas of sports, films, popular music, and television. After all, it is such extracurricular interests that allow for sociability among students, not the lonely mastering of irregular verb forms in French or benzene rings in chemistry.

Sports and games have supplied a small set of allusions in the slang of college students. *Tubular* 'excellent' alludes to a kind of wave that provides an exciting ride in surfing. *Use up all one's letters*, which means 'demonstrate intellectual superiority', is from the board game Scrabble. *Do 12-oz. curls* 'drink beer' expands *curl*, a movement in weight lifting in which a barbell is lifted in the hand. *Table zamboni* 'a rag for wiping spills from a table or bar top' alludes to the Zamboni, a tanklike machine that resurfaces the ice at hockey games. Academic year 1990–91 saw the popularity of *do the Heisman* to mean 'leave, spurn, reject', an allusion to the running figure on the top of the Heisman trophy presented annually to the outstanding collegiate football player. The expression was popularized by the song "The Heisman" by the group Johnny Quest. The new sport bungee jumping made its way into college slang in 1990–91 as *bungee*, meaning 'very', as in "Jody has a bungee awesome smile."

Since the beginning of the talkies, motion pictures have been a source of popular expressions, some of which have persisted in informal usage with their allusions intact for decades, like *Here's looking at you, kid* from the 1942 film classic *Casablanca* or *an offer you can't refuse* from *The Godfather* of 1972. Part of getting the full flavor of the expression is being aware of the allusion.

The tough characters portrayed in films by Humphrey Bogart in the 1940s gave rise in 1970s college slang to the verb *bogart* 'to steal, take an unfair share', as in "Emile bogarted my sweats." A term for 'female breasts' used in college slang in 1983, *bodacious ta-tas*, was taken directly from the film *An Officer and a Gentleman*.

During the 1980s a new genre of teen exploitation films, as exemplified by *Animal House* and *Porky's I* and *II*, featured racy and often raunchy new vocabulary that was eagerly snatched up and passed along, particularly by high school and junior high school students who were supposedly too young to gain admission to these sexually explicit films. *Fast Times at Ridgemont High* in 1982, for instance, popularized the term *gnarley* 'disgusting'. In 1987 *to pull a Ferris Bueller* became a way of saying 'to cut class, take time off from studies', in allusion to the film *Ferris Bueller's Day Off*. Actors who had acquired a following from their sketches on the television program *Saturday Night Live*, like Chevy Chase and Eddie Murphy, continued to set trends in vocabulary in their films. Among the items used in Eddie Murphy's 1984 *Trading Places*, for instance, are *scumbag, jive turkey, Hey—what it is!*, and *Let's kick some ass/some butt*—all of which are now well recognized in colloquial varieties of English. *Bill and Ted's Excellent Adventure* in 1989 gave new and trendy intonation and meaning to the English word *excellent* and probably influenced the "Wayne's World" sketch on *Saturday Night Live* and a 1992 film of the same title that proved to be an important source of allusions for teenage and college slang in the early 1990s.

It is often through films that the American public is exposed to the distinctive vocabulary of African Americans and homosexuals, and it is likely that borrowing from these groups takes place more through films or television than by personal association. For instance, the expression *throw shade* 'humiliate exceedingly' moved beyond gay and African American usage and into the slang of college students in 1991 after the appearance of the film *Paris Is Burning*. Likewise, *jelly roll* 'sex' and *a dick thing* 'something typically masculine or macho' cropped up in college and adolescent slang right after the release of Spike Lee's films *Do the Right Thing* in 1990 and *Mo' Better Blues* in 1991.

Most college students of the past twenty years could not imagine life without listening to music and in this age of microelectronics are never far from their favorite kind. It is commonplace to see students walking across campus wearing earphones or even studying in the library in their own personal musical worlds. For some, it is even difficult to pay attention in class for fifty minutes straight without the reassurance of their background music. It is not surprising that from time to time lyrics of songs or references to musical entertainers become incorporated into the linguistic code they use with their peers.

Here is a sampling from UNC student slang from the field of music from across the years. In 1972 *pink floyd* meant 'immensely enjoyable', an allusion to the British rock group of that name. *Bozo*, 'a foolish, outrageous, or ridiculous person', ultimately from Bozo the Clown, was in vogue around the same time because of a popular album "We're All Bozos on this Bus." In the spring of 1979, *brick house* referred to 'a good looking girl' because of the Commodores' hit song "She's a Brick House." The old phrase *bite the dust* got a new life in the fall of 1980 and became a cheer at football games because of the song "Another One Bites the Dust" by the rock group Queen. In the early 1980s the New Wave group B-52's provided *private Idaho* 'one's own little world' and *limburger* 'a girl no one else would date'. Perennial favorite Bob Dylan was the source of *bring it all back home* 'have a great time' in 1986, and the Rolling Stones' "Stray Cat Blues" gave popularity to the expression *It's no hanging matter* in 1989. College students acquired yet another synonym for 'engage in sex' in 1990 from the dance and song "Doing the Humpty-Hump." And the African American expression *straight up*, meaning 'honestly', became widely used in 1990 because of a hit song by Paula Abdul. The late 1980s and early 1990s also carried rap music from black inner-city contexts to the world. Expressions like *Audi 5000* 'good-bye', *O.P.P.* 'a male or female who is romantically committed to someone else', *posse* 'friends', and *word up* 'a signal of agreement' entered the slang of college students, both African American and white, directly from the lyrics of rap music.

A five-minute single record by fifteen-year-old Moon Unit Zappa of San Fernando Valley started the phenomenon of Valley Girl talk that spread throughout the nation during the summer and fall of 1982. Valley Girl talk promulgated a distinctive style of delivery as well as a southern California teen vocabulary, based in large part on surfer slang. Among the words that achieved national distribution and showed up in college slang as a result of the Valley Girl fad were *awesome, gag me with a spoon, geek, goober, grody, rad, totally, tubular,* and *zod.*

The debut of MTV in 1981 made song lyrics even more accessible, for young people could indulge in their two favorite pastimes at once, music and television. On MTV the latest hit music is performed and interpreted dramatically by the musicians who recorded it—often with innovative camera work, elaborate sets, special effects, and trend-setting styles in clothing, jewelry, and hairdos.

The most frequent source of allusions in college slang of the past twenty years has been television. Reruns of *The Andy Griffith Show,* which originally aired from 1960 to 1968, have given *otis* 'drunk', a reference to the town drunk, and *nip it* 'stop', from *nip it in the bud,* Deputy Sheriff Barney Fife's solution to the crime of jaywalking in Mayberry. *Sure, I knew you could,* which alludes to Mr. Rogers's gentle assurances to children in his neighborhood, became a sarcastic expression of doubt when used by college students to one another. *Star Trek,* which originally ran from 1966 to 1969, inspired Trekkie fan clubs that have developed their own ingroup slang. But not only Trekkies appreciate *Star Trek* allusions. Because of reruns, a series of *Star Trek* films, and a new television series, the old familiar phrases like *Beam me up, Scotty* and *There's no intelligent life here* are always liable to crop up in college slang. *Star Trek: The Next Generation* is leaving its mark too; it has given *level 1 diagnostic* for 'observation', as in "I'm going to run a level 1 diagnostic on the refrigerator." The 1992 expression *pull a Mac-Gyver*—which means 'do something mechanically clever', as in "Dad pulled a MacGyver and used paper clips to fix the clutch"—alludes to the ability of Special Agent MacGyver to use his brains and manual dexterity to get himself out of life-threatening situations every week.

Names of television characters and personalities can generalize in slang. In the early 1980s a *jetson* was a synonym of *space cadet* 'someone who is unaware of what's going on', an allusion to the title characters of a cartoon set in the space age. The stone age predecessors of *The Jetsons, The Flintstones*, provided the noun *wilma* for 'a female who acts stupid' from the name of Fred Flintstone's wife in the earlier cartoon. *Leave It to Beaver*, which originally aired from 1957 to 1963, in the late 1980s was still being tapped for *Beav* and *Wally*, names that college males called each other in jest when caught acting the role of either a little brother or a big brother. In 1991 a *wally* was also 'a nerd accepted into a social group because he is needed for his good looks, athletic ability, or high grades'. In 1987 when the series *Moonlighting* was popular, a *Bruce* was 'a male who thinks he is cool but really isn't'. *Bruce* is from the actor Bruce Willis, who played the bungling private investigator David Addison in the series. In 1991 a *claven* was 'a know-it-all', from the character in the series *Cheers*.

The television program that has consistently provided allusions for college slang since its initial airing on 11 October 1975 is *Saturday Night Live*. *SNL* was the first television show targeted specifically for the first generation raised on television. Critic Leon Wieseltier has called it "an anthropological masterpiece" and "national television for insiders" (1986, 50). And, in fact, some knowledge of what is current on *SNL* is a must for college students who have any aspirations of fitting in with their peers. The Coneheads sketches, which depicted a family of aliens with cone-shaped heads living in suburbia in the late 1970s, contributed *parental units* for 'parents', from which also developed *units, rental units*, and *rents*. *Gumby*, meaning 'a large quantity', and *gumbyhead*, meaning 'someone who does something stupid', allude to Eddie Murphy's *SNL* characterization of the green clay doll Gumby. Gumby had first appeared on *Howdy Doody* in 1956 and then for a few years starred in a half-hour children's show before being brought to life again by Murphy in the early 1980s. *Could it be . . . Satan?* in 1987 became on campus a humorous response to something naughty, in imitation of the favorite saying of *SNL*'s Church Lady. In 1991 three mock honorifics were in use among college students, *meister* and the suffixes -*ster* and -*san*, as in 'the Kenmeister,' 'Kenster,' and 'Kensan.' This pattern was inspired by the Rickmeister on *SNL*. *Like buttah*, meaning 'smooth, soft, beautiful' or 'executed or performed smoothly or well', entered college slang in 1992 from the Coffee Talk sketch.

The most linguistically influential *SNL* sketch has been "Wayne's World," which began in 1989 and by 1992 had been expanded to a feature-length film of the same name. In "Wayne's World," Wayne (played by the creator of the sketch, Mike Myers) and his high school friend Garth (played by Dana Carvey) do a public access television show from Wayne's basement in Aurora, Illinois. Their theme song is "Wayne's World, Wayne's World, Party Time, Excellent," and their programs are often spoofs on cultural phenomena like television commercials or sitcoms like *Laverne and Shirley*. There is plenty of talk of *hurling* 'vomiting' and of women — *babe-a-licious girls, babe-a-lonians*, and just plain *babes* — who, Wayne and Garth hope, *walk the way of a trollop* 'signal sexual availability'. Two linguistic usages in particular made their mark on colloquial American English because of "Wayne's World," *Way!* and *Not! Way*! is a positive response to someone else's incredulous *No way*, as in X: "I just won two tickets to the ACC Tournament." Y: "No way." X: "Way!" Wayne and Garth's characteristic method of negation by placing *not* after an affirmative statement by 1992 had become a national in-joke, used by elementary school children and showing up in magazine headings and television commercials. For example, "This cereal is just for kids — N OT." The affirmative statement is delivered seriously with falling intonation and no hint of the reversal to come. Then after a brief pause, *not* is said with rising intonation. In its placement after a seemingly serious declarative sentence and in its effect on meaning, *not* is similar to *psych!* made popular by Eddie Murphy in the mid-1980s.

An African American counterpart of *SNL, In Living Color*, was also a source of allusions in college slang during the early 1990s. The controversial half-hour, weekly variety show was built around a recurring set of sketches that parodied African American stereotypes — Antoine the homeless bum, Homey the Clown, the gay critics of the arts, and others.[6] It poked fun at such prominent African Americans as the Reverend Jesse Jackson, Oprah Winfrey, and MC Hammer (Benton 1991). During the 1990–91 season, college students appropriated from *In Living Color* the expressions *go on, girl, homey don't play dat*, and *two snaps up. Go on, girl* is a signal of encouragement from a bystander for someone else to continue in a verbal confrontation. *Homey don't play dat*, the favorite expression of Homey the Clown, is a retort that expresses lack of agreement or cooperation, as in X: "Everyone in the dorm is rushing." Y: "Homey don't play dat." The subject *homey* can be replaced with another noun phrase, as in "This North Carolina girl don't play dat." *Two snaps up*, accompanied by finger snapping, is a sign of approval, as in "Dr. Hall's course gets two snaps up." The expression alludes to the favorable rating *two thumbs up* made popular by television film critics Roger Ebert and Gene Siskel.

Television commercials also provide allusions for college slang. *Know what I mean, Vern?*, meaning 'Do you understand, do you agree?', became a part of college slang and general American vernacular during the 1980s because of a series of commercials that varied from region to region only in the product or service being promoted. The alliterative *Maalox Moment* from Maalox commercials of the early 1990s refers to 'a time of stress'. *Chester* for 'someone who is *cheezy* (socially unacceptable or unfashionable)' comes from a cartoon character in a Cheetos commercial who keeps saying *cheezin'*, as in 'Steve's new haircut makes him look like a Chester.' *Beef-a-roni* 'good looking male' is formed on a product of the same name. *Cram-o-matic* 'to study hard at the last minute for a test' is patterned on the commercial for the Ronco Veg-o-matic.

Expressions picked up from films, musical lyrics, and television are not necessarily created by their writers. For instance, *Sure, I knew you could* is ordinary colloquial English, and appropriately used by television's Mr. Rogers, it is an assurance to young children. In slang, however, it is given an ironic interpretation and is used to belittle, to treat an adult like a child. Lexical items appropriated from television are subsequently susceptible to ordinary changes in meaning. For example, an allusion to the Lone Ranger, *masked man*, in 1985 slang meant 'homosexual'. It no longer referred to an individual defender of justice concealing his identity behind a mask for some sort of romantic reasons but instead to someone wishing to keep his identity concealed for fear of social sanctions.

Regardless of who invents them, expressions used on television can be disseminated nationally in a single night. Programs like the 1985 hit series *Miami Vice* make available to a large portion of society a vocabulary of vogue that allows them to identify with a style rather than with a group. *Miami Vice* exuded the latest in style—in photographic technique, music, flashy cars, fast boats, and clothing. The two main characters were undercover policemen with a vast knowledge of the criminal element of Miami, not the least part of which was their knowledge of the vocabulary and linguistic style needed to survive in that hostile setting. Slang items that had previously been popular among pockets of speakers such as college students or drug users now reached the ears of the public at large. Their meanings were usually immediately apparent from the context.

On *Miami Vice*, no activity ever happens; it *goes down*: "The deal is going down right now." Instead of *hello* and *good-bye*, characters say *What's happening?*, *What it is, blood?*, and *Check you later*. Terms of disdain abound: *lowlife*, *slimebucket*, *scum*, *pig*, *sleeze* (often submitted by students with the spelling *sleaze*). *History* means the ultimate good-bye. "You're history," reads a death threat; "Ten minutes and thirty seconds and we're history," says Crockett while trying to detonate a bomb. *Attitude* is 'a negative or uncooperative attitude', as in "This guy has an attitude, a real attitude." *Boogie* and *book* both mean 'leave', as in "Lombard's going to boogie" and "Why did you book from custody?"

Although the mass media provide a natural source for culturally determined slang, college students and other groups draw from the media selectively. In college slang, allusions to various cultural phenomena are more random than representative. The popularity of a musical entertainer, television program, or film does not guarantee that it will provide a source of allusion for slang. For example, despite their long-standing following among college students, Elton John, Paul Simon, the Beatles, Led Zeppelin, Sting, and many others are all missing from the allusions of North Carolina college slang.

Not all allusions in college slang are inspired by the entertainment media. *Barbie* and *Ken* 'painstakingly fashionably dressed college female/male' allude to the ever popular children's dolls, whose wardrobes and accessories are essential to their identities. *From Chicago* is a synonym of *airhead* 'someone who is unaware' and alludes to Chicago's nickname as "The Windy City." *Land's End* is an all-purpose exclamation, as in "Land's End! The phone is ringing again." It is the name of a mail order clothing company. *Egg-a-muffin*, an enthusiastic response of agreement altered from *Egg McMuffin*, and *McPaper* 'a quickly or poorly written paper' allude to the fast-food chain McDonald's.

Associations that are part of the meaning of slang items sometimes depend on knowledge of cultural stereotypes and values. Such associations can sometimes be verbalized as a little scene or vignette in which characters act out a cultural stereotype. For instance, a *cowboy question* means a 'dare', as in "Jump the median. It's a cowboy question." *Cowboy question* takes its meaning from the implicit command "assume the character of a cowboy and act like one." It is a challenge to someone's bravery or honor. Its interpretation relies on the television and movie image of the good cowboy—unwillingly drawn into a shootout by a wicked gunslinger, usually to uphold the honor of the law-abiding citizenry, womenfolk, or other defenseless persons. The interpretation of the slang item focuses on the daring of the action rather than on a noble reason for it.

It is the knowledge of the cultural stereotype of appropriate female behavior that makes *He could make me write bad checks* an understandable favorable comment on the good looks of a male. Traditionally, a woman who financially supports an able-bodied and healthy man or who pays for his attentions is looked down upon. Even worse, if she writes a check on an account with insufficient funds because of him, she breaks the law. The inference is that a man whose mere physical appearance could drive a woman to such wreckless behavior must be handsome indeed.

To *beer goggle* or to *have one's beer goggles on* is to 'find someone attractive because of the influence of alcohol', as in "You think he's hot? You must be beergoggling./You must have your beer goggles on." In this scene someone has drunk enough alcohol to be in a euphoric, friendly, or uninhibited mood in which the ability to discern or to react critically is diminished. Viewed from that perspective, all potential objects of affection seem attractive.

The walk of shame is 'the walk home in the morning after having spent the night out with a member of the opposite sex', as in "Did you see Sherry in her formal from last night? No doubt she was taking the walk of shame." Although males too return home disheveled after a romantic night out, students report that this expression applies only to females—as did curfew rules once upon a time. *The walk of shame* alludes to earlier times when such behavior on the part of a female college student would have occasioned not simply notice and knowing smiles as it does now but disgrace and possibly suspension from school.

The daisy chain is a flippant term for the 'connection between people who have had sex with the same partner at different times', as in "So, Chris, I guess you and I have slept together on the daisy chain." What makes this image of contemporary, unrestrained sexual relations incongruous is the association of daisies strung together into a festive garland with innocent children and school-approved ceremonies like May festivals and baccalaureate services.

Slang is sometimes disparaged for lacking in meaning and indicating a shallow mind. The vagueness of some slang is the result of sudden and widespread application to a wide range of referents or in a large variety of situations. Slang *sweet*, for instance, signals nothing more specific than positive value. Vagueness can result for the same reasons with standard vocabulary—for example, the word *aspect*. But not all slang is vague. As shown here in Chapters 3 and 4, the pairing of form to meaning in slang is often the result of multiple and complex processes as cognitively sophisticated as those that give rise to the most formal and cultivated levels of the standard vocabulary.

5: Use

Previous chapters describe the nature of slang, the forms slang takes, and the meanings slang evokes. This chapter examines the use of slang, noting where slang typically occurs and showing how its use is consistent with the social functions of slang.

Slang can occur at almost any point in a sentence — as the subject, or the predicate, or a modifier. In a conversation that incorporates several items of unfamiliar slang, it may seem that the speakers are using a different language. Because the lexical items are unknown, the conversation is incomprehensible. To the uninitiated, then, conversations using slang are comparable to a sentence containing nonsense words. A sentence like *The spakes brockered the musiles on the jeet*, for example, makes no sense because its nouns and verb are not recognizable words. Substitute familiar English words, and the sentence is fine: *The children watered the flowers on the deck*. For hearers who are outside the group, slang is like the nonsense words *spake, brocker, musile,* and *jeet*. A sentence of the same grammatical structure using slang might be *The gweebs dissed the granolas on the yard*, which translates into 'The people entirely lacking in social skills showed a disrespectful attitude toward the people dressed in styles of the sixties who were gathered in front of the undergraduate library'. Although the sentence containing slang may be incomprehensible because the slang meanings of *gweeb, diss, granola,* and *yard* are unknown, the speaker is not using a foreign language. The sequence of sounds and the grammatical structures are English. Once the hearer knows the words, the hearer understands. Slang, then, consists of words and phrases that fit into the established grammatical patterns of the language.

Even though college students could plug slang words willy-nilly into and throughout a discourse, they don't. In fact, the sentence *The gweebs dissed the granolas on the yard* is a contrived one, overloaded with slang for the purpose of illustration. It is possible that North Carolina students in the early 1990s could say and understand this sentence, but an utterance so saturated with slang items is not typical and would likely be taken as self-parody.

If slang does not occur at every opportunity, where, then, does slang occur in the conversational structure and why? Judging from citations that students submit as part of their assignment, two positions within a sentence are most hospitable to slang: (1) for nouns, after the demonstrative *that*; (2) for adjectives, in the predicate position after a form of the verb *be*.

1. That *airhead/goober/hunk* gave me a ticket to tonight's game.
2. That teacher is so *cheezy/clueless/def*.

This is not surprising, for nouns after *that* assign membership in a particular class and adjectives after *be* assert an identifying characteristic. Both structures facilitate the judgmental quality of slang. Flexner calls many of the words that fit into these two slots *counterwords*. "These are automatic, often one-word responses of like or dislike, of acceptance or rejection" (Wentworth and Flexner 1975, xi). Negative counters "merely say that the person is rejected— he does not belong to the group. In uttering the counter we don't care what the person is; we are pledging our own group loyalty, affirming our identity, and expressing our satisfaction at being accepted" (xi).

The frequent occurrence of the demonstrative *that* before slang nouns is consistent with the social functions of slang, particularly when *that* precedes a noun with unfavorable connotations, like *goober* 'a socially inept person'. *That*, as opposed to *this*, establishes distance between the speaker and the undesirable referent.

In the second pattern, *so* typically occurs before adjectives that designate qualities that can occur in degrees—like *cheezy* 'out of fashion', *clueless* 'lacking in awareness', and *def* 'excellent'. The pronunciation of *so* can be prolonged to show intensity or amount.

Perhaps more instructive is the use of slang words and expressions to facilitate conversation. The college slang lexicon shows several sets of words and phrases whose main use is just that—to establish verbal contact, to get a conversation going, to keep it going, and to end it.

Beginning and ending conversations gracefully is an acquired social and linguistic skill, and the potential for social awkwardness is great. The language in general and college slang in particular provide formulaic or ritualistic greetings and farewells. At any one time, college students have in their repertory many greetings that correspond to the standard *hello* and *how are you?* and to the informal *hey* and *hi*. *Yo* is probably the most frequently used long-standing slang equivalent of *hello* on campus. Over the years it has alternated with others like *check in, chello, come in, Berlin,* and *like hi.* Question forms such as these versions of *how are you?* signal that a response is in order: *how's it going? what does it look like? what it is? what's going down? what's happening? what's jumping? what's shaking? what's the deal? what's up? 's up? what's up, G? what you know? where it's at?* and *qué pasa?*

Expressions used to end conversations are more varied in form and are more likely to refer to knowledge shared by the speakers (Eble 1983). Unlike greetings, farewells are not questions, for a question provides the opportunity for the conversation to continue. Standard farewells tend to take the form of polite commands like *take care of yourself* or elliptical statements like *see you on Friday* (from *I'll see you on Friday*). They often use positive adjectives, as in *nice to see you,* and refer to the future welfare or meeting of the participants, as in *hope you feel better* or *I'll call you next week.* The parting remarks of college students follow the same patterns, as in the long-standing *check you later,* an elliptical statement that refers to a future meeting. Variations are *catch you later, check you on the flip side, catch you on the flip flop, check you, smell you later,* and *smell you. It's been real* comments positively on the time spent together. The frequently used *later* is a shortening of something like *see you later*; it gives rise to *latro* and to the humorous rhyming expansion *later, tater. G.B.* is an initialism of *good-bye,* and *hand* is an acronym of *have a nice day. Chbye* is the counterpart of the greeting *chello,* both pronounced with an initial *ch* sound. Many college slang farewells are foreign terms or deliberate alterations of foreign terms: *luego; ciao, chow for now; hasta la vista, baby* (from the lyrics of a rap song), *hasta hasta pasta, hasta la bye bye, hasty bananas; sarajevo; Paul Revere* (from *au revoir*); *adios, amoebas* and *osmosis, amoebas* (from *adios, amigos*); and *my feet are stay-ing* (from *auf wiedersehen*). Farewells are often the equivalent of *I must leave now* and use various slang substitutes for *leave*. For ex-ample, *I'm outta here* and its shortened version *outta here* both can end conversations, as well as *gotta* plus *bogart, bolt, boogie, book, break, cruise, dust, jet, motor, motivate, roll, slide, split*, or *troop*, all of which mean 'leave, depart'. *I'm history*, a parting phrase modeled on an underworld expression referring to death, has inspired the formation of *I'm archives* and *I'm art*. *Audi 5000* and its shortened variants *5000* and *A.D.* come from the lyrics of rap music. *Peace up* and *peace out* were likewise made popular by rap. The 1989 film *Bill and Ted's Excellent Adventure* popularized *party on* as a fare-well. *You're so tan I hate you, bye* pokes fun at sorority stereotypes and *kiss, kiss* at the superficial social custom of kissing good-bye.

College slang has many expressions that help to keep commu-nication and conversation going. They are typically empathetic responses to the good or bad news of another. Some express agree-ment, for example, *given, gotta love that, I'm down with that, I'm into that, no doubt, word*, and *word up*. Affirmative adjectives like *awesome, decent*, and *rad* used as exclamatory responses convey an element of admiration and approval as well as agreement, as do numerous exclamations like *cool beans, cool deal, get off, hot ticket, loved it*, and *victory*. Reactions of sympathetic disbelief in-clude *as if, get outta here, gimme a break, jump back, no way*, and *whatever*. *I'm hating it, I'm serious, sucks to be you, tell me about it, that bites, that bites the big one, you know it*, and *you're hating it* are various ways of expressing commiseration in the face of mis-fortune. Expressions of reassurance or support tend to be spatial: *gotcha back, gotcha covered, I'm there, we here*. One set of words gently gives advice to calm down: *chill, chill out, ease, let go, jell*, and *mellow out*. Other advice is harsher and more impatient, for example, the set of imperatives containing *get* — *get a clue, get a job, get a life, get a manual, get with the program*, and *get real*.

In-group vocabulary often occurs in the optional form-of-address slot in a sentence, as in the use of *rooms* 'roommate' in "Rooms, will you take the trash out?" This nonrequired part of an English sentence conveys social information about the participants in the conversation — for example, age, office, or awareness of the cultural norms of politeness. An expression of address makes ex-plicit the I/you relationship implicit in face-to-face conversation.

The use of an address form makes the claim that the speaker is not engaging in communication with a stranger; the speaker knows in some way the person being addressed. Because social factors are so important to the linguistic choices of college students, it is not surprising that they use address forms frequently (Eble 1991).

Many nouns used as address forms are, loosely speaking, kinship terms and identify the addressee's relationship to the speaker, as with the example *rooms* above. Other nouns of address used by college students are *bro* and *broth* from *brother*, *blood* from *blood brother*, *cuz* from *cousin*, *sister girl*, and *Beav* and *Wally* from the little brother/big brother relationship on the television series *Leave It to Beaver*. *Homeboy, homegirl, home, homebiscuit, homechop, homeslice, homey*, and *sherlock* are all developments of the notion of kinship between people from the same hometown, even though the terms have generalized in meaning to include people one is close to in other ways. It is notable that several of these kinship terms entered college usage from the dialects of African Americans.

The most generalized and frequent nouns of address — and most neutral with respect to connotations — are *man* and *dude*. They allow speakers the familiarity implied by the use of an address form, even though the speaker may not know the addressee. As a matter of fact, *man* and *dude* are often used merely as attention getters, as in "Man/Dude, you should see the line at the cashier's office." Although both forms originally referred to adult males, both are generalizing toward all ages and both sexes. As an attention getter, *man* can certainly be generally applied. *Dude* is not so far along in the process. With the popularity of the television cartoon character Bart Simpson, *dude* is certainly used by, to, and about children. But every year, students at North Carolina debate about whether or not *dude* can be unself-consciously used to address or refer to females. As of 1993, usage of gender-neutral *dude* was divided.

Almost any evaluative term from the slang repertory can be converted to an address form suitable to a particular situation by using it in conjunction with nouns like *boss, captain, master,* and *meister*, which indicate a degree of proficiency or leadership. For example, "Slack Meister, how did you manage to pull a C in English 36?" Or "Captain Cool, what did you do with my shades that you borrowed?" The suffixes *-ski* and *-wad* can be added to any proper name for a censuring effect: "Say, *Mikewad*, you left the door open and the cat got out." Or "*Toddski*, get a life. Fall break is next week, not this week."

Almost any derogatory noun can be used as a noun of address —*asshole, bitch, butthead, dickhead, hosebag, roadwhore, skank, sleezebag, slimebucket, slut,* and *whore,* for example. Many are laden with sexual connotations. In college student usage, potentially offensive nouns of address such as these are much more likely to be endearing than hostile in intent and are used by people on friendly terms with one another. For the most part, they are used only among peers and directed only to a member of the same sex. *Hello, bitches* is a common greeting among residents in female dormitories, and derogatory terms that refer to sexual promiscuity, like *hose bag* and *slut puppy,* are even used playfully as nouns of address among females. But a male can safely use such expressions to address a female only if he is certain that she will interpret them as affectionate; to have that certainty, a secure friendly relationship must already be established.

Not all forms of address in the speech of college students signal affection in the crass way illustrated by many of the examples cited so far. College students of both sexes still address one another with traditional terms of endearment like *baby, honey, sweetie,* and *pooh bear.* Nicknames, which often betoken shared experience and knowledge, are also common fillers of the optional form-of-address slot (Eble 1991).

The study of slang reported in this book, and thus far in this chapter, focuses on words.[1] However, words are not uttered in isolation. They are always embedded in contexts. Even one-word sentences that seem to evoke meaning all by themselves—like *Amen, Please, Careful!,* and *Stop!*—require context to be completely understood. The purposes and the situations that trigger the use of language as well as the identity and relationship of the users affect the choice of words and their meanings. Speculation about the use of slang, then, cannot merely focus on the slang items themselves but must be based on observation of slang in context.

Anthropologist Michael Moffatt from 1977 through 1987 studied undergraduate life in a large, public American university. At the beginning of the project, he even "passed" as a student, living in a student residence hall for several days. Part of student life that Moffatt observed was student language. In his 1989 *Coming of Age in New Jersey* he estimates that "the average time spent on friendly fun on weekdays in the middle of the semester was a little over four hours a day," with a large portion of this time spent in "endless verbal banter" (33). To gain access to some of the endless verbal banter of students at the University of North Carolina at Chapel Hill, I asked for the help of students enrolled in my English 36 class during the spring semester of 1989. The excerpts of conversations reported in the remainder of this chapter were either written down or tape-recorded for me by Elizabeth Barden, Lori Bell, Chris Carter, Anne Hoover, and Lori Ward. Their good will and cooperation were essential in obtaining these data, because my presence in a group of college students, even as a welcomed observer, would undoubtedly have altered the conversation.

About two hours of conversation were tape-recorded, one hour in a lounge in one residence hall, with the television blaring in the background, and one hour in two dormitory rooms in another residence hall. The students in the lounge, with the exception of one late arrival, knew that one of their group was recording them for a project about conversation for her English class. The occupants of the dormitory rooms knew that a tape recorder was running, but the visitors who dropped in did not.[2]

The recordings support Moffatt's observation that much of the friendly fun among college students consists of verbal banter. Here is a brief sequence from the lounge in which the fun relies on playing with the idea expressed in *like a big dog* 'with intensity'. Rick has just come in from playing volleyball and joins Beth, Mack, and others who are playing cards.

> RICK: You're not sweating like a big dog?
> BETH: I'm sweating.
> RICK: Like a big dog?
> BETH: But I've got a flannel shirt on.
> RICK: Like a little chihuahua maybe?
> MACK: Irish setter?

This playful, teasing, good-humored type of talking for fun is typical, particularly in groups of four or more with both male and female participants. Typical also is the low incidence of slang in this conversation. Although the imagery of the slang expression *like a big dog* serves as the catalyst for the interchange, neither Beth's nor Mack's responses contain slang.

The most surprising feature of the entire two hours of talk is how infrequently slang is used, even in situations for which slang items are readily available. For instance, Beth could have responded to the volleyball player's contention that the card players were not sweating by using various slang expressions current in 1989 — by retorting *you're bust* ('you're wrong'), by calling him *clueless* ('uninformed'), or by denying his right to know with *Who put the quarter in your slot?* ('It's none of your business').

Another discussion in the lounge is likewise deficient in slang — even though the topic is an unattractive female, an appraisal for which college students have numerous slang equivalents.

TIM: Chet must have, Chet must have — the ugly girl must have been home. I can't imagine him talking — maybe — I can't imagine him talking to her that long.

MIKE: Why does he have to read it — that poem? Why does he have to read that poem?

TIM: It's this incredibly romantic poem, and the teacher's trying to be a matchmaker between the two. He's got to present it in class, and she's got to help him cause he didn't get ready. . . .

TIM: We'll ask him when he gets back if he had fun doing it with the ugly girl? That would be terrible. . . .

MIKE: The unendowed.

TIM: Huh? Unendowed?

MIKE: You left out unendowed.

TIM: Yes. She is quite unendowed — she has no natural blessings, let's say.

JAN: Who is it you're talking about?

TIM: This ugly girl Chet has to read a poem to.

JAN: What does he have to read a poem to?

TIM: For his late drama class, or something. Maybe it's speech — one of the classes.

It is puzzling why the males never refer to the ugly girl with slang, like the perennially popular *dog*. Perhaps the presence of a female and the knowledge that the conversation was being recorded served as inhibitors.

In the two hours of student conversation, I find only twenty-five items I would classify as campus slang. Most occur only once — for example, *jump* for 'seduce', *shotgun* for 'drink beer straight down', and *stranger mixer* for 'a party to bring together men and women who do not know each other'. Only *awesome, cool,* and *sweet* occur in both the lounge and room settings. *Awesome* occurs most frequently by far, with thirteen instances in all. Even if the background noise and the distance from the microphone of some of the participants prevented me from recognizing another dozen or so slang items, a total of fewer than fifty instances of slang in two hours of conversation involving about a dozen participants seems low. This quantitative evaluation is, of course, subjective, as there is no established index of what constitutes a low or high concentration of a particular type of vocabulary for various sorts of discourse. However, these student conversations suggest that the option of using slang rather than ordinary colloquial vocabulary is exercised sparingly.

What is not surprising is where the slang occurs in the two hours of student talk. Slang occurs where language serving mainly social purposes is expected to occur — in talk about social life and at points in a conversation where rapport between the participants is established and reinforced.

Here are two excerpts about anticipated social events from the dormitory room tape.

The first is an enthusiastic report by Amy of the annual building of a cardboard tunnel for a party at a fraternity house.

Amy bursts into the room.

AMY: Y'all — awesome shirt. Y'all, the tunnel is out of control. It's already halfway over the house. They're expecting five hundred to eight hundred people.

JILL: My God.

AMY: They had five to eight hundred last year, and they're expecting more tonight. [Unclear murmur.] It's Friday night.

JILL: Cool.

KIM: That's awesome.

AMY: And I've already gotten the cup. And they have the . . . some cups from last year, the cream one.

JILL: Whatever.

[Chorus of voices as JIM and SARAH walk in.]

AMY: Y'all. They're expecting five to eight hundred people at this tunnel party.

SARAH: When is it?

AMY: Tomorrow night. And this tunnel is already over half the house.

SARAH: O my God.

AMY: They said y'all come out tomorrow and we're going to make it bigger and better than ever. They have cardboard everywhere. It's gonna be—it's just—you know, d.j.'s—I mean, it's gonna be awesome. Y'all really need to come.

In this segment, Amy uses the popular superlative evaluations *awesome* and *out of control* to assure her friends that the tunnel party will be an important social event that they should not miss. The other participants, all females, give Amy approving feedback by also using slang—*awesome*, *cool*, and *whatever*. Three of the twelve instances of *awesome* in the dormitory room setting occur in this conversation.

Another conversation that uses slang takes place as Mindy gets ready for a party.

SUE: What you doing tonight, Mindy, writing this paper?

MINDY: No, see, that's the deal. I've got a mixer tonight. And this guy that I'm lusting with is going to be there.

SUE: Who are you mixing with?

MINDY: Umm. Phi Kappa Sig. It's really small. They don't have a house. They're just a bunch of E-hogs[?].

SUE: Let me think. We had a mixer with them one time. Them and one of the frats out on the golf course. We mixed . . . and it was in a—house. I'm pretty sure that's who it was. Are you excited?

MINDY: Yeah. It's a secret drink.

SUE: Secret drink?

MINDY: Yeah. It's this drink they have concocted—it's like called a cruising something something, and the whole theme is like a spring break luau, and so it's like coconut and rum and all this stuff.

SUE: That's nice.

MINDY: Yeah.

SUE: So who's the guy you're madly—madly in love with?

MINDY: His name is Andy. And he's just so—

SUE: Cute.

MINDY: —cute. He's got a great body, and so nice and he's

funny. I mean just like every characteristic you could want, you guys.

SUE: And a potential husband — more qualities of a potential husband.

MINDY: Definitely. I bet he fulfills all of them. Oh I'd like to find out some of them tonight.

SUE: Oh great. You gonna jump him?

MINDY: Yeah. If I get over there and take a shower and stop looking like garbage.

In this conversation, the terms *mix* and *mixer* are part of the slang used to talk about social gatherings. *Lust with* 'feel sexual attraction toward' and *jump* 'seduce' are from the vocabulary of romance. But in talking about this potentially important social event, one that might lead to finding an appropriate partner, the conversation is not saturated with slang. For example, Sue uses *That's nice* and *Oh great* as feedback rather than any of numerous slang equivalents.

Slang functions at the opening of conversations as a way to establish rapport. If the participants do not address each other by name, they often use a slang expression or a nickname, for example, *homegirl*, *dudette*, or *Jim-bo*. One way that slang can be used at the beginning of a conversation is commented on by a male student. Matt reports this interchange between himself and a female acquaintance on campus:

FEMALE: Hey, Matt!

MATT: Howdy, chick!

Afterward Matt wrote out these comments on his greeting: "Whereas the normal greeting would be *Hey, Linda, Sally, etc.*, in this instance, though, I could not remember the girl's name. So I had to stray from the conditioned response and go with a not-so-often-used expression, an energetic tone of voice, and a smile overemphasized for the situation."

Slang can also serve as an icebreaker in situations in which strangers find themselves in the same space. In a paper she wrote on the topic of complaining, one female student supplies the following two examples of in-group language being used to get a conversation going.[3]

I stepped onto the elevator. I looked up. Standing there in front of me was that incredible hunk I had been passing on the way to my eight o'clock class every day for the past two months. I smiled up at him. He smiled back. It was just me and him in the elevator. He shifted his weight nervously from one foot to another as he intently studied the slowly illuminating floor numbers. I really wanted to strike up a conversation with him. He glanced at me out of the corner of his eye. I knew he wanted to communicate too! But—there was a problem. I didn't know him. He didn't know me. The two of us, as of this moment, had absolutely nothing in common to converse about. The tension built. The elevator descended. I had to say something soon. It was now or never! What could I do? *"God, this weather sucks,"* my hunk, still studiously studying those fascinating flashing numbers, calmly stated.

She agreed, they introduced themselves, and "the conversation continued as [they] slid, slushed, and slimed [their] way towards campus."

The fact that slang can sometimes be humorous strengthens its function as an icebreaker. Here is another example from the same student.

Two days ago in the bathroom of the Student Union, I found myself crammed into the small waiting area with four other girls. We all stood in silence studying the intricate dirt designs imprinted on the tile floor. Finally one of the girls, whom I recognized from my History 57 class, glanced up and around at the rest of us. Then she turned to the mirror and promptly stated, "My hair looks so awful. I hate rain. It always makes my hair friz out. I look like the reject French poodle queen from hell!" All of us burst out laughing and "the queen" got to giggling too. Then I assured her that she did not resemble a French poodle, while the other two girls began to discuss the havoc the rain and wind had played with their hair and makeup.

In both scenarios above, slang was used—*sucks, the reject French poodle queen from hell*—to acknowledge in speech a common awkwardness that the participants felt.

Another uncomfortable social situation in which students use slang is in responding to compliments. Politely accepting praise is difficult for speakers of American English in general (Herbert 1986), and particularly so for young people trying to find security among their peers. In a paper on compliments written for a class in 1991, student Jennifer Cox gives these examples.

MARCY: You are so sensitive.
BETSY: Shit, you're the sensitivity daddy-dog.

Here *shit* is an expletive of negation or denial. Betsy reverses the compliment and insists that it is Marcy who is the most proficient (*daddy-dog*) at being sensitive.

PATTY: Your hair looks so beautiful today.
GINA: Scare.

Gina handles the compliment by expressing a fear (*scare*) of accepting the good lest it turn bad — like not telling a birthday wish or else it won't come true.

Cox points out that college students are particularly likely to use slang to deflect a compliment about academic accomplishments or to ally themselves with the anti-intellectual stance of the group despite their own hard-won academic achievements. Here is a transcript of a telephone conversation between Cox and a good friend, in which Peter responds to her enthusiastic compliments with the slang word *dude*, a term sometimes associated with smoking marijuana. According to Cox, Peter uses flat intonation in imitation of the mellowness achieved by smoking pot.

JENNIFER: You are so amazing. I had no idea you had placed out of that many classes here. That is so impressive to me.
PETER: [Quietly] Dude.
JENNIFER: I mean, you really are incredible. Is there anything you can't do?
PETER: Dude.

Students who might be labeled *geeks* because they put their studies first can compensate for this antisocial behavior and maintain status among their peers by using the slang of the group to criticize themselves. Cox gives these examples of the use of *geek* in self-deprecating remarks about studying made by a member of Phi Beta Kappa.

"I'm geeking tonight, so I can't go out."
"I'll probably geek over to Davis Library around 7."
"Let me geek down these last few notes, and then I'll go out."

Students also use slang to extract themselves from a serious conversation or to close or change the topic. Here is a conversation between two female students from the dormitory room tape.

WENDY: How are you doing? Studying?
BECKY: I'm just getting my room back in order from my tirade this morning.
WENDY: From your what?
BECKY: From my tirade this morning.
WENDY: Tirade?
BECKY: Yeah, I started throwing stuff.
WENDY: Why?
BECKY: Pissed at David so.
WENDY: Are you OK?
BECKY: Yeah — OK. It's like my crate things like — no, not crates but you know how they stuck em — since, they're not crates — but they stuck em. You put stuff in em like this and I was like — yes — something like that but they're not as sturdy and they just, you know, like they sit in little slot things — and that — started to fall and I was flustered anyway by other things that were going on. Started to fall and I was trying — go like this — and they were leaning up against my knee. And I was trying go like this, and they you know, one kept falling inside the other — and everything — like that — I went and they just went — why? And everything. All over my room. So now I'm just going through everything. Nothing is in the right place. So now I'm like taking this opportunity just to throw stuff out.
WENDY: Hee-hee [nervous laugh].
BECKY: It's such a mess — before I start in on any studying. So well anyway.
WENDY: Anyway?
BECKY: Anyway?
WENDY: Does David know this?
BECKY: Umm. We were going to have a study session. We started talking and we decided that we'd have like a major study session on Sunday afternoon.

WENDY: That's awesome.

BECKY: He's really good.

WENDY: You have the awesomest study habits here.

This sample is highly colloquial, but only four words—*pissed*, *major study session*, *awesome*, and *awesomest*—occur in the collection as examples of college slang. Notice that the evaluative *awesome* and *awesomest* come only at the end with a change in topic.

A second conversation between two different females about a misunderstanding with a boyfriend lapses into slang only with the intrusion of a third person.

MARY: Are you going to be here?

LAURA: We'll probably think about—or whatever.

MARY: Are you still fighting right now?

LAURA: Like I was just mad at him—cause he just came at the wrong time.

MARY: Oh?

LAURA: He like came unexpectedly, woke me up.

MARY: This morning?

LAURA: Yes. And I was getting up early to study. I had this stuff. I had a pop quiz. I had to finish my Spanish lab which I'm not now even finished and I'm getting a zero on.

MARY: Oh.

LAURA: And just, I mean. And he knew that and he persisted in talking to me. I can't stand people who interfere with my privacy and my responsibilities.

[At this point another female voice chimes in, apparently on entering the room.]

PENNY: Pictures!

MARY: Awesome pictures!

The intrusion of the third person signaled the end of the intimate situation, and Mary, who had been listening to her friend's troubles, then changed the situation to a more group-oriented one by using the slang item *awesome*.

An important factor governing the use of slang items in a particular conversation may well be register—the varieties of language used by a single speaker in response to different occasions and situations of use. Michael Moffatt identifies at least three different peer-group speech styles used by undergraduates, which he calls "Undergraduate Cynical, typically spoken in the dorm lounges; Locker-room, typically spoken in all-male groups (and, to an increasing extent, in all-female groups); and Private-Sincere, typically spoken in rooms or in other private contexts to friends" (1989, 234). Moffatt's Private-Sincere style is part of the intimate register, in which the participants in a conversation know each other well and are willing to confide in and give comfort to each other. Several portions of the dormitory room conversations exemplify the intimate register, for example, the conversations between Mary and Laura and Wendy and Becky reported above.

In the following conversation, three suitemates talk about a disruption to their solidarity caused by the fourth suitemate's love life. They do not use slang.

TRICIA: Where did B.J. go?
PEG: She disappeared.
KATE: I think B.J.'s gone to Charlotte.
PEG: Yeah.
TRICIA: I wish she would.
KATE: Are we going to talk to her about getting her priorities straight? Like choose her roommates or Steve?
TRICIA: Haha.
PEG: Yeah, look B.J. We've had enough of this shit — it's him or us. Make a decision.

In another conversation, Sarah tells her suitemates about a misunderstanding with her boyfriend.

SARAH: Umm — y'all. I'm so glad that Jim came up here, y'all. It was like the best thing.
NANCY: Yeah.
SARAH: And I didn't think I could be mad about this, this pledging thing. But I mean it's already, it's like a couple of times, you know, he's been a lot later calling me or this or that. And I didn't think it was gonna come out but it did come out like I was kinda upset. But it's cool because like I didn't like lose it or anything or get mad. But we just, we just talked you know. We communicated quite well. We got a lot of points across. You know, it was good. And then, uh,

Jim got his hair cut which was great. And then we went to
dinner—K&W—which we always do.

NANCY: Uh. A lot of food for a little money.

SARAH: So what are you doing tonight, Jenny?

Except for *it's cool* and *lose it*, Sarah does not use slang. She does,
however, use jargon of current popular psychology to talk about
her relationship with Jim—for example, *communicate quite well*
and *get points across*. Perhaps this is to convey to her friends, and
herself, that she is trying to handle her romantic life in a rational
and adult way.

Slang vocabulary is not characteristic of the intimate register,
even for people who share a common slang vocabulary that they
use in other contexts. Further evidence of the lack of slang in
intimate situations is shown by telephone conversations between
lovers. Here is an example of two Carolina undergraduates' nightly,
long-distance conversations with their boyfriends as reported by
their roommate. We hear, of course, only the female's side of the
conversation.

Hey . . . [soft voice] What are you doing? . . . Nothing. Talking
to you. . . . How was your day? . . . I did okay. Probably a C. . . .
Uh, huh. . . . Uh, huh. . . . You already told me this story. . . .
[starts to raise her voice] Yes you did! . . . I'm not mad. . . . I'm
sorry. . . . Nothing's wrong. . . . No, there is nothing wrong. . . .
Stop badgering me! . . . Darling, nothing is wrong. . . . No, there
is nothing wrong. . . . Yes, I promise . . . [skip to end of conver-
sation] I love you too. . . . I miss you too. . . . Yes, I'm sorry for
yelling. . . . I love you too. . . . I love you too. . . . Talk to you
tomorrow. . . . I love you too. . . . I love you too. . . . Bye.

Hey. How are you? . . . How was the game? . . . How's your knee?
. . . Sweetie, why didn't you take it easy like I told you? . . . Okay.
Okay. Whatever. It's your knee. . . . Did you talk to Paula today?
. . . What did she say? . . . Yes, she could be right. . . . How does
that make you feel? . . . No, I don't ever think about ending it
all. . . . Honey, don't cry . . . [whisper] You know I love you. . . . Yes,
I mean it. . . . Yes, I'm sure I know what love is. . . . Well, don't you
think I deserve an equal chance? . . . How would you feel if you
were in my situation? . . [This continues consistently for hours.]

Nothing in this telephone conversation is identifiable as college slang, even though some of the vocabulary items definitely have college slang equivalents. As a matter of fact, the vocabulary in the phone calls could be used and understood by just about any speaker of American English regardless of age, social class, or other group-related factors. In these conversations, group membership is irrelevant. Only the relationship with one other person is important. Thus slang, used to negotiate one's identity in a group, is irrelevant here.

In these intimate situations — between female friends or between male and female lovers — the group to which the participants belong is for the moment unimportant. They need to assure each other not of their group identity but rather of their individual and personal loyalty. The aim of intimacy is loss of affiliation with a group in favor of unity with a person. Thus slang, which is social, is not the norm in the intimate register.

The samples of student conversation on which this chapter is based are surprisingly deficient in slang. Perhaps additional data will prove the sample atypical. Or perhaps college students do not rely on their ever changing slang vocabulary as pervasively as the size of the vocabulary would suggest. Nevertheless, this examination of slang in context does confirm the essentially social function of slang: slang items occur most frequently in talk about social life and at the margins of conversation where the imparting or exchange of new information is not the main goal — for example, as nouns of address, icebreakers, feedback signals, and topic shifters. Slang is almost absent in the private and sincere talk of intimacy.

6: Effects

From the outset, this book has maintained that slang is in many ways ordinary—in its sounds, in the sources of its meaningful units, in the way it fits into sentence structure, and so on. But in other ways, it is not ordinary. What distinguishes slang from other types of vocabulary lies in the effects of its use. Although investigators emphasize different effects, three general effects of slang are consistently pointed out: (1) Slang changes the level of discourse in the direction of informality. (2) Slang identifies members of a group. (3) Slang opposes established authority. These three general tendencies are not the only effects of slang. Doubtless there are others, and they are not entirely separable from one another. Moreover, the language does not need slang to accomplish these effects. The general, nonslang lexicon of English is filled with specific colloquial, descriptive, and judgmental vocabulary. However, these three effects of slang have been consistently remarked on for decades by many observers, both professional and amateur, and they provide convenient and reasonable categories for approaching the topic.

INFORMALITY

Slang changes the level of discourse in the direction of informality. It contrasts stylistically with a general vocabulary that reveals little about the speaker or the speaker's attitudes toward the subject matter or audience. This latter, neutral type of vocabulary, which does not call attention to itself, is illustrated by the first version in the following pairs of sentences. In the second version a slang word substitutes for a neutral term, and the resulting sentence is less formal.

1a. We *left* at three o'clock.
1b. We *split* at three o'clock.

2a. The president appeared *uninformed* about the bill.
2b. The president appeared *clueless* about the bill.

3a. I saw the defendant at 11 A.M., and he was already *drunk*.
3b. I saw the defendant at 11 A.M., and he was already *polluted*.

The sentences labeled *a* may well be informal even without slang words. But the presence of slang words in the *b* versions makes the sentences blatantly and deliberately informal and restricts the situations in which they may prudently be used. For instance, professional caretakers who have left the bedside of an invalid are more likely to chose 1a rather than 1b, for *split* may convey an inappropriate attitude of laxness or levity. And a public announcement on the evening news is more likely to occur as 2a rather than 2b, even though news reporters may use *clueless* in talking about the president with one another off the air or on talk shows.

Informality in language use is a slippery concept because informality is both a relative and a scalar notion. An utterance is informal by contrast with what is deemed formal, that is, suitable to serious and important occasions and subject matter. When testifying in court, I would probably not say 3b, "I saw the defendant at 11 A.M., and he was already polluted." To do so would indicate that I either did not understand the seriousness of courtroom proceedings or that I was deliberately flouting propriety.

Formality in language is also a matter of degree. The sentences below range from most formal (4a) to least formal (4d); the least formal uses the slang items *totally wasted* and *crash*.

4a. I'm extremely fatigued — I require sleep.
4b. I'm really exhausted — I need to sleep.
4c. I'm really tired out — I need to get some sleep.
4d. I'm totally wasted — I need to crash.

The most formal and least formal are the most restricted in use. The sentences in the midrange (4b and 4c), though certainly not formal in diction or structure, are fairly neutral in connotation and can be used without calling attention to themselves in the greatest number of contexts. In this set of sentences, the most formal sounds overly serious and aloof. At the opposite end of the scale, the most informal sounds overly relaxed and chummy. People are sensitive to the formality scale in vocabulary choice. Recently, for example, some scientists have questioned the appropriateness of the term *big bang* for 'the origin of the universe', because they feel that the phrase *big bang* is not suitable for the importance of the event.

Even though slang words almost always convey informality, a few judiciously chosen slang words in a longer discourse that is otherwise serious may be rhetorically effective. Thus a formal academic lecture on irresponsible government spending could make sparing use of slang without rendering the lecture informal — for example, cleverly playing on the slang expression *pork barrel* and including other slang expressions like *pork out* and *pig out*.

The criterion of informality as a defining characteristic of slang is probably of limited value in current American culture, where the appearance of informality is considered by many to be chic. Planners of serious and important occasions strive to eliminate old rituals and forms — such as calling cards, hats and gloves for women, receiving lines, and equal numbers of men and women for a dinner party. First names on first meeting, jeans and jogging suits, paper plates and plastic cups are the new norms — and the new forms. Language use reflects this more comfortable approach to social interaction. Rarely in spoken English is formal discourse more appropriate than informal. When it is, as on ceremonial occasions such as inaugurating or burying public officials, the speakers usually read from a prepared written text.

Slang words and images reinforce the positive values of informality in American society. It is good to be *laid back, mellow,* or *maxin' and relaxin'*, 'showing a calm, easygoing attitude'. Coolness is the semantic field for the relaxation of strictures, for the abandonment of controlling forms, as is shown by these terms from UNC-CH student slang: *cool, cool out, cool your jets, chill, chill out, take a chill pill,* and *chilly. Everything's chilly* means 'Everything's fine'.

Among the forty most frequent lexical items in the UNC-CH corpus (Appendix 1), three pertain to an easy approach to life or an appearance thereof: *cool, chill/chill out,* and *veg/veg out*.[1] In shape, most of the top forty slang terms exhibit characteristics associated with less formal vocabulary. Half are one syllable, as illustrated by the most frequent adjective, *sweet* 'excellent', and the most frequent noun, *slide* 'easy course'. The only top forty slang words that exceed two syllables are *granola* 'one who follows the lifestyle of the 1960s', from a cereal trademark, and *Sorority Sue* 'a stereotypical member of a female social organization'. The Latinate *sorority* was no doubt chosen originally instead of *women's club* or *sisters' club* precisely because it appeared more serious and learned. In form, several of the verbs show variants with a particle: the most frequent verb, *chill/chill out* 'relax'; *hook/hook up* 'locate a partner for sex or romance'; *trip/trip out* 'have a bizarre experience'. In general English, this verb pattern is often considered informal because for many two-word verbs there are more formal, one-word synonyms acquired by borrowing. For example, *throw out* and *turn down* are less formal than *discard* and *reject*.

GROUP IDENTIFICATION

Slang identifies members of a group. This is its most important function for college students. Slang has always been associated with groups. But with the possibility of instant and widespread communication in recent years, the group-identifying functions of slang for the population at large may have been diminishing. Instead, speakers may be using slang to identify with a style or an attitude rather than a group. Robert Chapman calls vocabulary that serves this purpose *secondary slang*. Its use is "a matter of stylistic choice rather than true identification" (1986, xii). If items like *abs* 'exercises to strengthen abdominal muscles', *bag lady* 'a homeless woman who carries her possessions in a bag or a cart', and *fanny pack* 'pouch for valuables worn on a belt around the waist' can be considered slang, they are a kind of national slang and say little about group identification. Nevertheless, small groups that desire social solidarity—fraternities, dormitories, sports teams—continue to invent and maintain linguistic forms that serve as shibboleths—words like *chipsy* 'arrogant and superficial', derived from the name of the fraternity Chi Psi.

Speakers use slang when they want to be creative, clear, and acceptable to a select group. For American college students the overarching purpose of slang is to confirm a sense of belonging. Sharing and maintaining a constantly changing in-group vocabulary aids group solidarity and serves to include and exclude members. In this respect, slang is the linguistic counterpart of fashion and serves much the same purpose. Like stylish clothing and modes of popular entertainment, effective slang must be new, appealing, and able to gain quick group acceptance. It is normal for adolescents to seek a sense of belonging by being fashionable. Knowledge of the latest hit TV programs, films, and music is a sign of social awareness and an acknowledgment of the importance of relationships with others. So is the mastery of current slang. In 1901 philologist Hans Oertel noted the importance of social solidarity to language choices — a notion that has been explored extensively only since the 1960s. Oertel argued that the acceptance or rejection of a sound change in language may be parallel to the acceptance or rejection of a fashion: "In practice the individual is not free to accept or to decline a fashion if he is to maintain his place in the circle which has decided in favor of it. No one need follow a fad, because that is purely individual; but he who refuses to follow a fashion, which is social in character, will find himself isolated exactly as he who maintains or affects an unusual or disapproved pronunciation" (145). What Oertel observed with respect to pronunciation applies as well to the choice of words and particularly to the use of slang.

The raison d'être of slang is social. Slang provides users with automatic linguistic responses that assign others to either an in crowd or an out crowd. For example, someone whose dress, lifestyle, and concern for the environment are reminders of the 1960s is depicted in 1990s college slang as quaint and tolerable in a somewhat gentle set of labels that make reference by association: *crunchy (granola)*, *earth biscuit*, *earth muffin*, *granola*, *nut-n-berry*, *rice-n-beaner*, and *Woodstock wannabe*. Slightly harsher terms refer to contemporary environmentalists whose zeal or self-righteousness puts them on the outs with the in crowd, for example, *Birkenstock Buddy*, *earth cracker*, *eco terrorist*, *squirrel kisser*, *tree-hugger*, and *tree nymph*, as in "That tree hugger put me down for carrying a styrofoam cup." Far more condemning is the large set of negative evaluative terms available at any time in college slang to allow users to make a value judgment without really taking a stand or expressing their feelings. During 1990–92, all of the following nouns categorized someone as not attuned to the prevailing style or priorities of UNC-CH student life: *bourgie*, *butthead*, *cheddar*, *cheese*, *cheeseball*, *cheeser*, *dork*, *dorkus pretentious*, *dumbfuck*, *dweeb*, *geek*, *goob*, *goober*, *goombah*, *lamo*, *nerd*, *nimrod*, *queen ween*, *random*, *schmuck*, *shithead*, *un*, *wally*, *wannabe*, *zero*. By contrast, there is no noun for someone who fits in just fine — perhaps confirming how precarious social assurance is in a college setting.

Favorable assessment is commonly expressed by adjectives rather than by nouns, implying that admirable qualities are non-essential and temporary rather than inherent and defining. Current adjectives that convey the judgment of good, attractive, or admirable are *awesome, booming, brilliant, chicalean, cool, fresh, happening,* and *sweet*. Others require an ironic interpretation to be construed as flattering: *bad, bitching, killer* ("BMW is a bad/bitching/killer car"). The adjective *bitching* can have a positive meaning, yet the noun *bitch* remains negative only. Evaluative meanings tend to be generally positive (*sweet*) or generally negative (*cheezy*), with little possibility for fine discrimination. Thus a slang evaluative term can apply to a wide range of referents, like a *sweet foul shot*, a *sweet concert*, a *sweet grade*, or a *sweet BMW*. The lack of precision gives the slang user two choices only, positive versus negative, thereby reducing the likelihood of arriving at a judgment different from that sanctioned by the group.

Slang serves to demarcate smaller groups or subcultures within the college student community. Stereotypical fraternity and sorority members are called collectively *fratosororalingoids*, with numerous gender-specific synonyms like *Chads* and *frat rats* for males and *Suzies* and *sororites* for females. Minority students who act white are identified with slang, for example, *apples* for 'Native Americans', *bananas* for 'Asians', and *oreos* for 'African Americans'. Asians who have not yet been acculturated to American ways are called *F.O.B.*, from *fresh off the boat*. The group of students who dress in black and listen to avant-garde music are termed *Goths*. Christian students who actively proselytize have a variety of names, including *Bible beaters, born agains,* and *crusaders*. The growing national awareness of homosexuals in American society is reflected in an increasing number of terms in college usage. Most of these did not originate on college campuses; they have been in limited use nationally for decades. Almost all are derogatory. Males, for example, are called *fags* or *fudge packers* and females *dykes* or *lesbos*. Many groups on campus have names for themselves, like *band geebs* for 'members of the UNC marching band' or *teckies* for 'members of the Carolina Union technical services'.

Slang not only provides labels to set subgroups apart from the dominant student culture; slang also functions within such subgroups to validate and enhance internal solidarity. A special, shared vocabulary helps groups like technicians, student journalists, and sports teams to work together, often under stressful conditions. For example, teckies have alternative names for various staff, like *raildog* for 'technician who works on the catwalk with the ropes controlling the sets and lights', and for various sites, like *Great Hell* for 'Great Hall' and *Hell Hole* for 'Hill Hall'. Staff of the *Daily Tar Heel (DTH)* use journalistic jargon to talk about the job, but they also use slang to express their feelings and create the camaraderie that makes working together on a difficult task worthwhile and fun. Staffers are particularly fond of interjections to convey a range of emotions from frustration to elation. Typically the staff runs through a number of these interjections in one school year. In the fall of 1990, *dude, keg, scourge,* and *zoom* were in favor. During the same semester members of the cross-country track team were talking about *rigging* 'experiencing tightening of the muscles at the end of a strenuous race' (from Latin *rigor mortis*), *doing LSD* 'running long distances at a slow pace in practice' (from *long, slow, distant* and alluding to the hallucinogen LSD), and doing *time in jail* 'required time in study hall'. After a race they would replenish their energy by *carbo-loading* 'drinking beer'. It is not uncommon for members of the same intramural sports team, residents of the same dormitory, or just a group of friends to cultivate a vocabulary of very limited distribution, often based on inside jokes or names of people. The term *grant* for 'something annoying', for instance, was used frequently by all the members of a graduate student study group, based on the name of a particularly obnoxious fellow graduate student.[2]

Slang often achieves its effect by humor, a factor that sociologists have identified as a force in group formation and behavior. William Martineau proposes "A Model of the Social Functions of Humor" (1972), in which humor serves two major functions— social conflict and social control. Humor can be directed either inside a group or outside a group and can be either esteeming or disparaging. Humorous disparaging slang like *social donut hole* 'socially inept person', *coyote date* 'ugly female', *polyester princess* 'someone who dresses out of style', and *wide load* 'obese person' strengthens the self-approval of the in-group by making fun of the kind of people who are not valued and are thus excluded. Such terms are controlling because they reinforce the message that to have a secure place in the in crowd one must have social skills, be attractive and slim, and dress in style.

Another function of humor is safety—allowing a person to test his or her interests and values in relation to those of the group without fear of losing status or esteem (Kane, Suls, and Tedeschi 1976). Often humor is the device for masking discomfort in talking about subjects that have traditionally not been discussed casually in polite society. Referring to sexual intercourse flippantly as *bumping uglies, doing the big nasty, doing the naked pretzel, getting paid,* or *knocking boots* allows the speaker, at least in casual conversation among peers, to minimize the emotional commitment involved. A college woman who says that she has been *latered* 'jilted' by her high school sweetheart gives the appearance of taking the rejection lightly, though the breaking up of the relationship may actually be quite painful. Likewise, picturing the attractiveness of a female in fast-food terms like *burger, double burger,* and *triple burger with cheese* allows a male speaker the anonymity and lack of interpersonal involvement associated with eating at such establishments. The life-threatening AIDS epidemic has acquainted all college students with the condom and has quickly given rise to slang synonyms like *jimmy, jimmy hat, party hat, sheepskins,* and *raincoat,* which serve to distance the harsh realities that make the protective device a subject of public language. As the incidence and fear of rape on college campuses have increased, the term *rape* has been generalized to mean 'misuse; diminish the effects of; steal; defeat': "I just went to the mall and raped my VISA." "My dad phoned this morning and raped my buzz." "She raped my coat." "Michigan got raped by Carolina in the NCAA final." The extension of the term *rape* to such contexts ameliorates the word and appears a denial on the part of college students of the seriousness of the crime.

The humor of many of these slang expressions slightly masks an ulterior motive. Psychologists have found that humor is "a strategic tool to communicate sexual desire between men and women" (Fine 1983, 167). College males have invented expressions for 'finding a date' that are humorous reminders of childhood fantasy play—not "for real" in case they don't succeed. They *cruise, put it in cruise mode, lock it in cruise mode,* or *put it in overdrive* and zero in on their target with *12:00 high, check it out.* College females guard themselves in the quest as well, humorously referring to 'a good-looking male' as a *nice car, nail* (nice ass in Levi's), or *NTS* (name tag shaker) or with an expression like *He could make me write bad checks.*

The group-identifying functions of slang are not disputed, perhaps because they are so obvious. But they are seldom studied systematically either, perhaps for the same reason. However, in a 1992 article entitled "Social and Language Boundaries among Adolescents," sociologist Teresa Labov calls attention to the importance of slang to American adolescents. Labov identifies slang terms as "the feature of youth culture through which identity within a subculture is advertised, if not also guaranteed" (345). In her study of eighty-nine slang terms submitted by questionnaire to 261 respondents at three colleges, Labov found that sixty-five showed subcultural distribution by one or more of six social variables — gender, race, city versus suburban, public versus private high school, geographic region, and present year in college (357).

Group-identifying functions are not unique to slang. They are part of a general pattern in which social factors and linguistic variation go hand in hand. For the past quarter of a century, linguists have amassed evidence to show that various features of language are used to establish and maintain groups and networks based on class, ethnicity, nativity, and other social variables. What is surprising is that slang, which is a powerful social barometer, has not figured in these studies.

OPPOSITION TO AUTHORITY

Slang opposes the established authority. It is typically cultivated among people in a society who have little political power, like adolescents, college students, and enlisted personnel in the military, or who have reason to hide what they know or do from people in authority, like gamblers, drug addicts, and prisoners. Part of the identity of marginalized groups is their position as outsiders vis-à-vis the established structures of power — ordinarily a relationship of opposition rather than cooperation. Slang can be a verbal expression of this fundamental opposition, showing a range of attitudes from slight irreverence to downright subversiveness.

The irreverent effect of slang has long been noted. In an excellent overview chapter on slang published in 1923, George McKnight observed that "the spirit of slang is that of open hostility to the reputable" (46). In the early years of the use of the term *slang*, its antiestablishment quality was obvious, for the term was applied mainly to the special vocabulary of criminals, who by definition oppose the conventions and norms of established society. Over the centuries the term has been extended to apply to the vocabularies of other identifiable groups, such as jazz musicians, carnival workers, truck drivers, homosexuals, and college students, who by and large live within the law but who have developed a vocabulary in opposition to the standard language for reasons of group solidarity. Groups like these violate the conventions of propriety more often than they violate civil or criminal laws. Their cultivation of slang as an alternate vocabulary encoding their communal values is nonetheless an oppositional practice.

Educators have long recognized the natural tension between slang and the standard language, and English teachers at all levels have forbidden the use of slang in writing. At the turn of the twentieth century, Harvard professors James B. Greenough and George L. Kittredge expressed the attitude of the educational establishment to slang: "Now slang, from the very fact that it *is* slang, that it is not the accepted medium of communication, has a taint of impropriety about it which makes it offensive" (1901, 72). In the mid-sixties, a time more sympathetic to civil disobedience, linguist James Sledd berated English teachers for proscribing slang, precisely because in doing so they deny to students one avenue for criticizing society: "When a teacher warns his students against slang, he reaffirms his allegiance to the social order that created him.... Genteel pedagogues must naturally oppose it, precisely because slang serves the outs as a weapon against the ins. To use slang is to *deny allegiance* to the existing order, either jokingly or in earnest, by refusing even the words which represent convention and signal status" (1965, 699).

The irreverent edge to slang derives from the dual function of language to create and maintain as well as to reflect social reality. A concept that can help in understanding the antiestablishment effect of slang is M. A. K. Halliday's *antilanguage*, which is part of the larger consideration of how the forms and organization of language can be explained in light of its social functions.

An antilanguage is the language of an antisociety, which constructs by the use of language an alternate reality set in opposition to some established norm. Although the distance between the two realities need not be great, the relationship is always one of tension. Among the characteristics Halliday observes in antilanguages are overlexicalization in areas or activities that set the group off from established society, metaphor as the ordinary mode of expression, and the typical use of the antilanguage for contest and display (Halliday 1976).

Incarcerated prisoners offer the most accessible example of an antilanguage. An extensive study by Inez Cardozo-Freeman of the language of prisoners in Washington State Penitentiary in Walla Walla from 1978 to 1980 verifies the characteristics of antilanguages proposed by Halliday. Many synonyms exist for 'die', 'suicide', 'drugs', 'crimes', and forms of illegal behavior. Metaphor is ordinary, for example, *rock pile* 'any kind of job', *sewer* 'large vein for injecting narcotics', and *magic wand* 'police club'. Prisoners wield their common language much like a weapon—using it to release pent-up aggression, to express fear and terror, to retaliate against their treatment, and perhaps to diminish their sense of guilt. According to Cardozo-Freeman, "underground language expresses symbolically the reality of the prisoner's existential condition. Prison is obscene, profane, violent, terrifying, grim, cruel, inhumane, impersonal, ruthless, and dehumanizing. Underground language reflects these conditions" (Cardozo-Freeman and Delorme 1984, 27).

But what about college slang? Does it qualify as an antilanguage, creating its own reality at odds with the reality of the establishment? To be sure, college slang has some of the characteristics of antilanguages. As shown in Chapter 3, college slang relies extensively on metaphor and other kinds of figurative language. And its use has some characteristics of performance. In some subject areas, college slang also has a variety of words and phrases for the same notion; that is, it is overlexicalized. But overlexicalization in college slang is not equivalent to overlexicalization in antilanguages.

College students, for example, have a large vocabulary pertaining to drinking. Perhaps because excessive use of alcohol is both socially and legally unacceptable, getting drunk—or at least talking about it—is a favorite pastime. Beer is the beverage of choice, and it is variously called *brew, brewski, brewdog, barley pop, icy pop,* and *cornflakes in a can.* People who frequent various bars play *bar golf* or do *batting practice.* A hazard of indulging in *bar hopping* is to *beer goggle* 'find someone attractive because of the influence of alcohol'. Slang terms for drunkenness from just the two school years 1990–92 show great linguistic energy: *baked, blasted, blitzed, bombed, boohonged, caked, choked, crocked, fubarred, golfed, gone, hammered, lit, loaded, out of control, plastered, polluted, pummeled, ripped, ripskated, rocked, slammed, sloshed, smashed, tanked, toasted, toe, tore up, trashed, wasted,* and *zooted.* In the sentence "Joe got *drunk* at the party last night," the substitution of one of the slang words just listed makes the sentence more than a statement that Joe drank too much alcohol. The attitude toward drinking excessively conveyed by the use of slang is at least nonjudgmental, if not admiring, and allies the speaker with the person who has committed the social impropriety. However, this attitude toward excessive drinking seems motivated more by a desire not to offend a peer than by a desire to rebel against authority.

Moreover, overlexicalization in college slang tends to show up not in the areas that set students off most sharply from established society but precisely in those areas that are taboo in the standard language — sex, bodily functions, and death. For instance, Deborah Cameron (1992) lists 183 synonyms for 'penis' collected by two undergraduate students at the College of William and Mary in the spring of 1990. In accepting the categories of propriety reflected in the standard language, student slang honors the establishment in the breach. In addition, the slang of college students is not cautiously secret — though because of its rapid turnover and its cultural allusions it is often incomprehensible to outsiders. Thus college slang is not a full-fledged antilanguage.

Nevertheless, college slang does express opposition to what is generally acceptable in society and in academia. For the most part, the opposition manifests itself as a kind of flippancy or irreverence. Many college slang items have referential equivalents in the general vocabulary, but the slang item carries an additional element of indelicacy — like *brain fart* for 'mental error', *build a log cabin* for 'defecate', *goo food* for 'Oriental cuisine', *pork out* for 'eat', and *technicolor yawn* for 'regurgitation'.

Usually the irreverence of college slang is targeted at social mores; the opposition to authority consists of breaches of good taste, which are often sexual. Take, for example, the following terms for 'public display of affection': *go for sushi, go ninety, grope, grub, hook, maul, snack,* and *suck tonsils.* In an allusion to a Hallmark Card commercial, *the gift that keeps on giving* is 'venereal disease'. A farewell even makes light of childbirth: *make like a baby and head out*. Terms for 'sexual intercourse' are often belligerent, for example, *bong, bump uglies, hit gut, jump, knock boots*, and *lay pipe*. 'Penis' has many synonyms, including *Herman the one-eyed German, one-eyed trouser snake*, and *heat-seeking missile*. The expressions *a dick thing* 'excuse for males' behavior' and *cock deisel* 'strong, muscular, attractive male' are offensive not because of what they mean but because they contain slang words for 'penis', *dick* and *cock*.

A major target of college slang is, of course, the academic system. Slang pictures students as embattled, as in an athletic contest or war—always on the verge of being destroyed, for example, *wasted* by a quiz. The term *school* itself means 'to dominate, to prevail, to do something better than the opposition so that they learn from you', as in "Lynch really schooled Duke with his rebounding." The beneficiary of the schooling is thus humiliated. Interestingly, college slang does not appear to attribute humiliation in the educational process to individual members of the establishment, as my collection contains no slang terms for teachers, deans, librarians, or campus police—only for the parking monitors, who are called *parking Nazis*.

Not surprisingly, slang terms for courses, grades, and buildings are numerous. Courses in radio-television-motion pictures are called *rumptyvump*. The grade A is an *ace*; C is a *hook*; D is a *dog*; F is a *flag*. The undergraduate library is *The Ugly. Spencer* residence hall for women is called *Spinster*, and any women's dormitory can be the *virgin vault*. Nearby fast-food restaurants are *Toxic Hell* for 'Taco Bell' and *Pizza Slut* for 'Pizza Hut'. Other institutions of higher learning are *UNC at K-Mart* for UNC-Wilmington, *UNC at Tweetsie Railroad* for Appalachian State, *Redneck Tech* for North Carolina State University, and *The University of New Jersey at Durham* and *A Little Piece of New Jersey in Our Own Back Yard* for Duke University. A constant source of student linguistic creativity is *Student Health Services*, which has been renamed as *Stupid Health Services, Shitty Health Services, Stupid Health, Student Hell*, and *Student Death*.

Seldom is the opposition to authority in college slang political, as in the untypical example of *pulling a Ronnie* for 'doing something stupid', which was current during the administration of President Ronald Reagan.

Since medieval times students have developed vocabularies that picture themselves on the outs with the establishment and ally themselves with less respectable elements of society, like gamblers and drug users. In so doing, they have always borrowed from the language of subcultures. Today's American college slang borrows heavily from the language of African Americans, current examples including *cop a tude* 'act in an uncooperative or angry manner', *dap* 'respect', *fly girl* 'attractive female', *front* 'pretend', *ho* 'promiscuous female', *home slice* 'friend', *jam* 'have a good time', *knock boots* 'have sex', *phat* 'voluptuous', and *word up*, an expression of agreement or approval. On the surface these borrowings appear to depict a group of lower social status as appealing and worthy of imitation. Yet a closer look shows that borrowings from Black Vernacular English are limited in range and are filtered by the stereotypes of African Americans held by mainstream society.

Compared with groups that develop antilanguages, college students are in a relationship to the establishment that is only mildly and occasionally adversarial. First, they conduct their business of being students in the language of the establishment. Indeed, they are required to demonstrate some proficiency in the standard written language for admission to the group and to stay in it. Second, their group membership is temporary, for their goal is to relinquish their status as students in four years. Other shifting factors that influence their relationship to the establishment include their youth, their development of financial and psychological independence, and their aspirations for the future. College students are always aware of living up to the expectations of others—family, home community, and teachers, for example. Although slang may provide college students with a means of subtle rebellion against all these pressures, the opposition to authority appears to be rather playful and occurs in predictable areas, obligatory and automatic rather than heartfelt. Slang mainly provides college students with a means of feeling connected to other people subject to the same insecurities. Thus the irreverent quality of college slang is also a function of its social nature.

The social richness of slang makes it a means of expression suitable for traditional American college students, who are often more uncomfortable negotiating the social intricacies of attaining higher education than with meeting its academic challenges.

7: Culture

Like buildings, household utensils, and decorative artwork, words are indicators of human culture. They even offer an advantage over physical objects, in that words can communicate information about the intangibles of life—about the thoughts, beliefs, and values of their users. Even though the Indo-Europeans of five thousand years ago cannot be identified by a trail of physical objects, in a well-known essay in *The American Heritage Dictionary*, Calvert Watkins is able to speculate about their culture by examining their words. Watkins writes, "Though by no means a perfect mirror, the lexicon of a language remains the single most effective way of approaching and understanding the culture of its speakers" (1992, 2084). This chapter traces the slang lexicon of American college students over the years as a way of coming to a better understanding of their culture.

Good evidence of the use of slang by American college students dates only from the mid-nineteenth century. However, the creative use of language by students in grumbling to one another about their lot in life and about those in authority over them must date in western Europe from the earliest days of the medieval universities. To keep check on ribald, quarrelsome, and blasphemous speech among students, college statutes mandated a combination of silence and the use of Latin (Rait 1912, 59). Perhaps one of the first items of college slang was *lupi* (wolves), 'spies who reported students for using the vernacular instead of Latin' (108). Students undoubtedly did use the vernacular, or there would be no need for *lupi*, and most likely they developed slang in their own language too. The editor of a fifteenth-century Latin manuscript suggests that the English phrase *ars lyke* (*arse lick*) masquerading as a gloss above a Latin word may be "a naughty schoolboy's graffiti" (Ross

1984, 142). Five hundred years later students still maintain unflattering descriptions for 'one who curries favor', for example, *kiss-ass* or *brown noser*. But, because of the oral and ephemeral nature of slang vocabulary, a direct, unbroken line of descent from earlier usage cannot be taken for granted.

Our knowledge of college slang in the United States during the nineteenth century relies heavily on two sources, B. H. Hall's *College Words and Customs* (1856) and Lyman Bagg's *Four Years at Yale* (1871). Hall's work, the more valuable for linguistic information, is a five-hundred-page listing of words and customs and draws examples from British universities as well as from thirty-three U.S. colleges. *Four Years at Yale*, a memoir, contains a seven-page alphabetized list of words from the author's undergraduate years at Yale in the late 1860s. In addition, the novel *Student Life at Harvard* (1876) purports to "give a faithful picture of student life at Harvard University as it appeared to undergraduates there" during the 1860s. These three sources reveal a slang vocabulary concerned with campus landmarks, rivalry among the classes, making a fashionable appearance, eating and socializing, and studying as little as possible.

The campus landmark that inspired the largest number of slang synonyms was the 'privy', called the *joe, minor [house], coal yard, temple,* and *number fifty* and *number forty-nine* at Harvard and *number ten* and *number 1001* at Wesleyan, Vermont, and Dartmouth. 'To be absent from recitation or lecture' was to *bolt* or *cut*. 'To fail completely' was to *flunk*, but 'to fail partially' was to *fizzle*. At North Carolina in 1851, 'to fail in recitation' was to *fess* (Dickinson 1951, 182). 'To study hard' was to *dig, grind, grub,* or *pole*, and to study hard at the last minute was to *cram*, its noun form *cramination*. 'Someone who curried favor with teachers or others for advantage' was a *bootlicker, pimp, piscatorian, toady,* or *supe*. Other items were *scrub* 'poorly dressed, socially inferior man'; *beggars* 'rivals'; *chum* 'roommate'; *rough* 'tease'; *rub* 'give difficulty to'; and *squirt* 'attempt at recitation'. The use of a translation for recitation in Greek and Latin classes was commonplace, and the metaphor of riding a horse gave rise to *pony, horse, trot, taking a ride, riding a pony,* and others. Relatively few slang words for 'drunk' are recorded in these sources, and almost no terms have sexual referents; these depictions of college life were all written for polite society.

By current standards, the mid-nineteenth-century college slang lexicon is spare both in size and in meaning, reflecting a social reality: higher education was still rare. Most of the colleges were private or church affiliated and for young men. College students were younger then, usually entering at age fourteen or fifteen. Those who attended were ordinarily from privileged backgrounds or intended for the ministry. Even if they used slang to talk about sex and other delicate topics with their college chums, the norms of social interaction prevented their mentioning the topics or disclosing their slang in wider circles or, especially, writing such words down. As a rule, people then did not write about sex, even in personal letters and diaries.

During the 1880s and 1890s, college enrollments almost doubled. The number of colleges likewise increased, particularly public ones. Many were coeducational, admitting women as well as men. The children of small farmers, merchants, and immigrants now claimed seats in college classrooms. Public interest in college slang at that time is shown by the many short and usually anecdotal articles on the topic published in newspapers and magazines. *American Notes and Queries*, for example, in November 1889 carried a list of twenty slang expressions from Harvard and three weeks later a comparable list from Hampden Sydney College in Virginia. The cleverest item is *Hoi Barbaroi*, from Hampden Sydney, for 'members of no fraternity'. This Greek expression alludes both to the English word *barbarian* and to its source, the Greek word meaning 'foreigner, one who is not Greek'. In college social circles, fraternities and their members are called Greeks. One who is not Greek, then, is not a member of a fraternity — and by implication is also a barbarian.

In 1895 Willard C. Gore, Ph.M., of the University of Michigan undertook what I believe to be the first systematic and sizable study of American student slang at a single university.[1] In the spring and fall semesters of 1895, he asked two hundred second- and third-year students in a rhetoric course at the University of Michigan to collect and define current student slang that they heard or read. Anticipating my methodology by eighty years, he did not define slang for them but accepted an expression as slang "because it was so regarded by the students who handed it in" (1993, 23). Gore submitted the list of about five hundred words and phrases to the vote of a class of sixty-five students. "A large number were unfamiliar to many. Very few, however, were regarded by any as having emerged from the slang stage" (23).

Gore's collection seems contemporary in many ways. About 10 percent of the entries refer to types of people still familiar on college campuses: a *blug* is 'one who is very stylish'; *a little tin god on wheels* is 'a superior person (said ironically)'; an *ice wagon* is 'someone who is slow'; a *prune* is a 'disagreeable and irritable person'; a *huckleberry* is a 'sweet and agreeable person'; a *grind* is 'someone who studies too much'. Almost as many terms are evaluative adjectives: *chiselly* means 'unpleasant, disagreeable'; *rank* means 'unfair or arbitrary'; *skatey* means 'ill-bred, vulgar, cheap'; *woozy* means 'pleasant, delightful'; and *out of sight* means 'first-rate, superior'. Several are expressions of support, like *I should say* and *too utterly too too*. About one-fourth of the items refer to academic matters, like *flim* for 'to cheat'; *con* for 'to get the grade *condition*'; *tute* for 'tutor'; *fruit* for 'a lenient teacher'; *heathen* for 'an unreasonable teacher'; and *crust the instructor* for 'make a good recitation'. However, unlike more recent collections, the 1895 Michigan list contains fewer than ten items each that refer to females or to overindulgence in alcohol, and words with sexual implications are almost entirely absent.

Within five years of Gore's study, Eugene Babbitt and fellow members of the New York branch of the American Dialect Society conducted the most ambitious national survey of American college slang to date. After a pilot study that circulated thirty words to several leading colleges for confirmation and additions, an expanded list of three hundred items was sent to "all the colleges and universities in the country, as well as to a number of secondary schools" (1900, 5). The results of responses from eighty-seven schools are reported in a thousand-item word list accompanied by a perceptive seventeen-page essay.[2] "College Slang and Phrases," published in 1900 in *Dialect Notes*, is the baseline for the historical study of twentieth-century U.S. college slang.

About one-tenth of the entries in Babbitt's word list are printed here as Appendix 3. This selection consists of all of the items that are reported both by Gore at the University of Michigan in 1895 and by respondents to the American Dialect Society survey. The content of American college slang evidenced by the national survey does not differ much from that of the University of Michigan alone. What is more interesting is that in broad categories the college slang of the turn of the century is comparable to that of the 1850s and 1860s.

The privy continues to be a source of linguistic diversion, inspiring additional slang synonyms like *bank, chamber of commerce, domus, Egypt, poet's corner,* and *prep chapel,* as well as *Jake* for men and *Ruth* for women.

Fully one-third of the items in the national survey refer to the persons, places, requirements, rituals, and difficulties that students encounter in their role as students. The time-honored *horse* metaphor for 'using a translation' has elaborated into *animal, beast, bicycle,* and *wheel.* A 'user of a translation' is a *jockey* or *equestrian,* and 'a bookshelf for translations' is a *stable.* A *race course* is a 'meeting of several students to prepare a pony', and a *racetrack* is the site of such a meeting. Some synonyms for 'failing to attend class' are *adjourn, hook, skip, sneak,* and *snooke.* A *safety* is 'a slip of paper handed to an instructor at the beginning of a recitation stating that the student is unprepared', and attendance at recitation under those circumstances is called a *dry cut.*

Particularly plentiful are words for performing in classroom recitation or on examinations, with more terms for failure than for success. Among the verbs for 'to fail' are *bust, crash, croak, fall down, fall down under the table, fluke, pitch, slump,* and *smash.* On the other hand, 'to recite perfectly' is to *bat, do it bright, curl, kill, paralyze the professor,* and *twist.* Students who recite though unprepared *cheek it, go on general principles, muscle,* or *make a stab.* If they 'get through a recitation without aids', they *walk,* that is, they do not *ride the pony.* One who 'surprises an instructor by answering all the questions' *staggers.* 'A passing examination in every subject' is a *clean shave.*

There are several terms for using unfair means to pass examinations, for example, to *frog, rogue through,* or *shenannygag.* The various ingenious devices prepared for the purpose of cheating have their own names: *cribs, panoramas, rolls, skins,* and *winders.* A *winder,* for instance, is 'a crib constructed of a long strip of paper rolled on two pencils'. But more contemptible than cheating as a way to succeed academically is currying favor with a teacher or someone else in authority. A student who does this is said to *bootlick, chin, coax, drag, fish, suck,* or *swipe.*

The polite reserve noticed in the college slang dating from the

1850s and 1860s is barely broken at the turn of the century. The slang still contains few terms for drinking, women, or groups discriminated against in society at large. For example, only about a dozen terms refer to drinking alcohol and a comparable total to Jews, Italians, and African Americans. Babbitt thinks that the lack of such terms shows that college students have not developed a distinctive vocabulary of their own for talking about these topics (11). It is possible that the use of offensive slang among students was much more limited and cautious a century ago when rules for behavior were stricter. However, it is also likely that terms considered common or vulgar in general conversation are underreported in Babbitt's collection. I imagine that both students and faculty of the Victorian era would have felt uncomfortable writing down and mailing lists of such words to the American Dialect Society even if they knew or used them.

Nonetheless, the small set of slang words and phrases that refer to women and to relationships between men and women do give a hint of the collegiate culture then. A female domestic employed in college dormitories rates almost as many names as does a female student, being called an *Amazon, grace,* or *Venus,* as well as the less lofty *sheet-slinger* and *kitchen mechanic.* Bird names are the standard in referring to a female student, for instance, *canary, hen, pullet,* and *quail;* and a female residence hall is a *hen coop/ranch/roost, quail roost,* or *jail.* Another term for 'female student' is *calico* and its shortened derivative *calic,* which gives rise by synecdoche to *dry goods.* Synonyms for 'pretty girl' include *geranium, peach,* and *peacherine.* Several terms mean 'to call on, escort, or entertain a lady', including *buck, buzz, fuss, go double, pike, swing,* and *turf.* Keeping company with the opposite sex is viewed in the context of marriage: a *college widow* is 'a girl whom new men meet from year to year but whom no one ever marries', and to *take a cottage course* is 'to marry before graduation'. Some words, though, imply less respectable types of relations between the sexes. A *birdie* is a 'girl eager to make a man's acquaintance without introduction'; *bat, fruit, seed,* and *scrub* all refer to a 'loose woman'; and *cat* means 'to keep company with a bad woman'. The words *bitch* and *slut* are part of the American college slang around 1900, but they both refer to the queen in playing cards.

Babbitt's study in 1900 was the last major undertaking in the scholarly study of American college slang for seventy years, until

Gary Underwood's project (1975) at the University of Arkansas from 1970 through 1972. Mencken's admirable chapter on slang (1963) — which documents the in-group vocabulary of such diverse groups as aviators, jazz musicians, railroad workers, and prisoners — gives college students short shrift. To be sure, over the years journalists have continued to keep the public up to date on the latest zany expressions from college campuses. And beginning in 1925, the journal *American Speech* frequently printed brief word lists from various campuses and served as the primary outlet for the publication of scholarly studies of college slang, like that of Dundes and Schonhorn in 1963. The short-lived periodical *Current Slang*, which was issued quarterly from the English Department of the University of South Dakota from summer 1966 through winter 1971, focused mainly on college slang, documenting the sudden burgeoning in the college lexicon of terms from African Americans and from the drug culture.

During the period from 1900 to 1970, the scholarly collection and analysis of American college slang was at best sporadic. However, in these scattered treatments can be seen traces of the major changes that transformed college slang and college culture by the 1970s. By 1926–27, slang at Kansas University depicted not only "loose women" but also women students as having sex appeal, with terms like *hot-sketch* and *mean-baby* (Pingry and Randolph 1928). University of Missouri slang of 1931 called a 'chic, up-to-date coed' a *hot number* and 'one who necks on a date' a *giraffe* (Carter 1931). The collection from Johns Hopkins published in 1932 includes slang in three areas barely evident in student slang from 1900. An African American was a *smoke* or an *eight ball*. An effeminate male was a *birdie, fag, fairy, fluter, pansy*, or *queer*. But it is in the area of sexual relations between males and females that the greatest increases occurred. A 'loose woman' was a *bag, blimp*, or *piece*; and 'a woman who is easily possessed' was a *cinch, pushover*, or *sex job*. A 'sexually repressed male' was *horny*, and to 'have wandering hands' was to *develop* or *explore*. 'Women's breasts' were *big brown eyes*. To 'kiss' was to *mug, muzzle*, or *smooch*, and to 'copulate' was to *go the limit* (Kuethe 1932). By 1948 at North Texas Agricultural College students were talking about 'perfume' as *rape fluid*; about 'a girl who enjoys arousing a male' as a *p.t.* (from *prick teaser*); and about 'experiencing an orgasm' as *losing one's rocks* (Jarnagin and Eikel 1948). In 1955, at Wayne State University, students had a slang term for marijuana, *pod* (White 1955).

After World War II, the GI Bill altered the collegiate population of the United States and set into motion changes in higher education that are still being felt today. During the 1950s and 1960s American institutions of higher learning relinquished the philosophy of in loco parentis under which they had functioned in a parental role toward students. As a consequence, many college regulations for controlling student behavior outside the classroom were eventually abandoned—such as dress codes, curfews, and mandatory attendance at chapel or assemblies.

By the time Gary Underwood collected his lexicon of 750 slang items at the University of Arkansas, from 1970 to 1972, American college slang had taken on its current shape. For instance, in the Arkansas collection there are multiple synonyms for *drunk* and *vomit*, derogatory terms for minorities, explicit words for sex, words with sexual connotations for women, and numerous terms for drugs or derived from the drug culture. As a whole, the terms Underwood reports from Arkansas parallel in meaning and effect the terms in the University of North Carolina collection. Both collections show plainly that since the turn of the century drastic changes have taken place in what college students are willing to reveal about their talk with one another.

Many of the hundreds of items of North Carolina slang used as examples throughout this book suggest various facets of college culture in the late twentieth century. For instance, *bro, sister,* and *homeboy/homegirl/homey* are the primary kinship terms in the college lexicon—and also among the most frequently used nouns of address. This usage implies a speech community formed on peer relationships rather than on hierarchy. Another example is provided by admonitions like *get a life, get a job, get a real job,* and *get with the program* for instructing others to conform to the expectations that society holds for adults. These expressions show that, despite the need of college students to merit the favorable judgment of peers, it is ultimately the standards of the world of work beyond college that count. Other slang presented throughout this book confirms that the current college culture is firmly rooted in the general culture. Unlike an antilanguage, in which the lexicon is highly developed specifically in those areas that set the users apart from mainstream culture, college slang invests little in vocabulary pertaining to the users' status as scholars. Instead, the focus is on relationships with other students and on activities that reinforce those relationships. College student vocabulary about relationships echoes the discourse of American society at large. Ubiquitous popular discussion about openness and honesty in relationships, for example, is the context for college expressions like *DHC* 'deep, heavy conversation', as in "I'm afraid that when my grades arrive, I'm in for some *DHC*," and *DTR* 'defining the relationship', as in "It's time for John and me to have the DTR conversation." Current uneasiness about the changing role of women in society underlies college slang expressions like *PMS* 'be agitated, annoyed', from premenstrual syndrome, which is reinterpreted as Putting Up with Men's Shit, and *WHAM* 'a woman who harms men physically or emotionally', from Women Hate All Men, and its plural *WHAMS*, supposedly from Women Have All Men Scared. Increasing national fears about new immigrant groups are shown by *FOB* 'Asian who has not yet learned American culture' from Fresh Off the Boat and by *Nuprin*, a joking reference to 'Asians', from the brand name of pills for pain that are 'small, yellow, and different.'

Another approach is to generalize from a sizable and coherent subset of the corpus. Such a subset of the Carolina corpus is based on the number of submissions per item. Appendix 1 lists the University of North Carolina "top forty" — the lexical items that were submitted by a total of thirty students or more during the period extending from fall 1972 through spring 1993.

The "top forty" can be classified semantically with respect to the twenty-eight categories of meaning identified by Fiorenza (Appendix 2). Thirty-two of the forty fall into these nineteen categories:

'excellent': *sweet, killer, bad, cool, awesome*
'socially inept person': *dweeb, geek, turkey*
'drunk': *wasted, catch a buzz, trashed*
'relax': *chill (out), veg (out)*
'fads': *not!, word up*
'fraternity/sorority member': *bagger, Suzi*
'disregard': *bag, blow off*
'kiss passionately': *grub, hook (up)*
'attractive': *hot*
'attractive person': *fox/foxy*

'have a good time': *jam*
'do well': *ace*
'insult': *diss*
'leave': *book*
'fail': *flag*
'eat rapidly': *pig out*
'out of touch': *clueless*
'pursue for sex': *scope*
'worst situation': *the pits*

The remaining eight are *slide* 'an easy course'; *crash* 'to go to sleep'; *cheezy* 'unattractive, out of favor'; *trip (out)* 'have a bizarre experience'; *granola* 'one who follows the lifestyle of the sixties'; *homeboy/homegirl/homey* 'friend'; *dude* 'male, any person'; and *slack* 'below standard'. The meanings of these eight are not unusual or unexpected for slang; they simply do not fall into one of the categories of meaning Fiorenza identified as generating high-frequency synonyms.

Viewed by grammatical rather than by semantic categories, eleven of the top forty are nouns; eleven, adjectives; sixteen, verbs; and two, faddish interjections (*not!* and *word up*). Of the nouns, one means 'an easy course' and one means 'the worst situation'. The remaining nine are types of people. *Dweeb, geek,* and *turkey* are the most negative, as these sorts permanently lack social skills. *Baggers* and *Suzis* are the privileged types who join social organizations whose membership is by invitation only. A *granola* is the type who has chosen not to change with the times. On the positive side, a *fox* is a beautiful, well-groomed, fashionable woman. *Homeboy* and its derivatives name 'friends'. *Dude* is neutral in connotation, as it can apply to virtually anyone.

Of the adjectives, the two for 'drunk' are the passive participles *wasted* and *trashed*. *Clueless* indicates that the referent is not consciously aware of communal knowledge, and *slack* applies to someone who does not meet prevailing standards. *Sweet, awesome, bad,* and *cool* are all-purpose positive assessments, and *cheezy* is an all-purpose negative one. *Hot* is a positive evaluation of physical attractiveness. *Killer* means either 'excellent' or 'terrible'.

The sixteen verbs summarize what students do. On the high-energy end of the scale, they perform well (*ace*), have a good time (*jam*), have a bizarre experience (*trip (out)*), and engage in romantic pursuits (*scope*, *hook*, and *grub*). At the other end of the scale, they cease an activity or neglect a responsibility (*blow off*, *bag*) and fail (*flag*). To maintain themselves physically, they eat (*pig out*), drink (*catch a buzz*), relax (*chill [out]*, *veg [out]*), go to sleep (*crash*), and depart (*book*). Judgmentally, they criticize others (*diss*).

The forty most frequent lexical items imply a community of speakers concerned with relationships among people, particularly with judgments of acceptance or rejection. They divide almost evenly between terms with positive associations and connotations and those with negative ones. Those that convey negative judgments are rather mild. None of the most frequently submitted negative labels is as vivid, memorable, or offensive as low-frequency derogatory terms like sexist *hosebag*, racist *porch monkey*, and homophobic *fudge packer*. The sexual activity pictured in the top forty is the pursuit, not the consummation; although the collection has many graphic verbs that refer to the physical union of male and female, such as *bounce refrigerators* and *parallel park*, none was submitted frequently enough to make the top forty. Interestingly, the drinking terms focus on the unpleasant effects rather than on the convivial process. Only two of the top forty Carolina slang items give a hint that the users are students, *slide* and *flag*.

The narrow scope of this subset of college slang is actually a rather accurate reflection of the range of the corpus as a whole. The narrowness is, in part, a function of the fact that the vocabulary items are slang. Slang vocabulary is like an irregularly blinking signal that discloses someone's location to those privy to the code. The signal is deliberate, limited, and intended for a select audience. Slang vocabulary is likewise restricted; it does not give speakers the resources to talk about the full range of human experiences. One cannot go about the business of living using only slang. As a simple and blatant example, slang does not provide vocabulary for numbers, for personal pronouns, or for concepts of time such as before and after. The slang that college students use with one another is vocabulary for a special purpose. That purpose is sociability, a pleasurable sense of being in harmony with other people.

The studies of anthropologist Michael Moffatt (1989) and folklorist Simon J. Bronner (1990) both verify the primacy of social relations and activities in the lives of recent American college students. It is not academic concerns that shape undergraduate college culture or college slang—it is human ones. College students put more of their time and youthful spiritedness into figuring out who they are in relationship to others, what they like and dislike, what they can and cannot do, and what they will and will not tolerate than in trying to figure out their textbooks, lectures, and professors.

It is also possible that recent generations of college students are creating, appropriating, and using more slang than their counterparts did a century ago. This may be in part because in the United States colloquial vocabulary and slang are generally more widely used now than in the nineteenth century. Lighter notes a stylistic shift toward the highly informal with the advent of writing intended for mass circulation early in the century. The mass media explosion that began then has provided the context for an increase in slang: "for the tone of all current mass media, spurred by the demands of competition, plunges on in the direction of the breezy, the startling, the tough-minded and terse—attitudes that slang is born to impart" (1994, xviii). Undoubtedly because of the influence of the mass media, a type of national slang that conveys attitudes rather than identity with a group, what Chapman calls "secondary slang," has become more noticeable (1986, xii). Thus students arrive at college with a lifelong exposure to slang and its social functions. What's more, when first-year students join their newly forming speech community on the first day of registration, they have already survived an important sociolinguistic testing ground. As Danesi (1994) shows, they are already veteran users of the social dialect of their high school and the cliques to which they belonged. Slang, then, is not among the new and threatening features of college life.

What is the future for American college slang? What cultural phenomena will be lauded, supported, stereotyped, made fun of, or condemned in the slang at the turn of the twenty-first century? Currently, the two greatest sources of influence on college slang and on the linguistic style of college students are African Americans and gays. In a recent independent studies research project, UNC-CH senior Kenneth Levine analyzed the expressive styles and self-identifying vocabulary of these two groups and found common needs manifesting themselves in similar ways linguistically. Several of the lexical items Levine identified had already turned up in North Carolina student slang, like the verb *read* 'tell someone off' and *work someone's last nerve* 'annoy exceedingly'. College students who do not belong to these groups, and who do not care to belong to them, nonetheless find their verbal dexterity appealing and worthy of imitation. The influence of African Americans and gays on college slang will continue as long as members of the two groups remain popular in the arts and entertainment media and as the groups achieve more recognition on campus.

Early indications are that the national debate over the rights of minorities and disadvantaged groups, the issue of "political correctness," will manifest itself in interesting ways in college slang. More than any previous generation, students of the 1990s are the beneficiaries of textbooks, lectures, workshops, and conferences designed to analyze critically the assumptions and consequences of discrimination of all kinds. In their public and academic discourse, they can cite facts about differential wages for males and females, explain the high incidence of African American households without an adult male, and advocate the reasonableness of including gays in the military and women in the Roman Catholic priesthood. They have learned, and many believe what they have been taught. But in their casual discourse among friends, in the circles in which they vent their frustrations and express their opposition toward those they feel control their lives, the same students are uttering offensive, stereotypical slang referring to people unlike themselves whom they intellectually and morally support. This abandonment of political correctness among friends is perhaps a sign of trust in others, like telling a secret. It may also be a sign of the fear that in the increasing fragmentation of American society into groups demanding a fair share, they may wind up among the "have-nots."

Acquiring the kind of knowledge transmitted in books and classrooms is ultimately an individual experience and therefore potentially lonely. No longer apparent are the well-defined groups that were once a natural outgrowth of a rather simple academic system where everyone followed the same curriculum, had the same professors, and lived on the college grounds — and where the students were a fairly homogeneous lot. American college student bodies are now much more diversified in age, national and regional origin, race, ethnicity, social class, financial resources, and academic preparation. Institutions of higher learning are larger, with more bureaucracy than ever. As a result, contemporary college students must take greater personal responsibility for identifying and becoming a part of groups that can fulfill their needs for companionship during their college years. An increase in slang use in this would not be surprising.

I find myself in agreement with folklorist Simon Bronner, who studied the rituals, customs, legends, and jokes of college students in the 1970s and 1980s: "Students seek to strengthen their social identity, value system, and emotional growth, but find that the academic setting once noted for assisting this cultural passage has alienated rather than involved them. Increasingly students turn to one another for support, but struggle to create group harmony in a mass society stressing the uprooted, competitive individual" (1990, 239). A large part of that struggle for group harmony for college students is internecine verbal skirmishing; and the terms for negotiating the struggle are slang.

The Top Forty in Slang

University of North Carolina at Chapel Hill, 1972–1993

1 *sweet* 'excellent, superb'
2 *chill/chill out* 'relax'
3 *slide* 'easy course'
4 *blow off* 'neglect, not attend'
5 *bag* 'neglect, not attend'
6 *killer* 'excellent, exciting'
7 *jam* 'play music, dance, party'
8 *scope* 'look for partner for sex or romance'
9 *wasted* 'drunk'
10 *clueless* 'unaware'
11 *diss* 'belittle, criticize'
12 *pig out* 'eat voraciously'
13 *bad* 'good, excellent'
14 *crash* 'go to sleep'
15 *cheezy* 'unattractive, out of favor'
16 *hook/hook up* 'locate a partner for sex or romance'
17 *trip/trip out* 'have a bizarre experience'
18 *dweeb* 'socially inept person'
19 *buzz/catch a buzz* 'experience slight intoxication'
20 *cool* 'completely acceptable'
21 *grub* 'kiss passionately'
22 *geek* 'socially inept person'
23 *granola* 'one who follows the lifestyle of the sixties'
24 *homeboy/homegirl/homey* 'friend; person from home'
25 *not!* 'no', sentence negation
26 *ace* 'perform well, make A'
27 *dude* 'male, any person'
28 *the pits* 'the worst'
29 *bagger* 'fraternity member'
30 *flag* 'fail'
31 *hot* 'attractive, sexy'
32 *slack* 'below standard, lazy'
33 *trashed* 'drunk'
34 *veg/veg out* 'do nothing'
35 *word/word up* 'I agree'

36 *awesome* 'excellent, superb'
37 *book* 'leave, hurry'
38 *turkey* 'socially inept person'
39 *fox/foxy* 'beautiful, sexy'
40 *Sorority Sue/Sue/Suzi* 'sorority member'

Slang Items with at Least One Synonym Submitted by at Least Ten Students in One Semester, Fall 1976–Fall 1991

'excellent' (11)

awesome	killer
bad	solid
bitchin'	sweet
cool	tough
fresh	wicked
key	

'socially inept person' (10)

dork	nerd
dweeb	spaz
geek	turkey
goob(er)	whimp, wimp
groover	wus(s)

'drunk' (9)

blitzed	shitfaced
buzz(ed)	toasted
catch a buzz	trashed
fried	wasted
ripped	

'attractive person' (4)

babe	fox(y)
chick	hunk

'insult' (4)

diss	rag (on)
dog	slam

'relax' (4)

chill	cool out
chill out	veg (out)

'greeting' (4)

's up   what's up

what's happening   yo

'attractive' (3)

fine   phat

hot

'do well' (3)

ace   get off

blow away

fads (3)

not 'negation'   word up 'agreement'

psyche 'fooled you'

'fraternity/sorority member' (3)

bagger   Sue, Susie, Suzi

fratty bagger

'have a good time' (3)

jam(min')   throw down

party

'leave' (3)

blow   book (it)

bolt

'kiss passionately' (3)

grub   scrog

hook (up)

'disregard' (2)

bag (it)   blow off

'eat rapidly' (2)

pig out   scarf

'exhausted' (2)

beat   burned out

'fail' (2)
    bomb   flag

'farewell' (2)
    check you later   later

'get in touch with reality' (2)
    get a clue   get a grip

'intensifier' (2)
    ——— from hell   mega

'lose control' (2)
    freak (out)   wig (out)

'out of touch' (2)
    clueless   spaced (out)

'person out of touch' (2)
    airhead   space cadet

'pursue' (2)
    scam   scope, scoping

'study long and hard' (2)
    book (it)   cram

'worst situation' (2)
    bummer   (the) pits

Source: Data adapted from Elisa Fiorenza, "A Statistical Analysis of Patterns of Slang Usage at the University of North Carolina at Chapel Hill from Fall 1976 to Fall 1991," undergraduate honors thesis, Department of Statistics, University of North Carolina at Chapel Hill, 1992.

Some American College Slang circa 1900

Listed here are all of the items that appear in each of the two major sources of American college slang for the late nineteenth century, Gore (1993 [1895]) and Babbitt (1900).

ball-up 'to confuse'
beef 'a mistake'
biff 'a slap or punch'
bluff 'to make a false show of ability'
**bohn/bone* 'to study hard or diligently'
bolt 'to absent oneself from class'
bounce 'to eject forcibly'; 'to expel'
bum 'a pleasurable excursion'

cheek 'audacity or impudence, particularly when unprepared for class'
chump 'one possessing few social graces'
*co-ed 'pertaining to an institution that educates both sexes'
cold 'perfect, complete'
cooler 'jail'
corker 'a person or thing that is extraordinary'; 'severe or difficult'
*cram 'to attempt to store a great number of facts in the mind hastily, particularly before an examination'
*crib 'to cheat in recitation or examination'
crush 'to have an infatuation for someone'

dead 'perfect, complete'
dip 'diploma'
dough 'money'

easy 'innocent, simple, easily fooled'
exam 'examination'

fem-sem 'a seminary for females'
*fiend 'one who excels in something'
fluke 'an utter failure'
*flunk 'to fail in academic work; a failure'

flunker 'one who fails in academic work'
foxy 'sly; well dressed'
*frat 'a fraternity'; 'a member of a fraternity'
*freak 'a student who is exceptionally proficient in a given subject'
freshie 'a freshman'
*fruit 'a person easily influenced'

*grind 'a student who studies constantly'; 'a joke or takeoff, usually
   personal'; 'a demanding instructor'; 'a demanding course'; 'to
   devote an unreasonable amount of time and effort to studies'; 'to
   ridicule or satirize'; 'to cause to work hard'
gym 'gymnasium'

hen-medic 'a woman studying medicine'
*horse 'a literal translation used in preparing a lesson'; 'a joke,
   especially broad or humiliating'; 'a student of remarkable ability';
   'to study with the help of a translation'; 'to swindle or beat'
hot 'tip-top, excellent'

jay 'person who does something disagreeable or foolish'
jolly 'to have a good time'
josh 'to make fun of by teasing'
jump 'to absent oneself from a lecture'

kid 'to deceive'
K.M. 'a servant girl (from *kitchen mechanic*)'

law 'a law student'
*lunch hooks 'teeth'

math 'mathematics'
measly 'disagreeable, mean'
medic 'medical student'

peach 'one who has attractive qualities'
P.G. 'a postgraduate student (from *post graduate*)'
*play horse with 'to ridicule or make sport of'
*pluck 'to report a student as deficient in examination'
plug 'a silk hat'
plunker 'a dollar'

pony 'a literal translation'; 'to translate with the help of a translation'
prep 'a preparatory student'
prune 'a weird or irritable person'
psych 'psychology'
pull one's leg 'curry favor with'
push 'a crowd'

quiz 'a short examination'

ride 'to use a translation'
roast 'to censure'; 'to ridicule'
rush 'to entertain a freshman preparatory to taking him into a
   society'

scrap 'a fight'; 'a verbal quarrel, sometimes good natured'
shark 'one who excels in anything'
sheepskin 'diploma'
skin 'unfair'
slam 'unkind remarks about someone'
smooth 'excellent, pleasing'
snap 'a course requiring little studying'; 'an instructor who gives an
   easy course'
soph 'sophomore'
souped 'unsuccessful in a recitation or examination'
spout 'to declaim, harangue'
spread 'a banquet'
stab 'an attempt at recitation'
stick 'an uninteresting person'
stiff 'a cadaver'; 'a body for dissection'
sub-freshman 'a preparatory student'
swipe 'to steal'

tacky 'untidy, unkempt'
tear 'a protracted spree'
tin 'money'
trade-last 'an exchange of compliments'
trig 'trigonometry'
trot 'a translation'; 'to make use of a translation'
tumble 'to understand'

varsity 'university'

walk 'to go through a recitation without aid'
whale 'a phenomenal scholar'
work 'to gain favor, as of an instructor'

yap 'a contemptible person'

*On the original list of thirty items circulated as part of the pilot study by Babbitt et al.

Select Glossary of Student Slang

University of North Carolina at Chapel Hill, 1972–1993

Only the examples of slang from the University of North Carolina
at Chapel Hill collection (1972–93) that are used in this book are
listed. The date at the end of an entry is the date of the lexical item's
first occurrence in the collection. An asterisk (*) following the date
indicates that the item was submitted only once during the period of
time covered by the collection. Acronyms with periods are pronounced by naming the letters; for instance, *F.O.B.* is "ef-oh-be,"
not a rhyme of *cob*.

aardvark: to engage in sex 93
A-box: someone in an unpleasant mood (attitude box) 91*
ace: the grade A 73; of high quality 77; to perform well or succeed
    77; friend 92*
ace boon coon: best friend 81*
ace buddy: best friend 77*
-action: combining form denoting activity 82
A.D.: to leave 92*
adios, amoebas: a farewell 88*
-age: suffix forming an abstract noun 81
-aholic: suffix indicating one who indulges excessively in 81
airhead: someone who lacks common sense 77
air Hebrews: sandals 92*
all-nighter: session of studying or writing that lasts all night 80
alter ego: a form of identification, like a driver's license 90*
animal: athlete 72*
-animal: combining form indicating one who does something
    excessively 83
apple: Native American who acts white 92*
arbitrary: insignificant 86*
archives: a thing of the past, used in the farewell "I'm archives" 84
art: a thing of the past, used in the farewell "I'm art" 86*
as if: exclamation of disbelief 81
asshole: obnoxious or stupid person 73
attitude: an uncooperative, resentful, hostile, or condescending
    attitude 87
Audi 5000/5000: good-bye 91

Aunt Betsy's Cookie Store: Alcoholic Beverage Control store 74.*
awesome: excellent, worthy of admiration 79

babe: good-looking female 80
babe-a-licious: good-looking female 91*
babe-a-lonian: good-looking female 91*
bacon: good-looking, sexy 92*
bad: good, excellent, worthy of admiration 72; fault, as in "my
     bad" 86
bad bongos: situation in which things do not go well 74.*
bag: to neglect, stop, disregard 77
bagger: fraternity member 77
baked: drunk 87
balls to the walls: a tense or frantic time or situation that requires the
     ability to fight back 79*
banana: Asian who acts white 92*
banana factory: hectic, horrible, or futile situation 87*
band geeb: member of the UNC Marching Tar Heels 90
bang: to engage in sex 87*
bank: money 91*
Barbie: painstakingly fashionably dressed and groomed female 84.*
barf: to vomit 74
bar golf: practice of going from bar to bar drinking 88
bar hop: to go from bar to bar drinking and investigating the social
     possibilities 83*
barley pop: beer 92*
batcave: to sleep 81*
batting practice: the custom of going from bar to bar drinking until
     drunk 92*
Beam me up, Scotty: expression of the desire to be elsewhere 79
beam out: to daydream 84*
The Beast: Milwaukee's Best, a popular brand of inexpensive beer 87
beat the feet: to hurry 73*
beau: boyfriend 90*
beaucoup/beaucoups: a large quantity of 81
Beav: name that indicates that the referent is acting like a little
     brother 85*
beef-a-roni: sexy male 85*
beer goggle: to find someone attractive because of the influence of
     alcohol 87

Benny Mason: particularly strong marijuana 92*

B.F.E.: the middle of nowhere, a remote place (bum fucking Egypt) 92

Bible beater: evangelizing, fundamentalist Christian 73

big time: to a superlative degree 81

Birkenstock buddy: environmentalist 92*

bitch: shrewish female 73

bitch: to complain 77

bitching: excellent, admirable, good-looking; difficult 84/77

bite on: to imitate 87*

bite the dust: to be defeated, prevailed over 80

bizarre: beyond the norm 89*

blasted: drunk 74

-blatt: suffix of familiarity or endearment added to nouns 88*

blimp boat: obese person 81*

blimp out: to eat voraciously 79

blind: drunk 80

blitz: to perform well 80

blitzkrieged/blitzed: drunk 74/75

blood: fellow black 76

blow: to sing 77; to leave 81

blown out: drunk 75

blown up: drunk 78*

blow off: to miss class, ignore responsibility, disregard 82

blow out: to shock, embarrass 78

blow this popsicle stand: to leave 86

bod: body 72

bodacious ta-tas: woman's breasts 83*

boff: to engage in sex 86

bogart: to steal, take an unfair share 72

bogel: to do nothing 91*

bogus: objectionable, having negative qualities 81

boheme: bohemian, someone who identifies with the 1960s 84

bohemian: someone who identifies with the 1960s 83

boho: bohemian; someone who identifies with the 1960s 84*

bolt: to leave 73

bombed: drunk 76

bomb out/bomb: to fail, perform poorly 72/73

bone: to engage in sex 85

bong: to engage in sex 92*

bonk: to engage in sex 89
boogie: to move, dance, perform 73
boogie box: portable stereo tape deck 87*
boohonged: drunk 81*
book: to leave 77
booked: ugly 90
booming: excellent, worthy of approval 92*
bop: to engage in sex 89*
born again: a fundamentalist Christian 93*
boss: excellent 72
bounce refrigerators: to engage in sex 85*
bourgie/boojie: someone who is bourgeois, superficial, pretentious 91
bowhead: stereotypical sorority member 87
bowser: an ugly female 80
bow-wow: an ugly female 90*
box: a female; the vagina 91
bozo: foolish, outrageous, ridiculous person 72
brain: intelligent person 86
brain burp: random thought 92*
brain fart: temporary loss of memory; mental error 92
brary: library 80
brary dog: someone who studies in the library 86*
bread: money 74
break: to leave 84
brew: beer 73
brew dog: beer 88
brewski: beer 80
brick house: good-looking, well-built female 79
brilliant: excellent, worthy of admiration 92
bring it all back home: to have a good time 86*
bro: brother 76
broth: brother 73*
brown nose: to curry favor with 73
brown noser: one who curries favor 85*
brr rabbit: complaint about the cold 78*
Bruce: a male who thinks he is suave but really is not 87*
brutus: a mean, ugly person 84*
buddha: excellent, worthy of admiration 92*
buel: food; to eat voraciously 85
bug out: to act frantic or crazy 86

buick: to vomit 80*

build a log cabin: defecate 92*

bum: to feel depressed, in low spirits 80

bummer: unpleasant or depressing experience 72

bum out: to cause or experience unpleasant feelings or bad
reactions 74

bumping: exhilarating 88

bump uglies: to engage in sex 92*

bungee: extremely 90

bungo: to mistreat severely, to inflict injury on 84*

bunk you: euphemism for fuck you 80*

burger/double burger/triple burger with cheese: sexy female/very sexy
female/very, very sexy female 86*

burned out/burnt out: physically or mentally fatigued 74; suffering
the ill effects of drugs 77; of alcohol 81

burners on high: a state of sexual excitement 92*

burn out: to become mentally or physically exhausted 72

bust: fault, as in "my bust" 85

busted: arrested 77

butt: extremely, very 88

butthead: stupid or obnoxious person 89

buttloads: large quantity 88

buzz: pleasant, euphoric feeling from drugs or alcohol 74

buzz crusher: anything that destroys a feeling of euphoria 87

caf up: to drink coffee or eat something containing caffeine for
energy 82*

Cajun talk: imitation of certain stereotypical pronunciations of the
Cajun dialect of southern Louisiana 92*

caked: drunk 91*

call the dogs: to vomit 92*

candy: excellent, worthy of admiration 91*

capeesh?: do you understand? 89*

Captain Cheddar: cheezy male 88*

carbo-load: to drink beer 90*

Carolina crunge: contagious, flu-like illness that spreads throughout
campus a couple of times a year 78*

catch a buzz: to feel pleasantly intoxicated 76

catch you later: a farewell 73

catch you on the flip flop: a farewell 77*

cazh: casual 81

Chad: stereotypical fraternity member 92*

chbye: good-bye that pairs with chello 81*

check in: a greeting 77*

check it out: to look for a partner for romance or sex 84

check out: to look at, observe 73

check you: a farewell 86

check you later: a farewell 74

check you on the flip side: a farewell 77*

cheddar: someone who is cheezy, who does not fit in 92

cheese: someone or something unattractive, unappealing, undesirable 91

cheeseball: someone or something unattractive, unappealing, undesirable, or not attuned to group standards 91

cheeseman: socially inept person 87*

cheeser: someone who is not attuned to the prevailing group standards 92*

cheese whiz: someone who thinks that he or she is impressive but is not 89*

cheesy, sleazy, greasy: female of questionable reputation 88*

cheezy: out of fashion, unappealing, tacky 87

chello: a greeting 81*

chester: socially inept person 91*

chica/chiquita: girl 87*/91*

chicalean: excellent, stylish, worthy of admiration 92*

chick: female 72

chill: beer 76*

chill out/chill: to relax, calm down, gain composure 82

chilly: acceptable 85

chilly dog: beer 85*

chipsy: arrogant and superficial 86*

choice: excellent, worthy of approval 88

choked: drunk 91*

chow down: to eat voraciously 77

chow for now: good-bye 91*

chucks: athletic shoes 84

chutzpah: brashness 91*

ciao: good-bye 81

-city: combining form indicating a presence or abundance of 80

classic: excellent, worthy of admiration 90

claven: a know-it-all 91*

clean: well dressed 74

clueless: not attuned to what is going on, unaware 81

cock: penis 93*

cock-diesel: strong, muscular, attractive male 93*

coke: cocaine 72

cold busted: caught in the act 86

cold one: beer 87

come in, Berlin: exhortation to pay attention, a greeting 78*

cool: good, in the know, sophisticated, worthy of admiration 72

cool beans!: expression of approval, admiration 87

cool breeze: person who is sharp witted, athletic, well liked; person
    who thinks himself or herself to be cool but is not 89/91

cool deal!: exclamation of approval, admiration 90

cool out: to take it easy, relax 81

cool whip: something very new and appealing 89*

cool your jets: to calm down, relax 73

cop a tude: to act in an uncooperative or angry manner 87

corn dog: someone who is socially inept or acts weird 88*

cornflakes in a can: beer 92*

couch potato: person who lies around doing nothing except perhaps
    watching television 84

Could it be . . . Satan?: reaction to something naughty 87*

court party: party at Big or Little Fraternity Court 87*

cowboy question: dare 81*

coyote date: a woman who is so ugly that when her companion for
    the night wakes up the next morning and she is asleep on his arm,
    he would rather chew off his arm than wake her up 88

crack: funny or witty person 76*

cracker jack: fool, oaf 79*

cram: to study hard at the last minute 75

cram-o-matic: to study hard at the last minute 82*

crank out: to produce large amounts of work, energy, sound 78*

crash: to go to sleep 73

crash and burn: to sleep; to have a disastrous social experience
    89/86*

crasher: one who cannot tolerate alcohol 84*

cretin: obnoxious person 76*

crib: house; where one lives 75; easy course 88

crip course: easy course 74

crispy: drunk 88

critical: excellent, worthy of admiration 90*

crocked: drunk 80

crud: anything or anyone worthless, repulsive 73

cruise: to look for a partner for sex or romance 77

cruiser: one who is moving about seeking the company of another for sex or romance 83*

crumb: to feel sad or depressed 89

crumbsnatcher: dependent child or spouse 91*

crunch: females 76*

crunchy: someone who identifies with the styles and concerns of the 1960s 90*

crunchy granola: someone who identifies with the styles and concerns of the 1960s 86*

crusader: evangelistic, fundamentalist Christian 92*

cuz: cousin, friend 86

daisy chain: the connection between people who have had sex with the same person at different times 90*

dangling modifier: a single, long, flashy earring 84*

dap: handshake; influence, respect 84/90

daze: to daydream 77*

D.D.F.M.G.: exclamation on sighting a very attractive member of the opposite sex (drop dead fuck me gorgeous) 91*

dead soldier: empty beer container 87*

decent: excellent, worthy of admiration 77

deep six: to finish a six-pack of beer 81*

def: excellent, worthy of approval 87

D.H.C.: deep, heavy conversation 82*

dick: obnoxious person; to mistreat 87*/91*

dickhead: a term of affection for close friends only 85*

a dick thing: something characteristically associated with males 91

dig: to understand 72

dildo: someone stupid, dumb 74*

dimwit: someone stupid 76

dingleberry: someone stupid, dull, obnoxious 73

dip: a bore, dullard 76

diss: to criticize, belittle 86

diva: prima donna; excellent, worthy of admiration 90*/92*

do: all-purpose verb 72

do: hairdo 75

dog: the grade D 79

dog: unattractive female 72; male who chases females 76; to treat unfairly or defeat soundly 83; something unattractive or unappealing 87

dog it: for a female to act sexually available 86 *

dog out: to betray, neglect, treat with disrespect 91 *

-dom: suffix indicating the domain of 88 *

donut hole: someone with no social skills 90 *

dook: something unpleasant, worthless 85 *

dookie: someone obnoxious 91

dope: stylish, exciting, admirable 89

doper: anything associated with smoking marijuana 81

do-right: a helpful deed 86 *

dork: socially inept person, one who does not fit in 73

dorkus pretentious: fool 91 *

dorky: characteristic of a dork 87

doscus/dosc: fool, idiot 74 *

do the Heisman: to leave, spurn, reject 90 *

do the humpty-hump: to engage in sex 90 *

do the (big) nasty: to engage in sex 88

do the wild thing: to engage in sex 90

do time in jail: for athletes to spend the required time in study hall 90 *

do 12-oz. curls: to drink beer 85 *

double-bagger: ugly female 87

dough: money 90 *

dough-brain: someone who acts stupid or as if not thinking 82 *

down with: to be in agreement with 89

dressed to impress: well dressed 77 *

drive the porcelain bus: to vomit 83

droned: unaware because of alcohol and/or drugs 73

D.T.R.: defining the relationship 92 *

ducats: money 76

duckies: money 91 *

duck soup: something easy 91 *

dude: male; any person 72; expression of agreement, approval 90

dumbfuck: someone not attuned to the prevailing norms 92 *

dumptruck date: overweight female 87 *

dust: to leave 84

dweeb: someone not attuned to prevailing norms 85

dweezle: socially inept person 86 *

-dweller: combining form to indicate someone who frequents a
   particular place 83 *

D.W.I. Harley: moped 90 *

dyke: female homosexual 74

eagle flies: pay day 83 *

earl: to vomit 84

earth biscuit: someone who identifies with the styles and concerns of
   the 1960s 90

earth cracker: environmentalist 93 *

earth daddy: older-than-average college male with the values of the
   1960s 88 *

earth muffin: someone who identifies with the styles and concerns of
   the 1960s 90

ease: to leave 81

Easter bunny: benefactor, someone who does a favor 91 *

eat up: fatigued 72 *

eat your heart out: to be envious 72 *

eco-terrorist: zealous environmentalist 92 *

egg-a-muffin: enthusiastic response of agreement 82 *

emboosticated: embarrassed 79 *

escargot: male walking arm in arm with his date 84 *

exsqueeze me: excuse me 92 *

face rape: to kiss passionately 86 *

facial: an insult, rebuff 78 *

-factor: combining form that indicates an abundance of 77 *

fag: male homosexual 72

fag hag: heterosexual female who associates with gay males 76

fake!: expression that someone has been tricked or duped 89 *

fake and bake/fake bake: to get a tan in a tanning booth 88 */91

faux: a mistake; to make a mistake 86 *

feeb: dull-witted or absent-minded person 77

fern: someone who clings to the styles of the 1960s 86 *

-fest: a combining form indicating an abundance of 86 *

file: to show off, dress up 78

five-year program/six-year program: the time it takes to complete an
   undergraduate degree 92 *

flag: to fail, make the grade F 73

flipped out: crazed; drunk 73

fly: attractive, pretty, stylish in reference to females 80

flygirl: attractive female 85*

F.O.B.: an Asian not acculturated to American ways (fresh off the boat) 92*

fois: reminiscent of European style 89*

fox: attractive, beautiful, or sexy female 74

foxy: attractive, beautiful, sexy 74

frat: fraternity member 80

fratdom: the world of fraternities 88*

fratosororalingoid: obnoxious fraternity or sorority member 92*

frat out: to dress and act like a fraternity member 78

frat rat: member of a fraternity 73

fratty: pertaining to fraternity life 73

fratty-bagger: stereotypical fraternity member 78

-freak: combining form that indicates one who is extremely interested in or overly fond of 74*

freak: strange looking or acting 72

fresh: appealing, admirable 84

fried: drunk 82

friz: Frisbee 76*

fromage: cheezy, objectionable 90*

from Chicago: unaware of what's going on, an airhead 85*

———*from hell:* an extreme example of 87

front: to pretend 90

froyo: frozen yogurt 91*

fubarred: unattractive; suffering the ill effects of alcohol or drugs (fucked up beyond all recognition) 91

fuck: to mistreat, swindle 86

fudge packer: male homosexual 93*

future: unattractive male 79*

gag me with a spoon: expression of disgust 82

ganja: marijuana 83*

garden tool: sexually promiscuous female; whore 90

gator: to wallow in beer by doing a dance in imitation of an alligator 77*; fraternity member 84*

G.B.: good-bye 78*

geeb: member of Marching Tar Heels band 89*

geek: socially inept person 79; one who studies excessively 82

geek out: to study hard 88

geeky: socially inept; overly studious 90

get a clue: admonition to pay attention, become aware 82

get a grip: admonition to act in a responsible way, act in control 81

get a job: admonition to act mature 82

get a life: admonition to act mature 85

get a manual: admonition to find out what is going on 89*

get back: expression of admiration 89*

get down: to dance, have a good time 75

get it: expression of encouragement 89

get off: expression of admiration 77

get out of here: expression of disbelief 86

get out of town: expression of disbelief 84

get over it: admonition to adapt to a situation 82

get paid: to engage in sex 88*

get real: admonition to be serious, act mature 72

get some: expression of encouragement 90*

get the heck out of Dodge: to leave any place 85

get up: expression of admiration 89

get up with: to have a romantic encounter 86; to meet someone 89*

get with the program: admonition to act in a mature or responsible way 83

get you some: to engage in sex 85

G.H.: the soap opera *General Hospital* 81

ghetto blaster: portable stereo tape deck 83

the gift that keeps on giving: venereal disease 86

gig: male who dates many women 82*

girlfriend: noun of address among females 88

give me a break: request for consideration 77; exclamation of disbelief 91

given: expression of agreement 92*

gnarly: disgusting 85; excellent, worthy of approval 93

go commando: to go without underwear 74*

godsquad: people who evangelize on campus 85

go for sushi: to kiss passionately 85*

golfed: drunk 91*

gone: drunk 79

go ninety: to kiss passionately 92*

gonzo: drunk 80*

goober/goob: socially inept person, someone not attuned to the
   prevailing group norms 85/86
goob out: to cause repulsion or disgust 87*
goo food: Oriental cuisine 85*
goombah: someone not attuned to the prevailing group norms 90*
go on, girl: expression of encouragement used among females 90*
gorbachev: response to a sneeze, gesundheit 90*
gotcha back: expression of support 90*
gotcha covered: expression of support 93*
Goth: student who dresses in black and listens to avant-garde
   music 91
gotta love that: expression of approval of another's good fortune 91*
gouda, gouda, gouda: signal that someone or something is
   cheezy 90*
G.Q.: fashionably dressed (*Gentleman's Quarterly*) 81
Grand Vile: Granville Towers 77
granola: someone who identifies with the styles and concerns of the
   1960s 82
granola-groid: someone who identifies with the styles and concerns
   of the 1960s 90*
grape-nut: someone who clings to the styles of the 1960s 87*
grass: marijuana 72
gravy: easy 72
grazie: thanks 88*
grease down: to eat voraciously 76
Great Hell: Great Hall of the Student Union 91*
gril: affectionate noun of address to another female 92*
grody: repulsive, disgusting 83
groomed to zoom: well dressed 74*
groover: someone who is out of date or out of fashion 80
groovy: great, exciting 72; out of favor, unacceptable 83; good,
   fashionable 91
grope: to kiss passionately 80
gross: unattractive, unappealing 72
Grossville: Granville Towers 79*
group gropes: encounter groups 73*
grub: to eat a lot 77; to kiss passionately 79; to engage in sex 88
guido: someone acting macho 88*
gumby: a large quantity 84*
gumbyhead: someone who does something stupid 84*

gunslinger: female who rejects a male's attention rudely 91*
gut: easy course 75*
gweeb: person entirely lacking in social skills and style 86
gwimp: socially inept person 76*

ha-ha: beer 79
hammered: drunk 86
hand: a wish to have a nice day 91*
hang: to cope, endure; to do nothing in particular 76/90
happening: exciting, admirable 82
harsh: to mistreat 89
harsh on: to criticize, belittle 80
hasta hasta pasta: a farewell 90*
hasta la bye-bye: a farewell 90*
hasta la vista, baby: a farewell 90
hasty bananas: a farewell 90*
hat: fraternity member 91*
haul ass: to leave 74
have one's beer goggles on: to find someone attractive because of the influence of alcohol 87
hawk: cold wind 74; to participate in an athletic activity for fun 88*
H.D.: male who mooches off a female (husband dependent) 88*
head: beer 74
-head: combining form to signal a person who does something habitually 72
heat-seeking missile: penis 91*
He could make me write bad checks.: Comment by a female on the attractiveness of a male 83*
heinous: terrible 86
hell dwell: to have a good time drinking and partying at local pubs 84*
Hell Hole: Hill Hall 91*
hemorrhoid: annoying person 89*
Herman the one-eyed German: penis 91
hey-wow: someone who clings to the styles of the 1960s 83
history: a thing of the past, as in the farewell "I'm history" 84
hit a home run: to engage in sex 87*
hit gut: to engage in sex 93*
hit on: to make sexual overtures 83
hit one's head on the ceiling: to make a mistake 76*

ho: person indiscreet in sexual matters 86; promiscuous or
    seductively dressed female 89
hold: to possess marijuana 92*
hombre: male friend 91*
home: person from the same hometown, friend 81
home biscuit: friend 88*
homeboy/homey: male from one's hometown, friend, someone who
    appears friendly 81/84
homechop: endearing term for a close friend, usually of the opposite
    sex 88*
homegirl: female from one's hometown, friend 86
homeslice: friend 89
Homey don't play dat: refusal to cooperate, consent, or accept 90
hone out: to eat voraciously 88*
hooch dog: marijuana cigarette 86*
hook: the grade C 76
hook up/hook: to find a partner for romance or sex 85/91; to kiss
    passionately 88/89
hoops: basketball 80
hosebag: promiscuous female 79
hot: sexually attractive 79
hot ticket: the epitome of what is in style 80
hound: sexually aggressive male 77*
how's it going?: a greeting 90
hulked: angry 89*
hunk: attractive male 72
hunt: to search for a partner for romance or sex 90*
hurl: to vomit 90
hype: excellent, worthy of approval 92*
hyper: hyperactive, excessively energetic 76
hypnotist: crazy person 86*

icy pop: beer 91*
ID/I.D.: form of identification, like a driver's license 89*
I hate it/that: sarcastic expression of pleasure 84
I'm down with that: expression of agreement 89
I'm hating it/You're hating it: expression of sympathy 88
I'm into that: expression of agreement 91
I'm serious: expression of agreement 81
I'm there: expression of support 91

inch: to steal 90*

intellectual hour: soap opera time 80*

invertebrated: drunk 82*

It's been real: a farewell 77

It's no hanging matter: assurance that something is unimportant 89*

j: joint (marijuana cigarette) 72

jam: to make music; dance; have a good time; perform well
    72/76/77/80

jambox: portable stereo tape deck 82

James Earl Dog: marijuana cigarette 86*

jamming: excellent 82

jap scrap: motorcycle or appliance made in Japan 88*

jar pot: particularly strong marijuana 92*

jello: person whose brain is like jello; an older person 92*

jell out/jell: to relax by doing nothing; calm down 83*/90*

jellybeans: painkillers 90*

jelly roll: sex 91*

jerk: socially inept person 79

jerkface: foolish, dull person 78*

jet: to leave 90

jetson: someone who is unaware of what is going on 83*

jimmy/jimmy hat: condom 90/91

jimmy dog: marijuana cigarette 86*

jing: money 73*

jive: deceptive talk 74

jock: athlete 76

jody: the generic male that a husband or boyfriend accuses a female
    of cheating with 89*

joe: beer 79*

jones: craving for anything, originally drugs 74

juiced: drunk 79

jump: to seduce 89*

jump back: expression of astonishment 91*

the junk: great, the best 92*

keeva: excellent, worthy of admiration 92*

keg: exclamation of approval 91*

kegging: excellent, worthy of admiration 91*

Ken: painstakingly fashionably dressed and groomed male 84*

kick ass: to be difficult; prevail over something or someone 81
kicking: excellent, worthy of admiration 88
kicks: athletic shoes 83
killer: excellent, worthy of admiration 83
killer weed: extremely high quality marijuana 78*
kiss, kiss: a farewell 91*
knock boots: to engage in sex 90
knockers: a woman's breasts 76*
Know what I mean, Vern?: Do you understand? 83*
K.O.: to die (kick off) 76*

L7: loser, "square" (said with thumbs and index fingers forming a
    square) 80*
LaChaise: Chase Cafeteria 90*
laid back: relaxed, at ease 74
laid out: drunk 81*
laminite: a phony 86*
lamo: someone not attuned to the prevailing styles and priorities 93*
lamp: do nothing in particular 91*
Land's End!: all purpose exclamation 87*
late night: party, usually at a fraternity house, that does not start
    until after the bars close, around one in the morning, and usually
    gets very big 85
later: a farewell 77; to end a relationship, jilt 86*
later, tater: a farewell 78*
latro: a farewell 91*
la vogue: women's restroom 87*
lay out: to sunbathe 78
lay pipe: to enage in sex 87
legman: ladies' man 76*
legume: vegetable, one who lies around doing nothing 81*
Lenwah: Lenoir Hall Dining Room 87
lesbo: female homosexual 92*
let go: to relax 91*
level 1 diagnostic: observation 91*
lifer: someone who has committed a trivial offense 84*
like a big dog: with intensity 83
like buttah: executed or performed smoothly or well 92*
like hi: a greeting 91*
limburger: female no one else would date 84*

lit: drunk 78

A Little Piece of New Jersey in Our Own Back Yard: Duke. University 85*

loaded: drunk 83

lock it in cruise mode: focus attention on a stranger in a group for romantic or sexual attention 84*

lose it: be out of control of one's situation 77

lose move: stupid action 87*

love: trying, difficult 90*

loved it!: expression of elation 88

L.S.D.: a run of a long distance at a slower pace during cross-country track practice 90*

lude out: to become unable to function, usually because of drugs 80*

luego: a farewell 81*

lunchbox: someone who is out of touch with what is going on 84*

lunchy: unaware 74*

lust with: to feel sexual attraction toward 89*

Maalox moment: time of stress 90*

-machine: combining form that indicates an enthusiast, devotee 83*

macho: aggressively masculine 77

mad dog: cheap wine (Mogen David 20/20) 78*

main squeeze: best girlfriend or boyfriend 77

major: important, grievous 84

make like a baby and head out: to leave 85

mange: to eat 86

masked man: homosexual male 85*

matriculate: to start on a trip 73*

maul: to kiss passionately 93*

max: the highest degree 74

max and relax: to take life easy 93*

Maybelline waste: disappointing social event 90*

McPaper: a quickly or poorly written paper 91*

M.D.: cheap liquor (mad dog, Mogen David) 78*

M.D.G.: strong physical attraction (mutual desire to grope) 81*

mean: good, admirable 72*

mega-: prefix indicating a great amount or degree 80

-meister: combining form that indicates familiarity or mastery of 91

mellow: relaxed 74

mellow out: to relax 81

mercy buckets: thank you 90*

mercy buttercups: thank you 81*

mesc: mescaline 72*

messed up: drunk 80

Mickey D's Rainbow Steakhouse: McDonald's 91*

mickey mouse: trivial, cheap, easy 72

microbeer: seven-ounce beer 90

mine: my fault 89*

mix/mixer: informal party that brings together different groups for
   socializing 80

M.L.A.: passionate kissing (massive lip action) 81*

mommy up: to love, hug, comfort 88*

mongo: huge 85

mongolito: term of endearment 89*

motivate: to move around in a group socializing 79; to leave 85

moto: master of the obvious 90*

motor: to leave 87

motorvate: to leave 86

mountain climber: high induced by drugs 78*

mousse up: to use a foamy hair-care preparation 86*

mow on: to eat voraciously 87

M.R.A.: unsociable behavior (major reeb action) 81*

Mr. Mason: particularly strong marijuana 92*

mud puppy: an ugly female 83*

munch out: to eat voraciously 79

mutile: incapacitated, immobile person 81*

My feet are staying: a farewell (auf wiedersehen) 88*

nail: well-built male (nice ass in Levi's) 90*

naked pretzel: sexual intercourse 91

narc: narcotics agent 72

N.B.D.: expression of nonchalance (no big deal) 81

N.C.: a boorish person (no class) 80*

N.C.A.A.: a boorish person (no class at all) 82*

nerd: socially inept person 72

nice car: good-looking male or female 84*

nimrod: socially inept person, someone not attuned to the group
   norms, a loser 93*

nip it: to stop something 83*

nob: socially inept person 72*

no doubt: expression of agreement 88

nonschlock: avant-garde 86*

Not!: negative reversal at the end of a sentence 90

no way: expression of disagreement, disapproval, rejection 75

N.S.²: retort to a stupid question or statement (no shit, Sherlock) 87*

N.T.O.: date who does not come up to expectations (not the one) 91*

N.T.S.: attractive male that makes a female's heart beat so fast that her name tag shakes (name tag shaker) 79*

nuke and puke: microwavable meal 90*

Nuprin: Asian 92*

nut-n-berry: someone who identifies with the concerns and styles of the 1960s 91*

nutter butter: someone who is unaware or inattentive 91*

obliterated: drunk 87

obno: crude, obnoxious person 79*

O.D.: to overdose, an overdose 72

-omatic: suffix indicating intensity or repetition 82*

one-eyed trouser snake: penis 91*

O.O.C.: drunk, high on drugs, acting crazy (out of control) 81*

ook: to vomit 91*

O.P.P.: someone else's boyfriend or girlfriend (other person's property) 91

-orama: suffix indicating extensiveness 86

oreo: African American who identifies with whites 73

organic: fashionable 77*

O'River: a farewell (au revoir) 91*

osmosis amoebas: a farewell (adios, amigos) 83*

otis: drunk 84*

O.T.L.: not in touch with reality, inattentive, unaware (out to lunch) 79

O.T.R.: snappish, in a bad mood (on the rag) 81

out of control: drunk 87; extraordinary, excellent 89

out of here/outta here: a farewell 85

out of sight: excellent, extraordinary 72

out of state: excellent, extraordinary 73*

outpost: someone who is out of touch with reality, a daydreamer 84*

outrageous: excellent, worthy of admiration 91*

out to lunch: not in touch with reality, inattentive, unaware 73

ozone ranger: someone who is out of touch with reality 78

paper: money 91*

parallel park: engage in sex 86*

parental units: parents 82

parking Nazi: parking lot monitor 90

party hat: condom 91*

party on!: a farewell 90*

Paul Revere: a farewell (au revoir) 84*

P.D.K.: someone who is out of fashion (polyester double knit) 85*

peace person: someone who identifies with the concerns and the styles of the 1960s 91*

peace up/peace out: a farewell 90/91

perma-: prefix indicating permanence, continuity 81

perpetrate: to pretend 86

phase out: to become unaware, as if asleep 80*

phat: having a curvaceous figure, voluptuous (pretty hips and thighs) 73

P.I.B.: brooding, gloomy adolescent who wears dark clothes and listens to alternative music about death (people in black) 90

pie out: to become drunk 76*

pig dog: someone who eats a lot 82*

pig out: to eat voraciously 72

pill: basketball 80

pink floyd: something immensely enjoyable 72*

pissed: angry 74

pissoir: bathroom 86*

the pits: the worst situation 75

pit sit: to sit on the steps of the Pit between classes 92*

pit slut: female who sits around the Pit to meet friends and see people 92*

Pizza Slut: Pizza Hut 93*

plastered: drunk 73

plastic: artificial, fake 73*

plastic cow: nondairy creamer 87*

plastic out: to assume temporarily an artificial behavior or personality 73*

play tonsil hockey: to kiss passionately 86*

ploughed: drunk 85

P.M.S.: to feel irritable, anxious (premenstrual syndrome, or putting up with men's shit) 90

polislide: easy political science course 78

politico: campus political figure 74*

polluted: drunk 72

polyester: something out of style or fake 90*

polyester princess: female who dresses in out-of-date fashions 92*

pomp: someone who acts as if he or she is better than others 92*

ponch: noun of address for males 86*

poof: to leave 90*

poopbutt: undesirable person 91*

popsicle stand: current location 86

pop tops: to drink beer 81*

porch monkey: black person 81*

pork: to engage in sex 86

pork out: to eat voraciously 76

poser: someone who pretends to be something he or she is not 90

posey: pretentious 92*

posse: group of friends 90

potato: to lie around doing nothing 89*

pound: to drink heavily 72

power: extreme, extremely 86

P.Q.: someone who is out of date (polyester queen) 85*

preesh: expression of appreciation 86

presh: favorable, enjoyable 86*

private Idaho: one's own little world 81*

probably: probably not 88

pseudo-: prefix indicating phony, imitation 85

psyche!: exclamation that one has tricked or fooled someone else 85

published: very ugly 90*

pull a Ferris Bueller: to cut class, to take time away from studies 87*

pull a MacGyver: to do something mechanically very clever 92*

pull a Ronnie: to do something stupid 86*

pummeled: drunk 90*

punk: someone, something worthless, unimportant 79

put it in cruise mode: to seek a partner for romance or sex 84*

put it in overdrive: to seek a partner for romance or sex 84*

quad: stupid, clumsy person 77*

-queen: combining form indicating a female enthusiast 82

queen: male homosexual 73

queen ween: someone who backs out of a commitment 90*

qué pasa?: a greeting 85*

quick starts: athletic shoes 90*
quimp: socially inept person 76*

R.&I.: extremely exciting or enjoyable (radical and intense) 81*
rad: excellent, exciting, extraordinary (radical) 84
radical: excellent, surpassing expectations 79
rage: to engage in sex 92*
rag out: to become tired 73
raildog: technician who works on the catwalk with the ropes
    controlling the sets and lights 91*
raincoat: condom 91*
raise: parents 83*
ralph: to vomit 76
ramped: drunk 92*
random: stranger; someone who does not fit in 88
ranked: drunk 92*
rap: to converse 72
rape: to abuse 74; to diminish the effects of 86; to misuse, steal 91; to
    defeat 92
rape someone's buzz: to put a damper on someone's pleasure 86
rat bitch: an undependable lab partner 92*
raunch out: to offend by making sexual remarks or using offensive
    language 74*
Raw's: Roy Roger's Restaurant 78*
reach: someone who is out of touch with reality 86*
read: to tell someone off 89
redneck: stereotypical rural southerner 72
Redneck Tech: North Carolina State University 92*
redshirted: jilted 92*
reeb: socially inept person, outsider 81
rental units: parents 74*
rents: parents 74
rice-and-beaner: someone who identifies with the styles and concerns
    of the 1960s 92*
rice burner: Japanese motorcycle 84*
ride the E-train: to feel the effects of the drug Ecstasy 92*
ride the porcelain Honda: to vomit 90*
rig: to experience tightening of muscles at the end of a strenuous
    race 90*
righteous: excellent, worthy of approval 89

ripped: drunk 77

ripped off: cheated, treated unfairly 74

ripped out of one's gourd: drunk 73 *

ripped to the tits: drunk 83 *

ripping: excellent, worthy of admiration 91 *

ripskated: drunk 91 *

rip the rug: to dance 79 *

roach: the butt of a marijuana cigarette 72

road whore: promiscuous female 85 *

rock: basketball 80

rocked: drunk 88

rocket scientist: someone who is stupid 92 *

rock out: to play music loudly 81 *

rocks for jocks: easy geology course 79

rogue: to steal 84 *

roll: to leave 81

romper room: a place to get rowdy 85 *

rooms: roommate 92 *

rotic: romantic without the man 92 *

Rotsi: Reserve Officers Training Corps 79 *

rumptyvump: courses in radio–television–motion pictures 80

run with the big dogs: to do anything anyone else can 81

S.A.B.: social airhead bitch 86 *

-san: suffix that conveys familiarity 91 *

sarajevo: a farewell 84 *

saturated: drunk 86 *

scam: to look for a partner for romance or sex 85

schiz out: to lose emotional control, act crazed 81 *

schlock: out of fashion, trite 86 *

schlub: to fight 88 *

schmegma: any gross, slimy substance 90

schmiel/schmielage: female 88/88 *

schmiel on: to act nice in order to pick up a female 88

schmuck: someone who does not fit in 79

schnack: affection 92 *

schnicky-schnacky: public display of affection 92 *

school: to dominate, prevail, do something better than the opposition
so that he or she learns from you 84

scooby-doo: someone who eats a lot and never gains weight 92 *

scope: to look around, observe 73; to look in various public places for
    a partner for romance or sex 76

score: to obtain something desirable, usually sex 72

scourge: interjection used by *Daily Tar Heel* staff 90*

screw: to mistreat, swindle 73

screws me: excuse me 77*

scrog: to engage in sex 86

scrump: to engage in sex 83

scuzbag: sexually promiscuous female 80

seafood plate: please (s'il vous plaît) 84*

sergeant space: someone who is out of touch with reality 83*

sheepskin: condom 91*

shekel: to give, hand out 84*

sherlock: friend 86*

shit: expression of anger or disappointment 72; information 72

the shit: something superlative 86

shithead: objectionable person 83

Shitty Health Services: Student Health Services 91*

shocker: ironic exclamation that something is not surprising 91*

shoot cookies: to vomit 74*

shoot the pill/peel: to shoot baskets, play a pickup game of
    basketball 80

shotgun: to drink beer straight down 88*

shroom dog: someone who uses hallucinogens 88*

sick: great, fantastic 83

sieg heil: affirmative response to How are you? 74*

siesta: after-class nap 89*

sight delight: good-looking male 84*

silver plate: please (s'il vous plaît) 90*

sister girl: noun of address among female friends 89

skank: someone with a bad reputation 80

-ski: suffix added to names indicating stupidity 84*

skips: tennis shoes 89

slack: below standard, lazy 76

slammed: drunk 85

slamming: excellent, exciting 91

slampiece: sexual partner 90

slave: job 80*

sleaze: sexually promiscuous female 79

sleazebag: promiscuous female 82

sleazoid: promiscuous female 83

slickies: sorority members 92*

slide: easy course; to leave 72

slimebucket: objectionable or offensive person 92*

slop shop: any campus snack bar 81*

slorch: promiscuous female 91*

sloshed: drunk 79

slut: affectionate noun of address among females, a habitué 83

slut puppy: sexually promiscuous female 83

smashed: drunk 75

smell you later/smell you: a farewell 91*

smoke: to perform well 90

smoker: something difficult 76*

smoking: difficult 77

smuckered: drunk 77*

smurf: to steal 91*

snack: to kiss passionately 93*

snack bar: boyfriend or girlfriend 86*

snake: someone who steals something, particularly someone else's
    date; to steal 75

snatch 22: extremely ugly female 92*

snockered: drunk 77

snort out: to overeat, eat voraciously 84*

social donut hole: socially inept person 82*

soda cracker: white person 92*

sofa spud: someone who lies around doing nothing 86*

sofa yam: someone who lies around doing nothing 87*

S.O.L.: shit out of luck 83

solidement: affirmative response 80*

somnambulance: someone who is funny, likable, crazy 86*

sororite: stereotypical sorority member 93*

space cadet: someone who is out of touch with reality 73

space case: someone who is out of touch with reality 81

spacey: preoccupied, not aware of what is going on 76

spadet: student preoccupied with studies 81*

spaz: to act silly or strange 90*; clumsy person, usually said
    jokingly 80

spaz out: to lose mental control 82*

Spinster Dormitory: Spencer, residence hall for females 74

split: to leave 73

spork: eating implement (spoon + fork) 77*

square: person who is stupid or not up with the latest 74

squeek: to engage in sex 86*

squeeze me: excuse me 92*

squirrel kisser: environmentalist 92*

squirrelly: acting crazy, insane, nuts 74

sssss — : sound that an airhead emits 80*

-ster: familiarizing suffix on a person's name 92*

stone fox: beautiful woman 88*

story: an afternoon television soap opera 76*

straight: not under the influence of drugs; heterosexual 74

straight up: honestly 89

stranger mixer: party to bring together men and women who do not know one another 88*

stud: good-looking male 79

Student Death: Student Health Services 88

Student Hell: Student Health Services 91

study mongrel: someone who studies hard 92*

stupid: nice, good, popular 89

Stupid Health: Student Health Services 90

styling and profiling: fashionable and chic 88*

suck: to be unpleasant, stupid, objectionable 85

sucks to be you: expression of commiseration 91

suck tonsils: to kiss passionately 91*

suds: beer 86*

Sue: stereotypical sorority member 80

sue out: to dress, look, and act like a sorority member 81*

sugar: cocaine 89*

suit: properly attired businessman 92

's up: a greeting 81

Sure, I knew you could: sarcastic expression of doubt 81*

Suzi/Susie: stereotypical sorority member 77

Suzi sorority: stereotypical sorority member 74

sweave: swerve and weave 81*

sweet: pleasing, excellent, worthy of admiration 75

table zamboni: rag for wiping spills from a table or bar top 87*

take a chill pill: admonition to calm down, relax 82

talk to Ralph on the big white telephone: to vomit 77*

tan: tough as nails, macho 86*

tang: someone who puts a damper on things 74*

tang out: abandon, put an end to 74*

tanked: drunk 72

technicolor yawn: to vomit 81

teckies: members of the Carolina Union Technical Services 91*

ted: drunk 85

Tell me about it: expression of agreement 91*

That bites the big one/that bites: expression of commiseration 80/81

That's close: ironic comment that something is far from the truth 73*

That's fair: ironic comment that something is not fair 78

There's no intelligent life here: response to "Beam me up, Scotty" 79*

third world briefcase: portable stereo tape deck 87*

threads: clothing 72

three-dollar bill: strange person 72*

throw down: to eat voraciously 81; engage in sex 83

throwed: defeated, humiliated 91

throw shade: to humiliate exceedingly 92*

thunder thighs: overweight person 93*

tighty whities: men's briefs 91*

time in jail: required time in study hall (track team) 90*

tin: beer 80*

tives: relatives 74*

toast: in big trouble, the victim of misfortune 86

toasted: drunk 80

toe: drunk 92*

toke: drag on a marijuana cigarette 72

tom: computer (totally obedient moron) 90*

tool: socially inept person 74

tore out of the frame: drunk 76

torn up/tore up/tow up: drunk 81*/87*/86*

totaled out: drunk 86*

totally: to a great degree, completely 84

tough: good, attractive, admirable 72

Toxic Hell: Taco Bell 93*

toxic waste dump: person who uses drugs 88*

trashed: drunk 77

trash your act: to stop 73*

tree-hugger: environmentalist 90

tree nymph: environmentalist 92*

trendinistas: political or social activists who combine heightened political consciousness with stylish clothing 88; someone who champions trendy causes 90*

tres: very 81*

trip: experience that is overwhelmingly either pleasant or disgusting 72

trip/trip out: to strike as funny, crazy, or extraordinary; to be amazed, excited 84

troll: to search in the bars on Franklin Street for a partner for sex or romance 87

troop: to leave 91*

trough out: to eat voraciously 86*

T.S.H.: expression of commiseration (that shit happens) 83

tube: television 72

tubular: excellent 83

tude: resentful, hostile, uncooperative manner 92*

tunes: music 83

turkey: person who acts stupid or never seems to do anything right 72

12 o'clock high, check it out: to focus attention on someone in a group for the purpose of sex or romance 84*

twerp: someone who acts stupid 74

twink: someone unusual, crazy, dumb 74*

twinkie: Asian who identifies with Caucasians 92*

twize: Budweiser beer 79*

two snaps up: expression of approval 90

The Ugly: the undergraduate library 82

un: loser, someone who does not fit in 91*

U.N.C. at K-Mart: University of North Carolina at Wilmington 85

U.N.C. at Tweetsie Railroad: Appalachian State University 86

units: parents (parental units) 87*

University of New Jersey at Durham: Duke University 85

up the butt: in great quantity 91*

use: to prevail over an opponent, usually in basketball 74

use up all one's letters: to demonstrate intellectual superiority 76*

U.Y.B.: uppity Yankee bitch 86*

veg out/veg: to do nothing 80/81

velveeta: something or someone cheezy 83

vibes: inaudible signals that people and places emit 72*

victory!: exclamation of elation 91*

vid: videotape 85*

virgin vault: residence hall for females 92*

vomatose: disgusting 83*

V.P.L.: visible panty lines 82

-wad: suffix attached to a proper name to indicate that the person
 has acted in a dense or foolish way 82*

walk of shame: walk back to her residence hall by a female after
 having spent the night with a male 90

walk the way of a trollop: to signal sexual availability 91*

Wally: name that indicates that the referent is acting like a big
 brother 85*; nerd accepted in a social group because he is needed
 for his high grades, athletic ability, or good looks 91*

wank!: negative retort in imitation of a buzzer 73*

wanker: undesirable person, thing, or situation 73

wannabe: imitation of something better, a phony 90

waste case: drunkard 86

wasted: drunk; defeated 76/86

waste product: drunkard 85*

way: extremely, very 87; affirmative response to No Way 90

We be ——ing: report of an action, in imitation of Black English
 construction: "We be mowing on that salad bar" 81*

the weed: marijuana 72*

weegies: clothing issued by Wollen Gym 80*

ween: someone who is no fun 78*

we here: expression of support 93*

weird out: to feel confused or at a loss because of someone's or
 something's strangeness 72

welk: you're welcome 88*

WHAM: woman who harms men physically or emotionally (women
 hate all men; in the plural, women have all men scared) 86*

What does it look like?: a greeting 78*

Whatever!: exclamation of disbelief 92

Whatever floats your boat: expression of acceptance 87

What it is?: a greeting 76

What's going down?: a greeting 75

What's happening?: a greeting 73

What's jumping?: a greeting 81*

What's shaking?: a greeting 84*

What's the deal?: a greeting 81

What's up?: a greeting 76

What's up, G?: a greeting 90

What you know?: a greeting 86*

wheels: car 72

Where it's at?: a greeting 74*

whipped: drunk 84; unduly controlled by a romantic interest, usually a female 85

white bread: something good 81*; characteristic of white suburbia 91*

Who put the quarter in your slot?: sarcastic admonition to mind one's own business 89*

whooped: unduly controlled by a romantic interest, usually a female 85

whoredog: a lowlife person 83*; promiscuous female 87

whupped: unduly controlled by a romantic interest, usually a female 83*

wicked: good, admirable 74

wide load: someone with large hips and buttocks 90*

wig out: to become astonished, act crazy 81

wilma: female who acts stupid 87

wimp: weak, indecisive person, usually a male 77

wimp dog: male with little personality or assertiveness 87*

wimp out: to let someone down, fail to live up to a commitment 80

wiped out: drunk 72

Woodstock wannabe: reminiscent of the 1960s 91

word up/word: expression of agreement 86/88; a greeting or farewell 88

work someone's last nerve: to annoy exceedingly 90*

worship the porcelain goddess: to vomit 81

wounded soldier: partially empty beer container 91*

wrecked: drunk 72

wrought iron!: exclamation of approval (right on) 74*

wuss: a weakling, someone who cannot be depended on 76

X: to stop, eliminate 83

yak: to vomit 90

yam: to engage in sex 85*

the yard: area between the undergraduate library and Bingham and Greenlaw Halls where students congregate between classes 80

yernt: socially inept person 86*
yo: a greeting 73
you know it: expression of support or commiseration 91
You're so tan I hate you, bye: a farewell 91*
yo-yo: someone who acts strange 79
yuck: to vomit 91*
yuke: to vomit 91

za: pizza 79
zero: someone with no redeeming virtues 72
zod: person who is stupid or not up with the latest 83*
zoid: fan of punk rock music and styles 84*
zoo: the lowest grade possible 79
zoolooed: drunk 76*
zoom: interjection used by *Daily Tar Heel* staff 90*
zooted: drunk 84*
z-out: to go to sleep 81*

INTRODUCTION

1. Recently, in *Linguistic Variation and Change* (1992), James Milroy has raised the same objection with regard to explaining the nature of sound change by reference to the prestigious dialect only. Based on careful study of contemporary spoken vernaculars of Belfast, Northern Ireland, Milroy argues that both language maintenance and change are responses to variation inherent in language as a social phenomenon. He maintains that understanding ongoing variation and change can help to develop a more realistic account of historical change. Interestingly, Eugene Babbitt, in 1900, justified the study of slang in the same way: "It illustrates, as nothing else can do, the natural influences operating upon language and the natural effects to be expected, influences and effects which cannot be arrived at by *a priori* reasoning or with certainty from merely literary tradition. Besides, from seeing language as it actually exists, as it lives and grows, it is possible to make right inferences regarding language in the past, and to determine the probability or improbability of much that now rests wholly or largely upon conjecture" (18).

2. The figures in this description of the university are drawn from two university publications, *Teaching at Carolina: A Handbook for Instructors*, The Center for Teaching and Learning, 1991, and *UNC: Facts and Information*, University of North Carolina News Bureau, 1993.

CHAPTER ONE

1. Stanley Newman, in "Vocabulary Levels: Zuni Sacred and Slang Usage," has observed "low-valued words and expressions which enjoy only a brief period of currency" among the Zuni, a society without class or caste strata. "But status differentiation is applied to age groups; and the speech peculiar to young people is low-valued, while that associated with old people is prestigeful" (1964, 402).

2. This numerical account does not factor out the many terms that in each year turned out to be one-time submissions.

3. Cynthia Bernstein and Thomas Nunnally of Auburn University in Alabama in 1990 began a longitudinal study of student slang at

their university. An annual questionnaire solicits current items as well as students' judgment of the currency, scope, and meaning of campus slang items from the previous year. Preliminary reports at the meeting of the Southeastern Conference on Linguistics in April 1991 and in April 1995 suggest that this study will be valuable in understanding the rate and particulars of lexical change.

4. The particular challenges that slang presents to dictionary making are discussed in my essay "Slang and Lexicography" in the forthcoming Festschrift honoring Sydney Lamb.

CHAPTER TWO

1. John and Adele Algeo's *Fifty Years among the New Words* (1991) contains an excellent discussion of the formal processes responsible for new vocabulary in English over the past half century. Included is a table showing the consistent relative frequency of the various processes in three collections of new words in English. For their study of the neologisms recorded for fifty years in the "Among the New Words" section of *American Speech*, the Algeos found the order to be, from more frequent to less frequent, compounds, suffixes, prefixes, semantic shifting, grammatical shifting, shortening, blending, borrowing, creating, and unknown. In this chapter functional shift is the equivalent of grammatical shifting; semantic shifting is discussed in Chapter 3 on meaning.

2. Most American linguists put little trust in the claim that sounds evoke meaning directly, because such a claim violates the fundamental tenet of the scientific study of language — that in language the connection between sound and meaning is arbitrary. Yet native speakers of any language clearly do have personal attitudes about certain sounds that match the personal attitudes of other native speakers. Early in the twentieth century Otto Jespersen pointed out the diminutive force of the high front vowel sound for English in words like *teeny* (compared with *tiny*) and in the suffix on names like *Bobby*, *Dottie*, and so forth. Other prominent linguists have been interested in sound symbolism as well, among them Edward Sapir and J. R. Firth, who coined the term *phonestheme*. Most recently, the late Dwight Bolinger saw sound symbolism as support for the various mechanisms "that hold together the vast memory store that mature speakers lay up over a lifetime and from which — again with the aid of sound symbolism — they retrieve,

moment by moment, the forms that fit the subject of their talk" (1992, 29). For a clear overview of sound symbolism, see the essay by I. E. Reay in *The Encyclopedia of Language and Linguistics* (1994).

Wescott's claim that labial and velar sounds have a high correlation with derogatory meanings points out a tendency, not a rule, for many derogatory English words have no labials or velars (e.g., *shit*), and many words with labials and velars are not derogatory (e.g., *comb*).

3. The notion of semantic field is treated here rather than in Chapter 3 on meaning because such relationships between lexical items can help to explain form in slang. Although the description of meaning presented in Chapter 3 of this study does not explicitly use the notion of semantic fields, the fundamental view of the lexicon presented there is certainly compatible with recent explorations of lexical and semantic organization. A semantic field approach assumes that the lexicon of a language is highly structured, "a network in which each item is related to other lexical items in a variety of ways. There is no single semantic description which shows all of these relationships, and different approaches highlight different aspects of the network" (Lehrer 1974, 7). In semantic field analysis "the words of a language can be classified into sets which are related to conceptual fields and divide up the *semantic space* or semantic domain in certain ways" (15). Thus the meaning of a word depends, at least in part, on its relation to other words. This approach to the lexicon has been developed mainly over the past two decades. In 1989 a National Science Foundation conference brought together linguists, psychologists, and philosophers who were working on the lexicon and its relation to meaning. The resulting collection of essays, edited by Lehrer and Kittay (1992), reflects contemporary, multidisciplinary research into the principles of lexical and semantic organization.

4. An anonymous reviewer of the manuscript of this book suggests that *crib course* may not be an instance of folk etymology from *crip* but instead developed from *crib* 'pilfer, steal', attested from the eighteenth century and, in the twentieth, best known among students in *crib sheet* 'unauthorized notes used to cheat in an examination'.

CHAPTER THREE

1. For a more detailed and technical discussion of the types of semantic change, see Williams (1975), 170–93.

2. Both *queen* and *quean* are developments of the Old English noun *cwene*. *The Oxford English Dictionary* explains the difference in spelling: "In ME the word was distinguished from QUEEN by its open *e*, which in the 14–15th c. was sometimes denoted by the spelling with *ei* or *ey*, and later (as in other words of the class) by *ea*."

3. The cognitive and cultural nature of the classical figures of speech have been explored increasingly by contemporary linguists. Lakoff and Johnson's *Metaphors We Live By* (1980) is one of the earliest, most frequently referred to, and most accessible explanations of metaphor and metonymy as systematic processes that give structure to our conceptual system. For a discussion of the importance of metaphor in scientific thinking, see Papin (1992), 1253–65.

CHAPTER FOUR

1. See "Borrowing" in McArthur (1992) for a general discussion of the process and a select list of borrowings into English organized by source language. See "Foreign Elements in the English Word Stock" in Pyles and Algeo (1993) for a chronological treatment of borrowing in English.

2. Portions of the section on borrowing appear in Eble (1992a and 1993).

3. Collectively these dialects are referred to by a number of different terms. In linguist studies, Black Vernacular English is often used. In her 1994 book *Black Talk*, Geneva Smitherman also lists Black Talk, African American English, Black/African American Language, Ebonics, and Black/African American Lingo.

This discussion of African American contributions to general American slang based on the entries in Chapman (1986) is fuller than needed to show African American borrowing in college slang. It is warranted because of the increasing influence of African American verbal practices on the speech of all young Americans and because the information presented here about African American slang is not readily available in any other single source.

4. Lighter's earliest citation is 1944.

5. Gerald Cohen points out that, ironically, one of the best sources of the slang of African American musicians of this era is the autobiography of Mezz Mezzrow, a white jazz musician who identified strongly with his black colleagues. The April 1991 and November 1992 issues

of *Comments on Etymology* contain lists of black slang that Cohen has compiled from Mezz Mezzrow and Bernard Wolfe's *Really the Blues* (1946).

6. *In Living Color* received media attention when comedian and writer Franklyn Ajaye resigned because he felt that the image of African Americans projected by the program was too limited. Writing in the 14 January 1991 issue of *Black Ink*, the newspaper of the Black Student Movement at the University of North Carolina, staff writer James Claude Benton explained, "The problem is that for those who may not fully understand African Americans, a show that expresses part of the African American experience like this one has the potential to make them believe that African Americans are thieves, bums, clowns, or hoes. It has the potential to make others believe that is the norm for — or, worse yet, a common denominator that defines all of — Black America."

CHAPTER FIVE

1. Conjectures about slang in use based on a collection of lexical items like my UNC-CH corpus or on the results of a questionnaire like Teresa Labov's are not ideal. As Labov writes, "It would have been preferable to rely on ethnographic means to collect instances of slang in use" (1992, 347). However, participant-observer studies of language use among American college students are usually small projects for a speech or linguistics course, and at the end of the semester the data disappear with the students. The notable exception is *Slang U* (1990), compiled by students at UCLA in 1989 under the supervision of Pamela Munro. The analysis of social and linguistic networks among adolescents at school, such as the work of Penelope Eckert in Detroit (1989) and Boyd Davis in Charlotte (1986, 1993), clearly shows how valuable such an approach can be.

My observations about where in the stream of speech and under what social conditions slang is used are limited by my word-centered methodology. The generalizations that I offer in this chapter need to be tested by studying the use of slang in many hours of interaction among college students in a variety of typical social settings — in the locker room, waiting for the bus, in the dining hall, at parties, in all-female groups, in all-male groups, in groups of both males and females, and so on.

2. The names used to identify the participants in the conversations are fictitious.

3. In the elevator narrative, the point of view is edited to be consistently first person. In both narratives commentary about complaining and other words irrelevant to this discussion are eliminated.

CHAPTER SIX

1. In the portion of her questionnaire in which 261 students at three colleges were asked to define twenty-one slang items, sociologist Teresa Labov reports that the two terms meaning 'relax', *chill out* and *mellow out*, show the highest percentage of recognition. See Labov (1992).

2. I am indebted to Kirstin Reimer for the examples of teckie slang, to Lisa Lindsay for the slang of the *DTH* copy desk, and to Andy Pflaum for the terms from the cross-country team.

CHAPTER SEVEN

1. Although mentioned in Babbitt (1900) as "the most careful and complete" collection of the slang of a particular institution during the nineteenth century, Gore's twenty-nine-page collection with commentary was almost inaccessible until 1993, when Gerald Cohen reprinted it in *Comments on Etymology*—from a hand copy he made from a fragile original in the New York Public Library. If a history of American vernacular language is ever written, it will rely heavily on the careful work Cohen has done in tracking down, documenting, and publishing obscure sources like this one.

2. "College Words and Phrases" lists about one thousand items in the lexicon of American college students in 1900. Many of these, though undoubtedly part of the vocabulary of the academy, are not slang, for example, *alumni society, bursar, commencement, dean, faculty, regent,* and *thesis.* When I eliminate these, Babbitt's list contains slightly more than nine hundred items.

WORKS CITED

Algeo, John. 1980. "Where Do All the New Words Come From?"
    American Speech 55:264–77.

Algeo, John, and Adele Algeo. 1991. *Fifty Years among the New
    Words: A Dictionary of Neologisms, 1941–1991.* Cambridge:
    Cambridge University Press.

Allen, Irving Lewis. 1990. *Unkind Words: Ethnic Labeling from
    Redskin to Wasp.* New York: Bergin and Garvey.

The American Heritage Dictionary of the English Language. 1992. 3d
    ed. Edited by Anne H. Soukhanov. Boston: Houghton Mifflin Co.

Ashley, Leonard R. N. 1977. "Rhyme and Reason: The Methods and
    Meanings of Cockney Rhyming Slang, Illustrated with Some
    Proper Names and Some Improper Phrases." *Names* 25:125–54.

Babbitt, Eugene H. 1900. "College Words and Phrases." *Dialect Notes*
    2:4–70.

Bagg, Lyman. 1871. *Four Years at Yale.* New Haven: C. C. Chatfield &
    Co.

Banchero, Lawrence, and William L. Flinn. 1967. "The Application of
    Sociological Techniques to the Study of College Slang." *American
    Speech* 42:51–57.

Barber, Edwin. 1963. "The Treatment of Slang in *Webster's Third New
    International Dictionary.*" *American Speech* 38:103–16.

Barden, Elizabeth Anne. 1989. "Complaints—Greetings." Course
    paper, English 36, University of North Carolina at Chapel Hill.

Barnhart, Clarence L. 1978. "American Lexicography, 1945–1973."
    American Speech 53:83–140.

Baugh, Albert C., and Thomas Cable. 1978. *A History of the English
    Language.* 3d ed. Englewood Cliffs, N.J.: Prentice-Hall.

Benton, James Claude. 1991. "Endsights." *Black Ink* (Chapel Hill,
    N.C.), 14 Jan., 11.

Bloomfield, Leonard. 1933. *Language.* New York: H. Holt & Co.

Bolinger, Dwight. 1992. "Sound Symbolism." In *International
    Encyclopedia of Linguistics*, ed. William Bright, 4:28–30. New
    York: Oxford University Press.

Bolton, W. F. 1982. *A Living Language.* New York: Random House.

Brenneis, Donald. 1977. " 'Turkey,' 'Wienie,' 'Animal,' 'Stud':
    Intragroup Variation in Folk Speech." *Western Folklore* 3:238–46.

Bronner, Simon J. 1990. *Piled Higher and Deeper: The Folklore of Campus Life*. Little Rock: August House Publishers.

Brook, G. L. 1973. *Varieties of English*. London: Macmillan.

Brown, Penelope, and Stephen Levinson. 1978. "Universals in Language Usage: Politeness Phenomena." In *Questions and Politeness*, ed. Esther N. Goody, 256–89. Cambridge: Cambridge University Press.

Burke, W. J. 1965. *The Literature of Slang*. New York: New York Public Library, 1939. Reprint, Detroit: Gale Research.

Cameron, Deborah. 1992. "Naming of Parts: Gender, Culture, and Terms for the Penis among American College Students." *American Speech* 67:367–82.

Canine, Karen McFarland. 1986. "On the Outs." Conference paper, Southeastern Conference on Linguistics, Auburn University.

Cardozo-Freeman, Inez, and Eugene Delorme. 1984. *The Joint: Language and Culture in a Maximum Security Prison*. Springfield, Ill.: Charles C. Thomas.

Carter, Chris. 1989. "Some Observations on Conversation." Course paper, English 36, University of North Carolina at Chapel Hill.

Carter, Virginia. 1931. "University of Missouri Slang." *American Speech* 6:203–6.

Caso, Arthur Lewis. 1980. "The Production of New Scientific Terms." *American Speech* 55:101–11.

Chapman, Robert L., ed. 1986. *New Dictionary of American Slang*. New York: Harper and Row.

Cohen, Gerald. 1991. "Compiling the Black-Slang Items from *Really the Blues*, Chapter 1." *Comments on Etymology* 20:36–46.

———. 1992. "Compiling the Black-Slang Items from *Really the Blues*, Chapter 2." *Comments on Etymology* 22:24–36.

Covington, Michael A. 1981. "Computer Terminology: Words for New Meanings." *American Speech* 56:64–71.

Cox, Jennifer R. 1991. "I Am So Smart—Not!" Course paper, English 94A, University of North Carolina at Chapel Hill.

Current Slang (Department of English, University of South Dakota). 1966–71. Vols. 1–6.

Danesi, Marcel. 1988. "Pubilect: Observations on North American Teen-Ager Talk." In *The Fourteenth LACUS Forum, 1987*, ed. Sheila Embleton, 433–41. Lake Bluff, Ill.: Linguistic Association of Canada and the United States.

———. 1994. *Cool: The Signs and Meanings of Adolescence.*
Toronto: University of Toronto Press.

Davis, Boyd. 1986. "The Talking World Map: Eliciting Southern
Adolescent Language." In *Language Variety in the South:
Perspectives in Black and White*, ed. Michael Montgomery and Guy
Bailey, 359–64. Tuscaloosa: University of Alabama Press.

Davis, Boyd, M. Smilowitz, and L. Neely. 1993. "Speaking Maps and
Talking Worlds: Adolescent Language Usage in a New South
Community." Conference paper, Language Variation in the
South II, Auburn University.

Dickinson, M. B. 1951. "Words from the Diaries of North Carolina
Students." *American Speech* 26:181–84.

Dickson, Paul. 1990. *Slang!: The Topic by Topic Dictionary of
Contemporary American Lingoes.* New York: Pocket Books.

Drake, G. F. 1980. "The Social Role of Slang." In *Language: Social
Psychological Perspectives*, ed. Howard Giles, W. Peter Robinson,
and Philip M. Smith, 63–70. New York: Pergamon Press.

Dumas, Bethany K., and Jonathan Lighter. 1978. "Is *Slang* a Word
for Linguists?" *American Speech* 53:5–17.

Dundes, Alan, and Manuel R. Schonhorn. 1963. "Kansas University
Slang: A New Generation." *American Speech* 38:164–77.

Eble, Connie. 1980. "Slang, Productivity, and Semantic Theory." In
The Sixth LACUS Forum, 1979, ed. William McCormack and
Herbert Izzo, 215–27. Columbia, S.C.: Hornbeam Press.

———. 1981a. "Scenes from Slang." *SECOL Bulletin* 5:74–78.

———. 1981b. "Slang, Productivity, and Semantic Theory: A Closer
Look." In *The Seventh LACUS Forum, 1980*, ed. James E.
Copeland and Philip W. Davis, 270–75. Columbia, S.C.:
Hornbeam Press.

———. 1983. "Greetings and Farewells in College Slang." In *The
Ninth LACUS Forum, 1982*, ed. John Morreal, 433–42. Columbia,
S.C.: Hornbeam Press.

———. 1984. "Slang: Deviation or Norm?" *The Tenth LACUS
Forum, 1983*, ed. Alan Manning, Pierre Martin, and Kim McCalla,
409–16. Columbia, S.C.: Hornbeam Press.

———. 1985. "Slang: Variations in Dictionary Labeling Practices."
In *The Eleventh LACUS Forum, 1984*, ed. Robert A. Hall Jr.,
294–302. Columbia, S.C.: Hornbeam Press.

———. 1986a. "Slang: Etymology, Folk Etymology, and Multiple
Etymology." *SECOL Review* 10:8–16.

———. 1986b. "Slang and Cultural Knowledge." In *The Twelfth LACUS Forum, 1985*, ed. Mary C. Marino and Luis A. Perez, 385–90. Lake Bluff, Ill.: Linguistic Association of Canada and the United States.

———. 1987. "The Subversiveness of Slang." In *The Thirteenth LACUS Forum, 1986*, ed. Ilah Fleming, 477–82. Lake Bluff, Ill.: Linguistic Association of Canada and the United States.

———. 1988. "Slang as Poetry." In *The Fourteenth LACUS Forum, 1987*, ed. Sheila Embleton, 442–45. Lake Bluff, Ill.: Linguistic Association of Canada and the United States.

———. 1989a. *College Slang 101*. Georgetown, Conn.: Spectacle Lane Press.

———. 1989b. "The Ephemerality of American College Slang." In *The Fifteenth LACUS Forum, 1988*, ed. Ruth M. Brend and David G. Lockwood, 457–69. Lake Bluff, Ill.: Linguistic Association of Canada and the United States.

———. 1990. "College Slang in the Conversational Structure." In *The Sixteenth LACUS Forum, 1989*, ed. Michael P. Jordan, 451–59. Lake Bluff, Ill.: Linguistic Association of Canada and the United States.

———. 1991. "Forms of Address in the Speech of College Students." In *The Seventeenth LACUS Forum, 1990*, ed. Angela Della Volpe, 483–87. Lake Bluff, Ill.: Linguistic Association of Canada and the United States.

———. 1992a. "Borrowing in College Slang." In *The Eighteenth LACUS Forum, 1991*, ed. Ruth M. Brend, 505–10. Lake Bluff, Ill.: Linguistic Association of Canada and the United States.

———. 1992b. "Slang." In *The Oxford Companion to the English Language*, ed. Tom McArthur, 940–43. Oxford: Oxford University Press.

———. 1993. "African-American Contributions to Slang." In *The Nineteenth LACUS Forum, 1992*, ed. Peter Reich, 371–78. Chapel Hill, N.C.: Linguistic Association of Canada and the United States.

———. 1994a. "Lexicon and Culture: The Case of College Slang." In *The Twentieth LACUS Forum, 1993*, ed. Valerie Becker Makkai, 601–7. Chapel Hill, N.C.: Linguistic Association of Canada and the United States.

———. 1994b. "Slang and Usage." In *Centennial Usage Studies*, ed. Greta Little and Michael Montgomery, 15–18. Publications of the

American Dialect Society 77. Tuscaloosa: University of Alabama Press.

————. Forthcoming. "Slang and Lexicography." In *Functional Approaches to Language, Culture, and Cognition*, ed. James Copeland, Peter Fries, and David Lockwood. Amsterdam: John Benjamins.

Eckert, Penelope. 1989. *Jocks and Burnouts: Social Categories and Identity in High School*. New York: Teachers College Press.

Eschholz, Paul A., and Alfred F. Rosa. 1970. "Course Names: Another Aspect of College Slang." *American Speech* 45:85–90.

Fine, Gary Alan. 1983. "Sociological Approaches to the Study of Humor." In *Handbook of Humor Research*, vol. 1, *Basic Issues*, ed. Paul E. McGhee and Jeffrey H. Goldstein, 159–81. New York: Springer-Verlag.

Fiorenza, Elisa. 1992. "A Statistical Analysis of Patterns of Slang Usage at the University of North Carolina at Chapel Hill from Fall 1976 to Fall 1991." Undergraduate honors thesis, Department of Statistics, University of North Carolina at Chapel Hill.

Frost, Robert. 1966. *Selected Prose of Robert Frost*. Edited by Hyde Cox and Edward Connery Lathem. New York: Holt, Rinehart, and Winston.

Gibbs, Raymond W., and Annette Nagaoka. 1985. "Getting the Hang of American Slang: Studies on Understanding and Remembering Slang Metaphors." *Language and Speech* 28:177–94.

Gleason, H. A., Jr. 1961. *An Introduction to Descriptive Linguistics*. Rev. ed. New York: Holt, Rinehart, and Winston.

————. 1973. "Grammatical Prerequisites." In *Lexicography in English*, ed. Raven I. McDavid and Audrey R. Duckert, 27–33. Annals of the New York Academy of Sciences 211. New York: The Academy.

Gore, Willard C. 1993. "Student Slang." In *Contributions to Rhetorical Theory*, ed. Fred Newton Scott. 1896. Reprinted with index, ed. Gerald Cohen, in *Comments on Etymology* 22 (April): 1–47.

Greenough, James B., and George L. Kittredge. 1901. *Words and Their Ways in English Speech*. New York: Macmillan.

Grose, Francis. 1963. *A Classical Dictionary of the Vulgar Tongue*. 3d ed., 1796. Edited by Eric Partridge. Reprint, New York: Barnes and Noble.

Hall, B. H. 1856. *College Words and Customs*. Cambridge, Mass.: J. Barlett.

Halliday, M. A. K. 1976. "Anti-languages." *American Anthropologist* 78:570–83.

———. 1978. *Language as Social Semiotic.* Baltimore: University Park Press.

Hartmann, R. R. K., ed. 1983. *Lexicography: Principles and Practice.* London: Academic Press.

Herbert, Robert K. 1986. "Say 'Thank You'—or Something." *American Speech* 61:76–88.

Hockett, Charles. 1958. *A Course in Modern Linguistics.* New York: Macmillan.

Householder, Fred W., and Sol Saporta. 1962. *Problems in Lexicography.* In *International Journal of American Linguistics* 28, no. 2, pt. 4. Bloomington: Indiana University Publications.

Jarnagin, Bert, and Fred Eikel Jr. 1948. "North Texas Agricultural College Slang." *American Speech* 23:248–50.

Joos, Martin. 1967. *The Five Clocks.* New York: Harcourt, Brace.

Kane, Thomas, Jerry Suls, and James T. Tedeschi. 1976. "Humour as a Tool of Social Interaction." In *It's a Funny Thing, Humor,* ed. Antony J. Chapman and Hugh C. Foot, 13–16. New York: Pergamon Press.

Kittay, Eva. 1987. *Metaphor: Its Cognitive Force and Linguistic Structure.* Oxford: Clarendon Press.

Klaeber, Fr. 1926. "Concerning the Etymology of 'Slang.'" *American Speech* 1:368.

Kratz, Henry. 1964. "What Is College Slang?" *American Speech* 39:188–95.

Kuethe, J. Louis. 1932. "Johns Hopkins Jargon." *American Speech* 7:327–38.

Labov, Teresa. 1992. "Social and Language Boundaries among Adolescents." *American Speech* 67:339–66.

Lakoff, George. 1987. *Women, Fire, and Dangerous Things: What Categories Reveal about the Mind.* Chicago: University of Chicago Press.

Lakoff, George, and Mark Johnson. 1980. *Metaphors We Live By.* Chicago: University of Chicago Press.

Landau, Sidney I. 1984. *Dictionaries: The Art and Craft of Lexicography.* New York: Charles Scribner's Sons.

Laver, John, and Peter Trudgill. 1979. "Phonetic and Linguistic Markers." In *Social Markers in Speech,* ed. Klaus R. Scherer and Howard Giles, 1–32. Cambridge: Cambridge University Press.

Lehmann, Winfred P. 1976. *Descriptive Linguistics: An Introduction.* New York: Random House.

Lehrer, Adrienne. 1974. *Semantic Fields and Lexical Structure.* Amsterdam: North-Holland Publishing Co.

Lehrer, Adrienne, and Eva Feder Kittay, eds. 1992. *Frames, Fields, and Contrasts: New Essays in Semantic and Lexical Organization.* Hillsdale, N.J.: Lawrence Erlbaum Associates.

Levine, Kenneth. 1995. "A Comparative Study of African American English and Gay Argot." Course paper, Special Studies 90, University of North Carolina at Chapel Hill.

Lighter, J. E. 1994. *Random House Historical Dictionary of American Slang.* Vol. 1, A–G. New York: Random House.

Marples, Morris. 1950. *University Slang.* London: Williams and Norgate.

Martineau, William H. 1972. "A Model of the Social Functions of Humor." In *The Psychology of Humor: Theoretical Perspectives and Empirical Issues,* ed. Jeffrey H. Goldstein and Paul E. McGhee, 101–25. New York: Academic Press.

Maurer, David W. 1981. *Language of the Underworld.* Lexington: University Press of Kentucky.

Maurer, David W., and Ellesa Clay High. 1980. "New Words—Where Do They Come From and Where Do They Go?" *American Speech* 55:184–94.

McArthur, Tom, ed. 1992. *The Oxford Companion to the English Language.* Oxford: Oxford University Press.

McKnight, George H. 1923. *English Words and Their Background.* New York: Appleton and Co.

McMillan, James B. 1978. "American Lexicology, 1942–1973." *American Speech* 53:141–63.

Mencken, H. L. 1963. *The American Language.* 4th ed., rev. Raven I. McDavid and David Maurer. New York: Knopf.

Merriam-Webster's Collegiate Dictionary. 1993. 10th ed. Edited by Frederick C. Mish. Springfield, Mass.: Merriam-Webster.

Milroy, James. 1992. *Linguistic Variation and Change: On the Historical Sociolinguistics of English.* Oxford: Basil Blackwell.

Moffatt, Michael. 1989. *Coming of Age in New Jersey: College and American Culture.* New Brunswick, N.J.: Rutgers University Press.

Morse, William R. 1927. "Stanford Expressions." *American Speech* 2:275–79.

Muecke, D. C. 1973. "The Communication of Verbal Irony." *Journal of Literary Semantics* 2:35–42.

Munro, Pamela. 1990. *Slang U*. New York: Harmony House.

Newman, Stanley. 1964. "Vocabulary Levels: Zuni Sacred and Slang Usage." In *Language in Culture and Society*, ed. Dell Hymes, 397–406. New York: Harper and Row.

Nunberg, Geoffrey. 1978. "Slang, Usage-Conditions, and l'Arbitraire du Signe." In *Papers from the Parasession on the Lexicon*, ed. Donka Farkas, Wesley M. Jacobsen, and Karol W. Todrys, 301–11. Chicago: Chicago Linguistic Society.

Oertel, Hans. 1901. *Lectures on the Study of Language*. New York: Charles Scribner's Sons.

Olesen, Virginia, and Elvi Whittaker. 1968. "Conditions under Which College Students Borrow, Use, and Alter Slang." *American Speech* 43:222–28.

Palmer, A. Smythe. 1904. *The Folk and Their Word Lore*. New York: E. P. Dutton and Co.

Papin, Liliane. 1992. "This Is Not a Universe: Metaphor, Language, and Representation." *PMLA* 107:1253–65.

Partridge, Eric. 1970. *Slang To-day and Yesterday*. 4th ed. London: Routledge & Kegan Paul.

Peck, Richard E. 1966. " 'Out of Sight' Is Back in View." *American Speech* 41:78–79.

Pingry, Carl, and Vance Randolph. 1928. "Kansas University Slang." *American Speech* 3:218–21.

Pyles, Thomas, and John Algeo. 1993. *The Origins and Development of the English Language*. 4th ed. Fort Worth: Harcourt Brace Jovanovich.

Quirk, Randolph, Sidney Greenbaum, Geoffrey Leech, and Jan Svartik. 1985. *A Comprehensive Grammar of Contemporary English*. London: Longman.

Rait, Robert S. 1912. *Life in the Medieval University*. Cambridge: Cambridge University Press.

Random House Dictionary of the English Language. 1987. 2d ed., unabridged. Edited by Stuart Berg Flexner. New York: Random House.

Read, Allen Walker. 1973. "Approaches to Lexicography and Semantics." In *Current Trends in Linguistics 10*, ed. Thomas Sebeok, 145–205. The Hague: Mouton.

Reay, I. E. 1994. "Sound Symbolism." In *The Encyclopedia of Language and Linguistics*, ed. R. E. Asher, 8:4064–70. Oxford: Pergamon Press.

R. G. B. 1889. "College Slang, Harvard." *American Notes and Queries*, 9 Nov., 22.

Robertson, Stuart, and Frederick Cassidy. 1954. *The Development of Modern English*. Englewood Cliffs, N.J.: Prentice-Hall.

Ross, Thomas J. 1984."Taboo Words in the Fifteenth Century." In *Fifteenth Century Studies: Recent Essays*, ed. Robert F. Yeager, 137–60. Hamden, Conn.: Archon Books.

Schlauch, Margaret. 1959. *The English Language in Modern Times*. Warsaw: Panstwowe Wydawnictwo Naukowe.

Sebastian, Hugh. 1934. "Negro Slang in Lincoln University." *American Speech* 9:287–90.

Shidler, John Ashton. 1932. "More Stanford Expressions." *American Speech* 7:434–37.

Sledd, James. 1965. "On Not Teaching English Usage." *English Journal* 54:698–703.

Smitherman, Geneva. 1994. *Black Talk: Words and Phrases from the Hood to the Amen Corner*. Boston: Houghton Mifflin.

Sornig, Karl. 1981. *Lexical Innovation: A Study of Slang, Colloquialisms, and Casual Speech*. Amsterdam: John Benjamins.

Spears, Richard A. 1981. *Slang and Euphemism*. Middle Village, N.Y.: Jonathan David.

Student Life at Harvard. 1876. Boston: Lockwood, Brooks, and Co.

Tanaka, Ronald. 1973. "The Concept of Irony: Theory and Practice." *Journal of Literary Semantics* 2:43–56.

Thomas, Owen. 1969. *Metaphors and Related Subjects*. New York: Random House.

Underwood, Gary N. 1975. "Razorback Slang." *American Speech* 50:50–69.

———. 1976. "Some Characteristics of Slang Used at the University of Arkansas at Fayetteville." *Mid-South Folklore* 4:49–54.

Ward, Lori. 1989. "Lovers' Lingo: A Comparison in Styles." Course paper, English 36, University of North Carolina at Chapel Hill.

Webster's Ninth New Collegiate Dictionary. 1983. Edited by Frederick Mish. Springfield, Mass.: Merriam-Webster.

Wentworth, Harold, and Stuart Berg Flexner. 1975. *Dictionary of American Slang*. 2d supplemented ed. New York: Crowell.

Wescott, Roger W. 1971. "Labio-Velarity and Derogation in English: A Study in Phonosemic Correlation." *American Speech* 46:123–37.

——. 1977. "Ooglification in American English." *Verbatim* 3:5.

——. 1978. "'Zazzification' in American English Slang." *Forum Linguisticum* 3:185–87.

——. 1979. "Lexical Polygenesis: Words as Resultants of Multiple Linguistic Pressures." In *The Fifth LACUS Forum, 1978*, ed. Wolfgang Wolcke and Paul Garvin, 81–92. Columbia, S.C.: Hornbeam Press.

White, William. 1955. "Wayne University Slang." *American Speech* 30:301–5.

Whitman, Walt. 1885. "Slang in America." *North American Review* (Nov.).

Wieseltier, Leon. 1986. "Yupping It Up on *SNL*." *Vanity Fair* (June): 50–51.

Williams, Joseph M. 1975. *Origins of the English Language: A Social and Linguistic History*. New York: Free Press.

Woodworth, R. B. 1889. "College Slang, Hampden Sydney." *American Notes and Queries*, 30 Nov., 60.

Yates, Norris. 1981. "The Vocabulary of *Time* Magazine Revisited." *American Speech* 56:53–63.

Abdul, Paula, 90
Acronyms, 37; expanded, 37
Address forms, 101–3, 108
Affixation, 32–33
African Americans, 75, 80–86,
  89–90, 93–94, 141–42
Algeo, Adele, 38
Algeo, John, 18, 38
Alliteration, 42
Allusion, 73, 74, 86–88, 95–97;
  sports, 88–89; motion
  pictures, 89–90; music,
  90–91; television, 91–95
Amelioration, 58–59
American Dialect Society, 133,
  135
*American Heritage Dictionary
  of the American Language*, 5,
  23, 130
American Language (Mencken),
  3
"American Lexicology, 1942–
  1973" (McMillan), 22
American Notes and Queries
  (journal), 132
American Speech (journal), 13,
  136
Andy Griffith Show (television),
  91
Animal House (film), 89
Antilanguage, 125–26, 137–38
Argot, 11, 21
Armstrong, Louie, 84
Authority, opposition to, 116,
  124–29

Babbitt, Eugene H., 133, 135
Bagg, Lyman, 131
Barden, Elizabeth, 104

*Barnhart Dictionary of New
  English since 1963*, 18
Baugh, Albert C., 2
Bell, Lori, 104
*Bill and Ted's Excellent
  Adventure* (film), 85–86, 89,
  101
"Bishop Orders His Tomb at St.
  Praxed's" (Browning), 87
Black Vernacular, 80–86, 129
Blending, 38
Bloomfield, Leonard, 75
Body language, 21
Bogart, Humphrey, 89
Borrowing: from foreign
  languages, 38–39, 74–76;
  dialect, 74, 75, 80
Bronner, Simon J., 140, 143
Browning, Robert, 87
Burgess, Gelett, 25

Cable, Thomas, 2
Calloway, Cab, 84
Cameron, Deborah, 127
Cant, 11, 21
Cardozo-Freeman, Inez, 126
Carter, Chris, 104
Carvey, Dana, 93
Casablanca (film), 89
Catch 22 (Heller), 16
Chapman, Robert L., 18–19, 80,
  119, 141
Chase, Chevy, 89
Chaucer, Geoffrey, 16
Cheers (television), 92
Christmas Carol (Dickens), 53
*Classical Dictionary of the
  Vulgar Tongue* (Grose), 16–17,
  52

Clipping, 35–37
Coinage, 17–18, 25
Coleridge, Samuel Taylor, 87
"College Slang and Phrases"
    (Babbitt), 133
College Words and Customs
    (Hall), 131
Colloquialism, 20
Coming of Age in New Jersey
    (Moffatt), 103–4
Compliments, 109–10
Compounding, 26–32
Connotation, 58
Cool (Danesi), 72
Counterwords, 99
Cox, Jennifer, 110
Crane, Stephen, 15
Creswell, Thomas J., 20
Cultural borrowing, 74–76
Current Slang (periodical),
    136

Daily Tar Heel (newspaper), 8,
    122
Danesi, Marcel, 72, 141
Dialect borrowing, 74, 75, 80
Dialect Notes (journal), 133
Dickens, Charles, 53
Dictionaries, 3, 22–24
Dictionaries (Landau), 23
Dictionary of American Slang
    (Wentworth and Flexner), 3
Do the Right Thing (film), 90
Dumas, Bethany, 11–12
Dundes, Alan, 13, 136
Dylan, Bob, 90

Ebert, Roger, 94
Eliot, T. S., 87
Emptying, 56
English language: evolution
    of, 15; word-building in, 26,
    27, 32, 33–34, 35; borrowing

from foreign languages,
    38–39, 74–76
Etymology, 15, 46–48, 53, 130

Farewells, 100–101
Fast Times at Ridgemont High
    (film), 89
Ferris Bueller's Day Off (film),
    89
Figurative language, 61–62, 86
Fiorenza, Elisa, 51, 138, 139
Flash, 11
Flexner, Stuart Berg, 3, 23, 99
Flintstones (television), 92
Folk etymology, 46, 47–48
Foreign languages, 39, 74–76
Four Years at Yale (Bagg), 131
French language, 75
Frequency, 51–52, 118–19,
    138–41
Frost, Robert, 67
Functional shift, 33–35

Gay influence, 89–90, 121,
    141–42
Generalization, 54–56
Gleason, H. A., Jr., 2
Godfather (film), 89
Gore, Willard C., 132–33
Greenough, James B., 125
Greetings, 100
Grose, Francis, 16–17, 52
Group identification, 18, 116,
    119–24

Haley, Bill, 39
Hall, Arsenio, 85
Hall, B. H., 131
Halliday, M. A. K., 125–26
Hammer, MC, 93
Hampden Sydney College, 132
Hartmann, R. R. K., 23–24
Harvard University, 131

Trading Places (film), 89
Truth or Consequences
(television), 40

Underwood, Gary N., 135–36,
137
University of Arkansas, 135–36,
137
University of California at Los
Angeles, 22
University of Michigan, 132–34
University of Missouri, 136
University of North Carolina,
6–9; slang samples, 1, 4, 14,
137, 138; students, 7

Valley Girl talk, 91
Velars, 40
Vogue words, 20

Ward, Lori, 104
Washington State Penitentiary,
126
Watkins, Calvert, 130
Wayne State University, 137
Wayne's World (film), 93
*Webster's New Collegiate
Dictionary*, 16, 22–23
Wentworth, Harold, 3
Wescott, Roger W., 40, 46
Wieseltier, Leon, 92
Willis, Bruce, 92
Winfrey, Oprah, 93
Word formation, 25, 26

Yiddish, 76

Zappa, Moon Unit, 91

INDEX OF WORDS, EXPRESSIONS, & AFFIXES

Bar golf, 16, 126
Bar hop, 126
Barley pop, 126
Bat, 134, 135
Batcave (bat cave),
    31, 69
Batting practice, 71,
    126
Batture, 19
Batty, 69
Bazooms, 40
Beam me up, Scotty,
    91
Beam out, 30
Beanburger, 38
Bearish, 69
Beartrap, 28
Beast, 69, 134
Beat it, 23
Beat the feet, 41
Beau, 77
Beaucoup(s), 77
Beautiful, 15
Beauty queen, 60
Beav, 92, 102
Beef, 16
Beef-a-roni, 71, 94
Beerfest, 33
Beer goggles, 96,
    126
Bee's knees, 17
Beggars, 131
Behavior disorder,
    20
Being throwed, 50
Benny Mason, 64
BFE, 36
Bible beater, 42, 50,
    121
Bicycle, 43, 134
Biddy, 59
Bide, 17
Big bang, 118

Big brown eyes, 136
Big deal, 65
Big dog, 70, 104
Big time, 31
Big toe, 27
Big white phone, 72
Bill, 83
Bio-, 32
Biostatistics, 32
Birdie, 135, 136
Birkenstock buddy,
    42, 120
Bitch, 16, 50, 59, 67,
    103, 121, 135
Bitching (bitchin'),
    56, 59, 67, 121
Bite on, 44
Bite the dust, 90
Bizarre, 54
Black, 53
Blacktop, 27
Blanche, 63
Blasted, 45, 127
-blatt, 78
Bleach, 53
Bleed, 83
Blimp, 136
Blimp boat, 42
Blimp out, 31
Blind, 45
Blitz, 77
Blitzed, 45, 127
Blitzkrieg, 45, 77
Bloke, 19
Blood, 84, 85, 102
Blood brother, 84,
    102
Blow, 51, 84
Blown out, 45
Blown up, 45
Blow off, 30, 138,
    140
Blow out, 30

Blow this popsicle
    stand, 51
Bluebird, 83
Bluff, 17
Blug, 133
Blurb, 25
Bod, 36
Bodacious ta-tas, 89
Body, 36
Boff, 41
Bogart, 21, 89
Bogel, 13
Bogus, 41, 54
Boheme, 36
Bohemian, 36
Boho, 36
Bolt, 51, 101, 131
Bomb, 15, 44
Bombed, 45, 127
Bomb out, 14–15, 30
Bone, 84
Bones, 16
Bong, 41, 128
Bonk, 41
Boob tube, 41, 49
Boogie, 58, 84, 85,
    95, 101
Boogiebox, 31
Boogie-woogie, 58
Boohonged, 127
Boojie, 84
Book, 51, 95, 101,
    139, 140
Bookaholic, 33
Booked, 60
Booming, 56, 121
Boon coon (boon-
    coon), 81
Bootlick, 134
Bootlicker, 131
Booze, 17
Bop, 41
Born agains, 121

Bosom, 40
Boss, 23, 84, 102
Bottom line, 20
Bottoms, 81
Bounce
    refrigerators, 51,
    140
Bourgeois, 36, 84
Bourgie, 36, 84, 120
Bowhead, 31, 64
Bowser, 70
Bow-wow, 70
Box, 50
Box score, 28
Bozo, 90
Brain, 64
Brain burp, 42, 51
Brain drain, 41
Brain fart, 51, 127
Brary, 36
Brary dog, 70
Bread, 20, 23
Break, 101
Breakfast, 38
Breakneck, 28
Br'er Rabbit, 43
Brew, 63, 126
Brewdog (brew dog),
    70, 126
Brewski, 63, 78, 126
Brick house, 90
Brilliant, 56, 121
Bring it all back
    home, 90
Bro, 36, 102, 137
Broth, 36, 102
Brother, 36, 102
Brown noser, 131
Brr rabbit, 43
Bruce, 92
Brunch, 38
Brute, 46
Brutus, 46

Buck, 16, 135
Buckra, 80
Buddha, 56
Budweiser, 36
Buel, 38
Bug, 81
Bug out, 69
Buick, 40
Build a log cabin,
    127
Bull, 16
Bullish, 69
Bum, 40, 75
Bum fucking Egypt,
    36
Bummer, 14, 23, 33
Bumming, 50
Bum out, 22, 30
Bumping, 13
Bump uglies, 41, 51,
    123, 128
Bungee, 89
Bungo, 41
Bunk you, 40–41
Burger, 123
Burner, 80–81
Burners on high, 71
Burn out, 30
Burnt out, 44
Bus, 43
Bust, 134
Busted, 44
Butt, 50, 56
Butthead, 50–51, 59,
    103, 120
Buttloads, 51
Buzz, 55, 135
Buzz crusher, 31

Caffeinaholic, 33
Caf up, 64
Cajun talk, 79
Caked, 127

Calibrate, 49
Calic, 135
Calico, 135
Call the dogs, 70
Canary, 135
Candidate for the
    plumber's degree,
    16
Candy, 56
Canine, 38
Capeesh, 77
Captain, 102
Captain Cheddar,
    70
Caravan, 35
Carbo-loading, 122
Cardinal, 63
Careful, 27, 103
Careless, 27
Carolina Crunge, 42
Carry, 75
Case nickel, 81–82
Case quarter, 81–82
Cassette, 57
Casual, 36
Cat, 135
Cat-and-mouse
    game, 69
Catch a buzz, 138,
    140
Catch you later, 100
Catch you on the
    flip flop, 100
Catnap, 69
Cat's pajamas, 17
Catty, 69
Cautiously, 32
Cazh, 36
CDs, 17, 18
Cellar, in the, 21
Central, 32
Chads, 121
Chairman, 29

Chamber of
commerce, 134
Charbroiled, 38
Charge-a-plate, 17
Chase, 78
Chbye, 100
Check in, 100
Check it out, 51
Check out, 30
Check you, 100
Check you later, 95,
100
Check you on the
flip side, 100
Cheddar, 120
Cheek it, 134
Cheese, 70, 77, 120
Cheeseball, 70, 120
Cheeseman, 31
Cheeser, 120
Cheese whiz, 70
Cheesy, sleazy,
greasy, 41
Cheezy, 21, 70, 94,
99, 121, 139
Chello, 100
Chester, 94
Chica, 77
Chicago, from, 95
Chicalean, 56, 78,
121
Chick, 50, 108
Chicken, 61
Chicken colonel, 19
Chicken hawk, 51
Childless, 27
Chill, 63, 83, 101,
118, 119, 138, 140
Chill out, 30, 82,
101, 118, 119, 138
Chill pill, 42, 118
Chilly, 118
Chilly dog, 70

Chimney, 81
Chimpanzee, 74
Chin, 134
Chipsy, 119
Chiquita, 77
Chiselly, 133
Chivalrous, 58
Choice, 56
Choked, 127
Chow down, 23, 31
Chow for now, 100
Chromosome, 49
Chucks, 63
Chum, 131
Chutzpah, 77
Ciao, 77, 100
Cigarette, 40
Cigaroot, 40
Cinch, 136
-city, 29
Classic, 56
Claven, 92
Clean, 84, 85
Clean shave, 134
Cleaver, 52
Clip, 17
Clip joint, 21
Clockwork, 27
Close-captioned
programming, 27
Closed, 35
Close to the vest, 21
Clueless, 99, 105,
117, 139
Coal yard, 131
Coax, 134
Cocaine, 36
Cock, 128
Cock diesel, 128
Cockpit, 69
Cockroach, 47, 79
Coke, 36, 55
Cold busted, 85

Cold one, 63
Cold turkey, 21
College widow, 135
Colony, 53
Come again, 16
Come in, Berlin, 43,
100
Commando, 77
Committee to Re-
Elect the
President, 35
Communicate quite
well, 114
Compact disc, 18
Compu-, 25
Compucenter, 26
Compupaper, 26
Compute, 25
Computer, 25
Computered out, 28
Computerize, 25, 32
Con, 133
Concretely, 61
Conjecture, 68
Conk, 82
Conk-buster, 82–83
Contact, 34
Cool, 14, 56, 106,
107, 118, 121, 138,
139
Cool beans, 101
Cool breeze, 71
Cool deal, 101
Cool out, 118
Cool whip, 70
Cool your jets, 118
Cop a tude, 129
Corn dog, 70
Cornflakes in a can,
126
Cottage course, 135
Couch potato, 31,
70